From Norway to Burma

From Norway to Burma

The King's Own Yorkshire Light Infantry in the Second World War 1939–1945

Roger Holgate

Pen & Sword
MILITARY

First published in Great Britain in 2025 by
Pen & Sword Military
An imprint of Pen & Sword Books Limited
Yorkshire – Philadelphia

ISBN 978 1 03611 625 5

A CIP catalogue record for this book is
available from the British Library.

Typeset by Mac Style
Printed in the UK by CPI Group (UK) Ltd, Croydon, CR0 4YY.

The Publisher's authorised representative in the EU for product safety is Authorised Rep Compliance Ltd., Ground Floor, 71 Lower Baggot Street, Dublin D02 P593, Ireland.
www.arccompliance.com

For a complete list of Pen & Sword titles please contact

PEN & SWORD BOOKS LIMITED
47 Church Street, Barnsley, South Yorkshire, S70 2AS, England
E-mail: enquiries@pen-and-sword.co.uk
Website: www.pen-and-sword.co.uk
or
PEN AND SWORD BOOKS
1950 Lawrence Road, Havertown, PA 19083, USA
E-mail: uspen-and-sword@casematepublishers.com
Website: www.penandswordbooks.com

Contents

Illustrations and Maps

Introduction

The King's Own Yorkshire Light Infantry (KOYLI) was one of the many regiments that served in the Second World War. The British Army was divided into "regiments," which were often recruited from a particular geographic area, and which were responsible for the administration of a soldier's entire career, from recruitment, through training and subsequent service for as long as they remained in that regiment. The regimental system enabled each regiment to develop its own esprit de corps, based upon its history, traditions, sense of local pride, and military function. However, in active service, the regiment was usually subdivided into smaller, more flexible units called "battalions," which consisted of between 500 and 1,000 soldiers. Each battalion had its own headquarters and was, in turn, divided into "companies." It was extremely rare for battalions from the same regiment to fight in the same tactical unit. Hence, KOYLI battalions served as infantry throughout the world, from France to Norway, Iceland, Burma, Holland, Syria, India, Lebanon, Sicily, Italy, North Africa, Germany, and Greece. These were the 1st, 2nd, 1/4th, 2/4th,* and 9th Battalions, and this is their story.**

* The designation of a battalion reflected its lineage. For instance, when 4th Battalion KOYLI was expanded to twice its original size, the two resulting formations became 1/4th and 2/4th Battalions.

** Before seeing action in the war, three battalions of KOYLI had left the regiment to become anti-aircraft regiments within the Royal Artillery, and another had become an armoured regiment in Royal Armoured Corps.

Chapter 1
Norway 1940

1.1 Namsos

The German invasion of Norway began on the 3rd April 1940. It was not until the 14th that the first British troops began to arrive at the port of Narvik. 146th Infantry Brigade landed at Namsos in the north of the country, and comprised 1/4th KOYLI, 4th Royal Lincolnshire Regiment, and the Hallamshire Battalion of the York and Lancaster Regiment, under the command of Brigadier Charles Phillips.

Allied plans for the capture of Trondheim involved both a direct assault and an advance from smaller ports near the major city. Namsos is 127 miles north of Trondheim and in 1940 had a population of under 4,000. Although it had a stone harbour and two wooden docks, it could only be reached from the open sea along a 15 miles long fiord. Naval landing parties had been assigned to go ashore first, to be followed by 148th Brigade, but on the 14th, the force commander, Major General Adrian Carton de Wiart, was informed that, although 148th Brigade had been delayed, 146th Brigade, comprising 2,166 men, would be available next day. As a result, 148th was redirected to Åndalsnes, and the 146th were on their own.

The transport ships were originally destined for Namsos, but the commander of the flotilla of five destroyers who were to assist the landings, warned that the limited facilities at the port would mean that the disembarkations could take a long time and that this might place the transports in great danger, unless air superiority could be guaranteed. This, of course, could not be achieved, and so it was decided that the troops should be landed at Lillesjona, a remote inlet one hundred miles further north, where the German air force would have more difficulty in locating and attacking the ships. The destroyers would then pick them up and take them into Namsos.

By the evening of the 15th, the Lincolnshires and the Hallamshires had reached Namsos on board a small fleet of destroyers, but 1/4th KOYLI were

After the bombing of Namsos. British infantry search through the wreckage. Norway, April 1940. Keating (Captain) War Office official photographer. (*Wikimedia Commons*)

waiting at Lillesjona for the destroyers to return, so that they could follow. The German air force was keeping up a constant stream of attacks and it was decided that the Polish supply ship, "Chrobry," should set off alone to escape them. There was no time to load the 170 tonnes of stores that were needed by the battalion, and they left for Namsos at dawn.

The wooded hills were reflected on the icy surface of the River Namsen as the Chrobry approached the frozen quayside, and by late evening on 17th of April, the infantry were all ashore and struggling through the deep snow. Wrapped in heavy Arctic coats, each man carried three kitbags through the frozen streets, as the officers searched for local people who would be prepared to hire out their vehicles: the only other available transport being a single-track railway. The infantrymen were all territorials, part-time soldiers, who had little or no experience of firing mortars or any of the other weapons of modern warfare. In fact, the major general was heard to remark that none of them "really knew the Bren." Even so, a detachment of these frozen and bewildered soldiers were taken by train to the town of Grong, as another managed to collect enough transport to allow them to reach the Beitstadfjord.

The bombing of Namsos began at 10 am on the 20th and continued until 4.30 pm, destroying the wooden houses, the railhead and docks, together with water and electricity supplies. At the end of it, the town was a mass of flames from end to end, and Major General Carton de Wiart was already beginning to realise that the whole expedition was doomed.

He reported to the War Office the next day:

> "Enemy aircraft have almost completely destroyed Namsos, beginning on railhead target, diving indiscriminately … I see little chance of carrying out decisive, or indeed, any operations, unless enemy air activity is considerably restricted."

That afternoon, the German "Group Trondheim" left the town of that name, to advance towards Steinkjer. Under the command of Generalmajor Kurt Woytasch of 181st Division, the group was comprised of five infantry battalions, parts of two batteries of mountain artillery, and a company of engineers. As they set off, they had no idea that the British had already reached Steinkjer. In fact, 1/4th KOYLI had been taking part in the advance down the Beitstadfjord, and by that time they had taken up position at the village of Vist, having been designated as the first unit to meet the expected German thrust up the road from the south. The rest of the force had established a strong defensive position at the Straumen Bridge, which was the only way north through the Inderøya Peninsula. As the roads through Vist and Straumen seemed well guarded, it was considered possible that the Germans might take a secondary road that ran around the eastern shore of a body of water called the Leksdalsvatn, from Verdalsora to Steinker, and such a move would provide a route round the peninsula. But they seemed determined to take Vist first.

The Inderøya Peninsula is about twelve miles wide, and at that time it was covered by deep snow. On the morning of 21st April, a German destroyer landed elements of a mountain battalion at Kirknesvaag, on the western shore of the Inderøya, about fifteen miles from Steinkjer. At the same time, an infantry company landed from a torpedo boat at a point just north of Verdalsora, with the intention of taking the rail and road bridges in the town. The Germans on the Inderøya Peninsular were able to establish themselves on two areas of high ground, from where they could machine gun and mortar the British troops who tried to cross the open expanse of snow below them. Steinkjer was bombed, and both brigade and battalion HQs destroyed, leaving no communication with the KOYLI and Lincolnshires who were in direct contact with the main enemy force at Verdalsora, and had suffered a 20% casualty rate during three hours of house-to-house fighting with the German unit sent to secure the bridges there. When no instructions were received, the survivors began to withdraw to Vist on their own initiative, having managed to destroy the rail bridge. The Germans found that the road bridge, though damaged, was still passable. The two companies of KOYLI stationed at Straumen and Rora were forced to fall back to the main road just south of Sparbu. When a situation report was finally delivered to Brigadier Phillips, he immediately advised a withdrawal along the bank of the Snåasavatn, towards Grong. However, Major General Carton de Wiart was concerned that such a move would interfere with Norwegian operations in the area, so he changed the direction of the proposed move, to the northwest, before authorising it.

At 7.45 am, enemy aircraft began dropping marker flares onto the KOYLI positions south of Sparbu, and these guided the German mortar and machine gun sledges as they sped to outflank the two companies, who had to withdraw east, into the forest. There, they met up with the two companies from Stiklestad. Halfway to Steinkjer, they tried to organise another holding position, but as their commanding officer later reported, "the withdrawal, once commenced, was impossible to check." The battalion held on until 8.45 pm, when the enemy bombardment drove them back along the road to Steinkjer. The officer remained to reorganise the men of his battalion, but by 8.45 pm, the enemy, after shelling the town from the fjord, had begun to arrive there, as he then led his men northeast towards Sunnan. The now united 1/4th KOYLI were already exhausted when they left Henning at 9 pm to try to work around the flank of the Germans. Several miles up the bank of the River Steinkjerelva they came across an intact bridge, and after

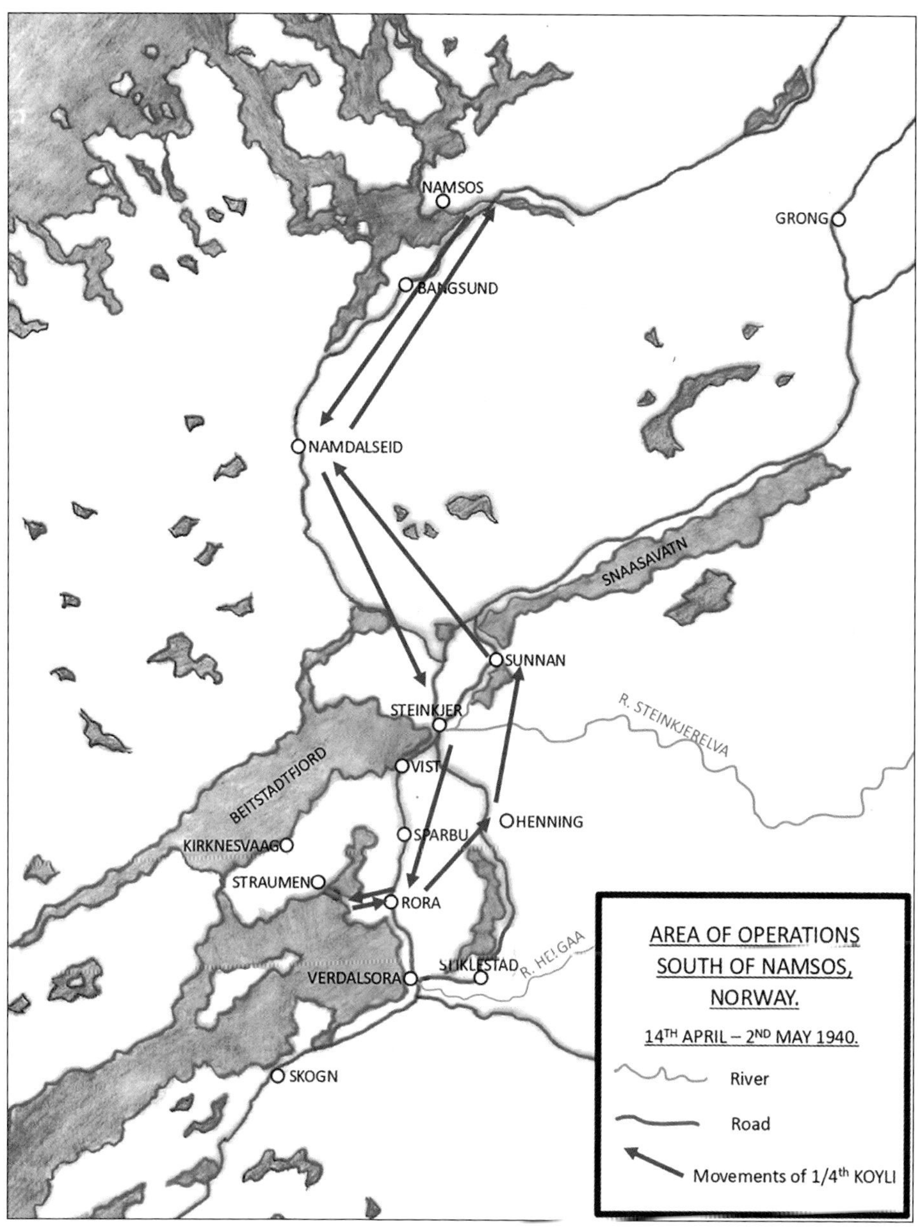

crossing it, completed a 58-mile trek to temporary safety, along winding, snowbound forest tracks, mostly by moonlight.

4th Lincolnshires had reached a point just south of Bangsund by the time the first members of the KOYLI passed through Namdalseid. The Hallamshire Battalion had been held in reserve throughout the action of the previous two days and were now called upon to protect the rear of the KOYLI, as they continued their retreat towards Namsos.

By the 26th, reinforcements of French Chasseurs Alpins had arrived on the scene as they went to relieve the Hallamshires, and along with Norwegian troops, carried out ski patrols to the east. The KOYLI would once again be in the rear area, and as this meant them being reinforced by the Chasseurs Alpins, they would be under the command of the French general for the operation, leaving Brigadier Phillips with two British and one French battalion to hold the area from Namsos to Grong.

The German forces in Steinkjer did not consider themselves strong enough to advance further without being reinforced by mountain troops, and this halt allowed the allies to put evacuation plans into action.

At the very rear of the allied column were the 13th Chasseurs Alpins, at a point about halfway between Namsos and Steinkjer. 1/4th KOYLI were next in the line, and in front of them were the Hallamshires and the 67th Chasseurs Alpins. The Lincolnshires were nine miles ahead of the column. The plan for the withdrawal involved the rearmost unit withdrawing through the next in line, who would withdraw through the unit in front of them, and so on until the whole column had reached Namsos. By the evening of 1st May, the plan had delivered both battalions of Chasseurs Alpins to the quayside of Namsos. Unfortunately, the ships sent to pick up the evacuees were severely bombed by German aircraft as they approached the Norwegian shore and had to take cover in a fog bank before making the difficult journey up the fjord, from the open sea. There, they found that the fog had cleared, and they had to turn back without embarking any troops, as the danger of air attack was too great.

The next night, they tried again, and five destroyers charged into the harbour at 10.30 pm. It was after midnight when the rear guard of the column destroyed the bridge at Bangsund and began to use up the last of their energy in a desperate attempt to get to the evacuation point before it was too late. 1/4th KOYLI straggled down to the dock as the last transports were being loaded, and at 4.30 am the sun rose. As they sailed, the ships were attacked by Stuka dive bombers that screamed down out of a clear sky, through the curtain of anti-aircraft fire sent up by the little fleet. The French destroyer Bison was sunk, and as HMS Afridi delayed picking up survivors, she was hit by two bombs. She capsized, and amongst those who went down with her were fourteen men of the Hallamshires, who had been

British troops arriving on the quayside at Namsos during the evacuation, 2nd May 1940. Keating (Capt), War Office official photographer. (*Wikimedia Commons*)

the last of the rear guard. The survivors of 1/4th KOYLI were evacuated to Iceland, where they became part of the garrison that was to protect the island from invasion. In August, 1942, when the threat of such a German move had receded, the battalion returned to England, to begin training for the invasion of France.

1.2 The Battle of Kvam

1st Battalion KOYLI were assigned to 15th Infantry Brigade at the outbreak of war, on 3rd September 1939, and as part of 5th Infantry Division, they seemed destined for France. However, following the German invasion of Norway on 8th April 1940, the brigade was detached from 5th Infantry Division, to join the reinforcements for "Sickelforce": part of the British Army's response. Commanded by Major General Bernard Paget, Sickelforce began landing in the Norwegian port of Åndalsnes, when 148th Infantry Brigade arrived on 18th April, but four days later they were engaged by German forces at Lillehammer and were soon in deep trouble. By the time 15th Brigade arrived to relieve the 148th, on 24th April, it was clear that the battle for Norway had already been lost.

The British forces were being pushed back along the Gudbrandsdal Valley, and Lieutenant Colonel Cass, in command of 1st KOYLI, rushed by train to the village of Kvam, only to be met by the sight of Norwegian and British soldiers in full retreat. The rest of the battalion arrived shortly after their commanding officer.

As the British and Norwegian forces had retreated up the valley, they had tried to slow up the German advance in any way possible, this mainly involved felling trees, or blowing holes in the road, but as they reached Kvam, they noticed that the road became very narrow as it passed through a steep-sided ravine. This seemed like the ideal place to try to cause a rock fall, and several men scrambled up the slope to set charges that would be blown as soon as the enemy approached. The KOYLI heard the explosion as they tried to establish the best place to set up an ambush, and they were hopeful that the Germans would now be stopped by the roadblock. However, on closer inspection, they realised that little damage had been done, and they stared after the departing column, as it disappeared towards the north. They were on their own.

After midnight, a few British aircraft were heard above. The KOYLI thought that they might at least be getting some air support, but they were to be disappointed: the aircraft had just escaped an attack from an armoured German unit that had smashed the thick ice on the lake they had been using as an airfield. They were on their way to safer landing sites.

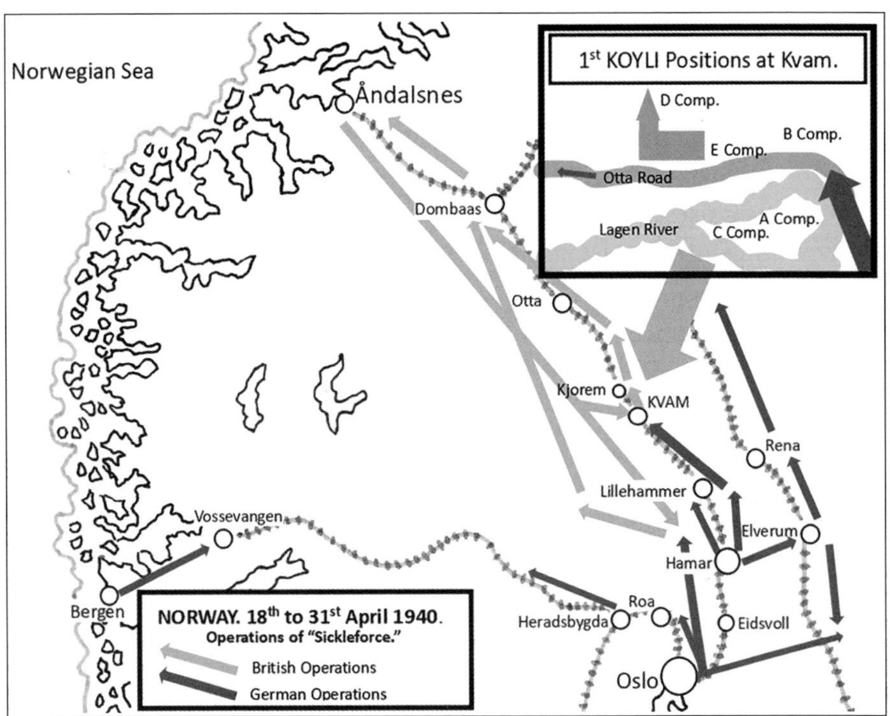

The River Lagen runs through Kvam, before bending sharply to the south at a point called "Kvam's Knee." The road down which the Germans were advancing, runs alongside the river as it enters the village, at a point called Kvamsporten: the gate to Kvam. On the day of the battle, the steep hills to the east were covered in deep snow, and ice floes floated down the river to collect at the point where it divides, to pass around an island called Storøya, which was now flooded.

Upon his arrival, Brigadier Smyth of 15th Brigade decided to set up his HQ in front of the church at the centre of the village, and one company of 1st KOYLI was sent to cover the road down which the Germans were coming. Two other companies were placed to the north of the road, as two more waded through the icy river, to take up position on the island.

A rearguard of Norwegian troops filed through Kvamsporten in the early morning light, dragging their wounded with them. They updated Brigadier Smyth about the strength of the enemy column that was following close behind, and it was not an encouraging report. He sent them on their way, promising to give them as much time as he could, but as the crunch of their footsteps faded into the frozen air, a new sound began to rumble along the valley: tanks. The Germans were on their way.

Under the command of Generalleutnant Richard Pellengahr, "Group Pellengahr" consisted of seven infantry battalions, two batteries of artillery, a motorised machine gun battalion, one company of engineers, and one platoon of tanks. Standing in their path were five companies of KOYLI, with five anti-tank guns, two mortars, a few light machine guns, and rifles with bayonets fixed.

The rumble of tank tracks grew louder, as the men of 1st KOYLI made their final preparations to meet them, and just before midday, the German advanced guard arrived. They seemed quite relaxed, as they ambled along behind the PzKpfw II tank that led the way through "the gate." They believed that they had the allies on the run, and they were enjoying the taste of victory. A second tank turned the corner at Kvam's Knee, and when it was less than 200 yards away from the first anti-tank gun, the leading company of KOYLI opened fire.

The air was rent by an ear-piercing explosion, as the tank erupted in flames. Then, the second company opened fire, and the leading panzer was ripped apart. As red-hot metal shards cut through the German infantry, the advance came to a shuddering halt, and the survivors turned to run for cover behind the walls of the ravine.

Then the mortars began to rain death onto the KOYLI positions, as the German infantry regrouped, and set up their machine guns in the snow drifts by the roadside. The Yorkshiremen were pinned down by a steady stream of gunfire, but it was not until late afternoon that the most advanced company was forced to pull back.

As night fell, the German infantry began to infiltrate the KOYLI positions, and with ammunition running low, the British pulled back into the village itself, where they were met by the newly arrived Hallamshires. A house-to-house battle took place throughout the hours of darkness, and when the enemy finally pulled back, the British thought they had gained at least a temporary reprieve. But then the artillery barrage began, and as the survivors of the two battalions crept into the shelter of the rubble that had been homes, the German air force put in an appearance, dropping bombs, and strafing any soldiers who tried to run between positions. Then, the infantry returned, and the fighting raged on. It was 5 pm before General Paget radioed Brigadier Smyth and told him to send 1st KOYLI and one company of the Hallamshires back through the rest of the brigade, to the village of Kjørem. The two battalions had lost fifty-four men in what was later discovered to have been the fiercest fighting in the whole of southern and central Norway. Also killed were three Norwegian soldiers and three civilians. British and Norwegian dead were buried in Kvam churchyard, where after the war, the townsfolk built a memorial to their bravery.

Despite the Luftwaffe's overwhelming air superiority making all movement seemingly impossible, 15th Brigade were ordered to secure a bridgehead on the road to Trondheim, to enable a build-up of forces that could block the German advance on the city. General Paget requested artillery, air support, anti-aircraft guns and a third infantry brigade. He received nothing.

The fighting continued at Kjørem, but the German pressure was inexorable, and General Paget decided to withdraw to a second position at Otta, which he hoped could be held until the arrival of his called-for reinforcements. Despite terrible losses, they held on in the face of constant attacks from both air and ground forces until nightfall, when they were ordered to withdraw across the river and begin the thirty-mile march to Dombås.

By 31st April, Sickelforce had been evacuated from Åndalsnes. Before their next experience of fighting, 1st KOYLI were to undergo a period of training in the UK, India and North Africa.

Chapter 2

France 1940

2.1 The Phoney War

At the outbreak of war, 2/4th KOYLI had been made part of 46th Infantry Division. They joined a unit made up of Territorials who came mainly from the north midlands area of England. To begin with, each battalion performed the function of a local defence force, in their

British troops move up to the front, June 1940. Malindine E G (Lt), Puttnam L A (Lt), War Office official photographers. (*Wikimedia Commons*)

own hometowns. The training was mainly centred around how to march in a straight line, and how to hold a dummy rifle; the full set of equipment required by a modern infantryman was not available at that time. A few weeks later, the part-time soldiers were summoned to the Corn Exchange building in Doncaster, where they were greeted by the sight of 800 fully equipped soldiers, filing into the building. The newcomers paraded before a desk, where their details were taken and various documents issued, before queuing up for tea and sandwiches, provided by the Co-Operative Wholesale Society. The training continued, and the supply of weapons slowly increased, until in March 1940, they received the order to join the British Expeditionary Force in France. Of course, they were not considered to be a front-line division and the area allotted to them was well away from the German border. They sailed from Southampton on 28th of April, and the 2/4th KOYLI were told that they would be put to work guarding the lines of communication from the Cotentin Peninsular to the area around Nantes. They had a small share of the guns and equipment that had been deemed to be reasonable for an infantry division at that time: four 2-inch mortars (without ammunition), eighteen Bren light machine guns, ten anti-tank rifles, one motorcycle, a four-seater car, eight 15 hundredweight lorries, three 30 hundredweighters, and a water truck.

When they landed at Cherbourg, they were immediately put to work on the roads that were now being flooded with men and vehicles on their way to the German border. They performed the duties of traffic police, and they repaired telephone lines and bridges, but mostly they did a lot of digging. The majority of them were not clear about the purpose of the digging, but the French people seemed to appreciate their efforts, and the steady stream of new customers into the cafes and bars must have been a welcome boost to the local economy.

"The Phoney War" was proving to be pleasant enough, but the threat from the east was always on the minds of the men who were now beginning to think of themselves as labourers, rather than soldiers. The local people seemed to place a great deal of trust in the "Maginot Line" that stretched along the border with Germany; it was, they said, impregnable. Even if the massive line of concrete forts and gun turrets was to prove insufficient to stop any German attack, the French army was the biggest in the world and would surely be too much for the cock-sure Nazis.

So, the men of 2/4th KOYLI spent the spring of 1940, stripped to the waist in the warm sun, digging for victory and counting on the strength of their allies.

2.2 Evacuation

On 12th May, the German army poured over the Belgian border, and 46th Division was sent as a reserve for the best units in the French army, who were opposing what appeared to be the main focus of the attack.

2/4th KOYLI were part of 138th Brigade, who were required to make their own way to Rouen, along roads where refugees flowed towards them, in an endless stream of misery. The 138th were forced off the road, into the fields, as they trudged through the shimmering heat of the French countryside. When they finally reached Rouen, they were immediately sent onwards, towards Amiens, and the flow of refugees became a tidal wave. The German fighter aircraft paid regular visits to these packed roads, spraying civilians and soldiers alike, with a rain of death that left the lanes and ditches littered with bodies and the smouldering wrecks of domestic cars and farm carts. There was no sign of the rest of 46th Division, and the KOYLI had little idea of what was happening in the area beyond their scope of vision, but they knew that the Germans were coming; the black clouds rising over the distant hills and forests were ample evidence that they would soon be involved in the first real fight of their lives.

The days were long, and the nights were longer, but they finally made contact with Divisional HQ, who allocated them to a stretch of the River Scarpe and Canal de la Deûle, from Arras to Douai. The names of the towns and villages that surrounded them were burnt into their memories, from tales of a previous war, and they looked out across the water towards Mons, Cambrai, and Saint-Quentin, where, in the next few hours, death and destruction would surely be raising its ugly head once more.

The bridges over these waterways provided the only route for military communication along the north-south axis, and the endless columns of refugees created a human roadblock. 2/4th KOYLI had the unpleasant task of pushing the exhausted civilians to the side of the road and clearing the bridges, whenever a military convoy wanted to pass. In the nick of time, they had been supplied with ten motorcycles that allowed them to scout along

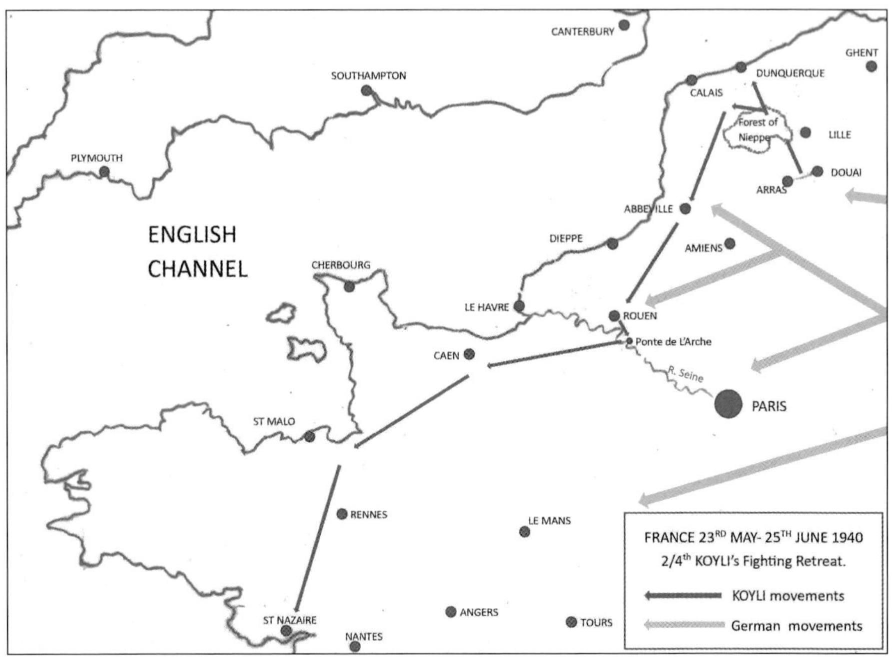

the river and canal banks, out towards the smoke-filled horizon. They had no maps, and little idea of where the German advance units might be, so every reconnaissance duty was a journey into the unknown. It was not long before the supplies began to run out. That the enemy was getting closer was not in doubt, and as they began to wonder just how they were going to stop the tanks that could be heard rumbling in the distance, they received a curt radio message that ordered them back to the Forest of Nieppe, to the south of Hazebrouck. There, they were told that the whole British Expeditionary Force was falling back to the port of Dunkirk.

The air attacks had become more frequent as the German spearhead punched its way towards the coast, and in the confusion of the withdrawal, 2/4th KOYLI became separated from the rest of the 138th. They were driven south by the direction of the German drive, and found themselves in the area of Abbeville, where they joined up with two battalions of the Duke of Wellington's Regiment, who had been isolated during the fighting there. Together, they fought their way to Dieppe but were soon forced from the town, in the direction of the River Seine. At Ponte de l'Arche they set up defensive positions on the bridges over which the German armour would come, as part of the scything advance that had been designed to cut off the main body of the allied armies. The fight was fierce and the German Panzergrenadiers were determined, but the KOYLI held on until news of an enemy landing further up the river made them realise that they were about to be flanked.

The roads to the south were still jammed with refugees, as the KOYLI marched towards their only hope of avoiding capture: a boat trip home. The closest port was Cherbourg, but as they approached, they were ordered further south. St. Malo, they were told, was their best hope. It was not.

Again, they were told to go south, and when they arrived at Rennes, they commandeered a train that took them to Radon. Here, they disembarked and marched the last few miles to Saint-Nazaire.

When they arrived on 16th June, they could see the queue from a distance, and estimated it to be about 5 miles long, curling down to the quayside, where ships were waiting to board them, or where smaller boats were busy ferrying out handfuls of tiny figures to the ships outside the harbour. Lines of stretchers, with nurses and civilians running alongside, snaked down to the sea and transport home, as German aircraft circled overhead, bombing and

A Boys anti-tank rifle unit on the beach near Étaples, south of Dunkirk,1940. Kessell (Lt), War Office official photographer. (*Wikimedia Commons*)

Troops on their way to the coast during the evacuation of British forces, June 1940. Puttnam L A (Lt), War Office official photographer. (*Wikimedia Commons*)

strafing the helpless crowds. All through the night, the KOYLI waited their turn, and at about 4 pm on the following day they heard a massive explosion from out in the bay. The RMS Lancastria had been hit by a bomb. She was a liner of the Cunard Line, built to carry 1,300, but today packed with well over 6,000, as the flotilla attempted to save the estimated 67,000 who still waited patiently on the quayside, beneath the storm of German bombs.

She keeled over as the few lifeboats were thrown into the water and people started to jump. The German aircraft dropped flares onto the widening pools of oil, burning to death many of those who had tried to leap to safety. The men of 2/4th KOYLI looked on in horror as the great liner slipped beneath the waves, taking with her two and a half thousand souls. They were amongst the last to be evacuated, and as their ship took them past the wreck of the Lancastria, they knew that they had changed. During the disastrous and often incompetent campaign in France, the men of 2/4th KOYLI, who had expected to be digging trenches and helping refugees, had fought against the most powerful military machine the world had ever seen, and survived. They had experienced war at its worst and would put that experience to good use in the very near future. When they had been brought up to full strength, re-armed, and provided with all the support necessary for a modern infantry unit, they would prove their worth on battlefields very different from the fields and beaches of France. The mountains of Tunisia awaited them.

Chapter 3

Burma 1941–2

3.1 The Burma Army

In 1941, today's Republic of the Union of Myanmar was known as Burma, and although this and many other place names within the country have now changed, I shall be using those that were in common use at that time.

Before the Second World War, Burma was part of the British Empire, and despite a growing sense of unease about the aggressive intentions of Japan, it was not considered that these would pose a major threat to the country.

The 17th Indian and 1st Burma Infantry Divisions that made up The Burma Army, under the command of Lieutenant General Thomas Hutton, were the only defensive forces in the area, and in the event of any unlikely Japanese incursion into the country, the support of General Chiang Kai-shek's Chinese Nationalist Army was expected, since they had been fighting Japan for many years.

1st Burma Division had been formed in July 1941 at the town of Toungoo, and Major General James Scott took command of three Infantry Brigades:

> 1st Burma Infantry Brigade: 2nd Battalion KOYLI; 1st Battalion Burma Rifles; 3rd Battalion Burma Rifles; 5th Battalion Burma Rifles.
>
> 2nd Burma Infantry Brigade: 2nd Battalion Burma Rifles; 4th Battalion Burma Rifles; 6th Battalion Burma Rifles; 8th Battalion Burma Rifles.
>
> 13th Indian Infantry Brigade: 5th Battalion 1st Punjab Regiment; 2nd Battalion 7th Rajput Regiment; 1st Battalion 18th Royal Garhwal Rifles.

1st Brigade had been formed from units based in the Maymyo area and was initially known as The Maymyo Infantry Brigade, before it was deployed to the Shan States, the area perceived to be the most at risk in the event of a Japanese attack. Brigadier Gerald Farwell was in command.

One of Japan's war aims was to take control of the raw materials from the European possessions in South-East Asia. They intended to impose their own dominance in what they referred to as a "Greater East Asia Co-Prosperity Sphere," comprising the Philippines, the Netherlands East Indies, and Malaya. Although Burma had significant oil deposits in the Yenangyaung area, the main purpose of launching an invasion there would be to protect the northwestern flank of the newly conquered territories, particularly Malaya and Singapore.

In 1941, the country was bordered by the Indian provinces of Bengal and Assam, Manipur, China, French Indo-China, and Siam. The relatively new Burma Road was the only route along which the Chinese armies could be kept supplied in their vital struggle against Japan, and if Burma were held, India's industrial heartland would be secure from invasion, but the geography of the country made its defence more difficult than was appreciated at the time. Covering a total area of 240,000 square miles, it was divided from India in the west, and China and Siam in the east, by mountain ranges which stretched down from the eastern end of the Himalayas. The range extended for three hundred miles to Imphal, where it reached its greatest width of about 100 miles, before turning south for another 400 miles, to the Bay of Bengal. This mountain range was known as the Naga Hills in the north, the Chin Hills in the centre, and the Arakan Yomas in the south, and formed a tangled and craggy barrier, cloaked by dense jungle, up to a height of 6,000 feet. In 1941, the few roads were mere dirt tracks that were constantly blocked by landslides, or flooded by the monsoon rains that swelled the waters of the three main rivers: the Irrawaddy, the Sittang, and the Salween. The capital city, Rangoon, lay in the Irrawaddy Delta, about twenty-five miles from the sea, and had a population of about 500,000. There were two monsoon seasons, and malaria was endemic in most parts of the country.

By the autumn of 1941, the political situation regarding the aggressive ambitions of Japan, has began to cause a greater degree of anxiety amongst both the military and political authorities concerned with the possible defence of Burma in the event of attack from the east. No one could have been under any illusions regarding the state of military preparedness, as the few forces present were almost completely inexperienced and undertrained. They had little equipment and no maintenance engineers to service the few vehicles that were available. It was, perhaps, the remains of an imperial force that was still rooted in the methods and mindset of the past. There were no artillery pieces, no anti-aircraft guns, no modern machine guns and a scarcity of rifles,

Buffalo Mark 1s of No. 453 Squadron RAAF, lined up at Sembawang, Singapore. Royal Air Force official photographer. (*Wikimedia Commons*)

no hand grenades, no mortars, no armour, insufficient medical facilities, and unsuitable uniform and body equipment. It was, to put it bluntly, a disaster waiting to happen, yet at the time, there seemed little that could be done about the situation, as the war against Nazi Germany was absorbing men and materiel like a sponge.

Japan, it was already known, had built up a modern professional air force, equipped with first-class bombers and particularly fighters. True, Britain had some of the best fighter planes in the world at that time, but all that could be spared for action in Burma were aircraft that had already proved themselves outmatched by the Luftwaffe. The Blenheim bombers that arrived in Rangoon in early 1941, had been withdrawn from action in

Europe, as they had become "flying coffins" when sent out to attack German troop movements during the 1940 Blitzkrieg through France and the Low Countries. There was no reason to believe that they would fare any better against the Japanese "Zero" fighters than they had against the Messerschmitt 109s, and their potential fighter escorts would probably be of little help; the outdated Brewster Buffaloes had been bought from the USA as a stopgap that was most certainly not going to stop any gap whatsoever. Unfortunately, one squadron of Buffaloes was the only RAF fighter unit in the whole of Burma.

3.2 Invasion

On 8th of December 1941, the Japanese threat to the whole of Asia became a reality, and four days later the Chiefs of Staff transferred the control of Burma from Far East Command to India Command, under the control of General Archibald Wavell.

The citizens of Rangoon were bemused by the sound of an air-raid siren as they gathered together outside their homes and workplaces to witness the Japanese Air Force making its first bombing raid on 23rd December. Christmas was in the air, and it seemed incongruous that bombers should be too. How could it be that a valued part of the mighty British Empire could come under attack without any sort of response whatsoever? It was out of the question, and yet, here it was happening, as the bombers came diving out of a clear blue sky, to smash the docks, warehouses, factories, and thousands of mostly wooden homes. As the sound of engines faded away and the dust began to settle over the devastated city, the search for casualties began and the result was inevitable: well over 2,000 civilians lay dead in the rubble.

The first attack was followed by others and the full attention of the authorities was focussed upon the chaos and destruction of the main administrative centre of the country, as Lieutenant General Shōjirō Iida set into action his plan for the full invasion across the Tenasserim Hills, from neighbouring Thailand where the Japanese had already imposed their authority after a devastating thrust through that country from the 2nd to the 7th of December. The Thais had been obliged to sign a treaty with the invaders on the 21st, and now the triumphant 15th Army was poised to confront the forces of the British Empire in their own backyard.

The Japanese were superbly trained and equipped, to say nothing of possessing a high morale, and a sense of invincibility that had been indoctrinated into them since birth, by the new generation of militarist leaders who saw the dominance of the Japanese people as the only way to achieve a settled world order that would free Asia from centuries of European control. This then, was the prevailing mentality of the men of 33rd and

Japanese machine gunners in Burma 1942. Unknown. (*Online Collection. National Army Museum, London*)

55th Infantry Divisions as they crossed the border and swept down upon the British garrison at Tavoy, in the toe of Burma. The 6th Burma Rifles and a battery of the Burma Auxiliary Force were helpless as the tidal wave burst upon them. Most were slaughtered before the invaders charged north, leaving the other garrison at Mergui, stranded in their wake.

Certainly, General Hutton had no real choice but to order that Moulmein should be held for as long as possible in order to delay the Japanese advance and so give the allied divisions time to think, and to prepare. But what forces were available to react decisively in such a situation, even if they had all the time in the world? The truth was that only one division would be available in the immediate future, and 2nd KOYLI were hurriedly sent from 1st Burma Division to bolster the extremely inexperienced men of the 17th Indian Division, who now looked on, transfixed, as the tsunami that was the Imperial Japanese Army, swept down towards them.

The first battalion to react was 3rd Burma Rifles, who fanned out along the edge of the mouth of the River Salween as soon as reports started to come in about Japanese troops building rafts, with the obvious intention of making an amphibious landing. On the landward side, the forward observation posts of 8th Burma Rifles began to report a major force advancing towards them, and on the 30th they were overrun. The rest of the battalion rushed forward to plug the gap, and the enemy was driven off, but as this was happening, the Japanese river crossing was completed through the thinly spread soldiers of the 3rd, and the defenders found themselves practically surrounded.

Moulmein fell, and with it the airfield, from which Japanese aircraft could now up their attacks on the capital city. There were few other forces between the Japanese Army and Rangoon, as they pushed towards the River Salween, and beyond that, the River Sittang. 17th Division was now responsible for the defence of a vast area.

On the afternoon of the 13th of February, the enemy began a 45-minute artillery and mortar bombardment of the town of Duyinzeik, which severely shocked the inexperienced and ill-trained troops of 17th Division as they took whatever cover they could find. Out of 16th and 46th Brigades, only one battalion, the 2nd KOYLI, was still in shape to meet the inevitable Japanese charge, as the dive bombers began to take their toll. Encouraging the others, they held on in the face of a devastating attack until, on the 15th they were forced to withdraw to the River Bilin.

When Wavell heard of the withdrawal, he telegraphed Hutton and spelt out the potential disaster that could result from any further retreat. He urged him to carry out a counter-offensive.

3.3 The Battle of River Bilin

As the Japanese thrust their way up the coast road towards Bilin, Brigadier Smyth, who was now in command, tried desperately to position the units of 17th Division to the best possible effect. To be sure, the situation was dire: the river was shallow enough to be forded, and however he organised his men, they would be open to flanking movements. 2nd KOYLI had joined 16th Brigade on the line of the river, so that they could meet the first attack, as 46th Brigade took up a waiting position at Kyaikto, to the northwest. 48th Brigade were held in reserve at Taung Sun, well behind the River Thebyu.

Brigadier Jones of 16th Brigade was instructed to hold the general line of the River Bilin, from the railway bridge south of Bilin to Paya. 1/9th Royal Jats were to take the sector on the right, covering the main road and railway, the survivors of 8th Burma Rifles were to man the centre, covering the village of Bilin itself, and 2nd KOYLI were to be positioned on the

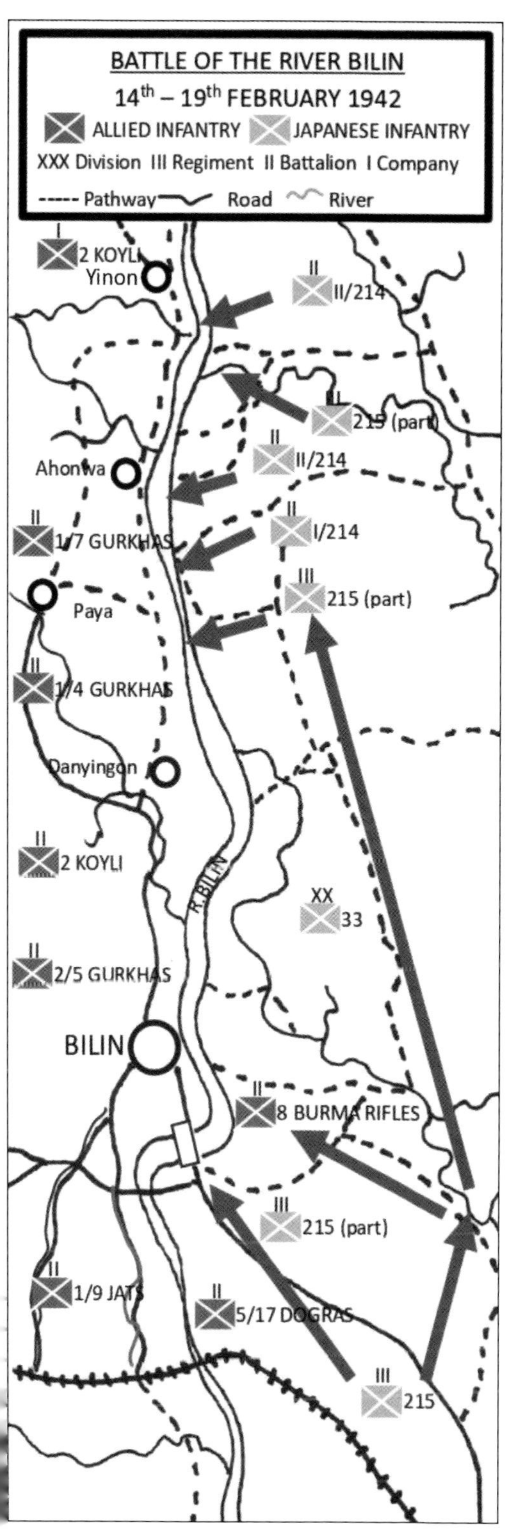

left, between Danyingon and Paya, with a detached company at Yinon. In reserve were 1/7th Gurkhas, and 5/17th Dogras were holding an outpost position on the Bilin – Thaton road, about four miles southeast of the town.

After taking Kuzeik, the Japanese 33rd Division sent 214th Regiment north, along tracks to the east of the Thaton-Bilin road, and 215th Regiment along the Duyinzeik – Thaton road, with the intention of capturing first Thaton, and then Bilin. 55th Division was ordered to hold back until Thaton had been cleared, before crossing the estuary of the River Bilin and advancing on Kyaikto. They intended to turn the right flank of the allied position on the river.

Using all their training and enthusiasm for battle, 214th Regiment sped north, to reach the River Bilin before 16th Brigade had managed to take up its positions along the riverbank, and by the time 2nd KOYLI arrived at Danyingon, on the morning of 16th February, they found the Japanese already in possession of the village. They darted amongst the trees and houses as they tried to infiltrate the enemy positions, but it was too late to move them. The single company went off to try to secure the town of Yinon, on the extreme left of the KOYLI's position.

At 9 pm, Brigadier Jones ordered his reserve battalion, the 1/7th Gurkhas, to join in the counterattack at Danyingon, knowing that since General Hutton's inspection of the positions at Kyaikto earlier in the day, there would be no possibility of withdrawing from the Bilin position until he had been able to organise a robust defence of the approaches to Rangoon. The die was cast, and all 16th Brigade could do now was hold their ground or die in the process.

Nevertheless, there was some possibility that the triumphant Japanese forces that held Danyingon could be made to think more carefully about continuing such a reckless charge into the interior of Burma, and the KOYLI led an attempt to do just that. At 8 am on the 17th, the counter-attack at Danyingon began. Both sides battled for possession of the town, in a bloody hand-to-hand fight that ebbed and flowed throughout the day. When, by late afternoon, the Japanese still clung to their positions, Smyth ordered 48th Brigade to load the men of 1/4th Gurkhas into the few available trucks and speed them to the front. At 5.30 pm they joined up with 5th Mountain Battery and joined the fight for Danyingon. The reinforced 16th Brigade swept through the village, driving the Japanese back towards the river, where they formed a tight beachhead and clung to that bank of the Bilin.

Scout units probing into the jungle, found that the advanced guard of the Japanese 214th Regiment had crossed the river between Yinon and Ahonwa during the 17th, and had built a roadblock on the Yinon Road, just south of Paya. 2nd KOYLI were sent to destroy it, and once again, the fighting was fierce and hand-to-hand, but the roadblock was well-constructed, and the defenders were able to hold their ground.

215th Regiment had meanwhile been investigating the area to the south of Bilin town bridge, and as Brigadier Jones was conscious that he had already used up his reserves, he called 5/17th Dogras back across the river. He had no idea that part of the 215th had already probed as far as the bridge itself, and as the Dogras started to cross, they were caught in a devastating crossfire that developed into a full-scale mortar barrage. The bridge was smashed to matchwood and the surviving Dogras were forced to swim to the relative safety of the west bank, leaving their weapons behind, and themselves out of the fight.

The rest of 215th were making their way along a jungle path that skirted the river without them coming within sight of the defenders on the far

Japanese soldiers make a river crossing. Unknown. (*Wikimedia Commons*)

bank. Before long, they spotted the small outpost that 8th Burma Rifles were holding on the east bank and began a powerful attack against it. The soldiers of the 8th had built shallow ramparts in the time that had been available to them, and now they tried to repel the Japanese charge with rifle fire and bayonet. Almost unbelievably, the enemy surge was held, and they started to fall back in the face of this last-ditch defence. In that moment of Japanese indecision, the men of the 8th plunged into the water and waded to the far bank. Within minutes, their former outpost was overrun. By now it was becoming obvious that defending a 15-mile front, from the mouth of the Bilin to Yinon, was beyond the capabilities of a single brigade, and for this reason, Smyth called for 2/5th Gurkha Battalion of 48th Brigade, to take over command of 8th Burma Rifles, 1/9th Jats, and the survivors of 5/17th Dogras, in the southern sector of the front. This combined force was now required to hold the line from Bilin to the mouth of the river, as the left flank of the position was secured by 2nd KOYLI, 1/4th and 1/7th Gurkhas. Although he still hoped to hold the Bilin position, Smyth was aware of the threat to his forces should they have to retire to the next defensive line, across the River Sittang. On the 17th he sent a message to Hutton, asking for assurance that 2nd Burma Brigade would send its best battalion to Mokpalin, to protect the Sittang Bridge.

Sure enough, that night, the enemy crossed the river near Bilin and attacked 8th Burma Rifles, forcing them to give ground and leave a gap in the line that exposed the left flank of the Jats. The Japanese were concentrating to the south of Zokali, on the north bank of the river estuary, whilst two battalions of 214th Regiment crossed the river near Paya and began to move west. A counter-attack by 2/5th Gurkhas had managed to close the gap near Bilin, as 2nd KOYLI again tried to clear the roadblock south of Paya, whilst trying to hold off a counterattack by the two battalions that were pushing down on Danyingon, from Paya. It was halted by a combination of stubborn grit by the KOYLI, an artillery barrage, and a rare bombing raid by the RAF.

At 4.45 pm Smyth radioed Hutton with the news that 16th Brigade, which had done most of the fighting, had been fought to a standstill by an enemy that was growing stronger by the hour. He ended: "Am taking chances on coastal landings and defence Kyaikto. Putting my last battalion (4/12th FF Regiment) into counterattack against concentration threatening left of 16th Brigade". He was now certain that his situation was rapidly becoming untenable, and after hearing that the Japanese had infiltrated the Zokali area and ordering 48th Brigade to send a company of 2/5th Gurkhas to Zothok to watch the right flank, he messaged Hutton again, with a request that any available support be sent. His report ended with an assessment of the strength of his forces: 1/7th Gurkhas, 400; 2nd KOYLI (less the detached company at Yinon), 350; 1/4th Gurkhas, nearly full strength.

In accordance with Smyth's request, Hutton ordered one company of 2nd Duke of Wellington's Regiment to protect the bridge at Sittang, and in his report to Wavell, he stated that, although the 17th Division had stopped the Japanese at the River Bilin, it was clear that the troops involved had suffered many casualties and were exhausted. He warned that, in the event of an attack by fresh enemy troops, it was likely that the Bilin position would be lost, which could lead to a retreat to the River Sittang. At that point, the best that could be hoped for would be to hold the Japanese there, with a few bridgeheads on the eastern bank, if possible.

On the 19th, Hutton was informed that 48th Brigade was beginning to identify enemy infiltration near its position, and other bad news was that the hoped-for counterattack by 4/12th Frontier Force Regiment on the left, had failed to materialise. The Japanese had penetrated the centre of the position, and it seemed highly unlikely that they could be pushed back now, as they were very well established on the west bank. The erratic reconnaissance reports all seemed to confirm that the enemy was flooding the southern areas of the current position, with the likely intention of threatening both flanks. In his forward HQ at Kyaikto, Hutton peered down gloomily at the situation map spread across the makeshift table. He knew that time was up for the men in the Bilin defence line. They had done all they could and had been badly mauled in the process. At least they had given the garrison at Rangoon some chance of preparing a defence, and now it was his duty to get them out. If they stayed any longer there was a strong possibility of them being cut off from the River Sittang, which was to be the next line of defence where 17th Division could be supported by 7th Armoured Brigade, in country suitable for armour. Smyth was given the authority to withdraw whenever he judged the time to be right.

The company of the Duke of Wellington's Regiment at the Sittang Bridge was to be relieved by 7/10th Baluch, as the rest of the regiment at Rangoon was placed under the command of 17th Division. 2nd Burma Brigade was to take control of a detachment of 2nd Indian Anti-Tank Regiment in its defence of the bridge, and they placed 3rd Burma Rifles and 7/10th Baluch around it: the only escape route for the 17th Division.

Smyth read the telegram from army headquarters, with a sense of relief:

> "G.O.C. gives permission to withdraw if necessary to keep the force intact. Heavy A.A. if still east of the Sittang is to be moved to west bank immediately."

As the counterattack by 4/12th Frontier Force Regiment, which had eventually started, was finally halted on the 19th, they were ordered to withdraw, and on the southern flank that afternoon, Japanese were encountered near Taungzun railway station. Air reconnaissance reported enemy landings on the coast to the north of the estuary, together with the arrival of enemy reinforcements in the Bilin area itself, and the danger was increasing by the hour. Smyth quickly issued instructions for an escape from the trap. 48th Brigade was to cover the withdrawal of 16th Brigade before acting as a rearguard, blowing up all the bridges in the immediate area and then withdrawing to the divisional reserve near Kyaikto.

At 11.30 pm the codeword was given and the withdrawal began. The Japanese had been held up on the Bilin River for 4 days and their best division had been made to use all its strength to finally break down the defenders in their dugouts. The advance had been stalled, and the time so gained, made it certain that 7th Armoured Brigade, due at Rangoon on the 21st, would be able to join the action on the Sittang River.

3.4 The Battle of Sittang Bridge

The frustrated Japanese Commander was determined to move his forces across country and cut off the retreating 17th Division, and on the night of the 19th February, they began to pour forward. Under cover of a thick river mist, 2nd KOYLI disengaged in the early hours of the 20th, and by nightfall, they had reached the Boyagyi Rubber Estate near Kyaikto, where they were joined later by 8th Burma Rifles and 1/9th Royal Jats. The withdrawal of 48th Brigade was blocked by a Japanese force that had managed to cross the river and infiltrate the positions of the retreating 1/9th Jats. At noon on the 20th, the RAF made another appearance with their few precious aircraft in an attempt to cover the withdrawal. Diving down towards the yellow lines that were the pathways through the forest, they sprayed the column of infantry and sent the survivors diving for cover. Unfortunately, the situation reports provided were, by necessity, very fluid indeed. Some strafing attacks were mistakenly directed against friendly forces, resulting in several fatalities. Nevertheless, the vast majority had managed to reach the narrow waters of the Thebyu Chaung (stream) by 6.30 pm.

Shortly after setting up his field HQ, Brigadier Hugh-Jones, of 48th Brigade, received a message from Smyth. This gave the Brigadier full authority

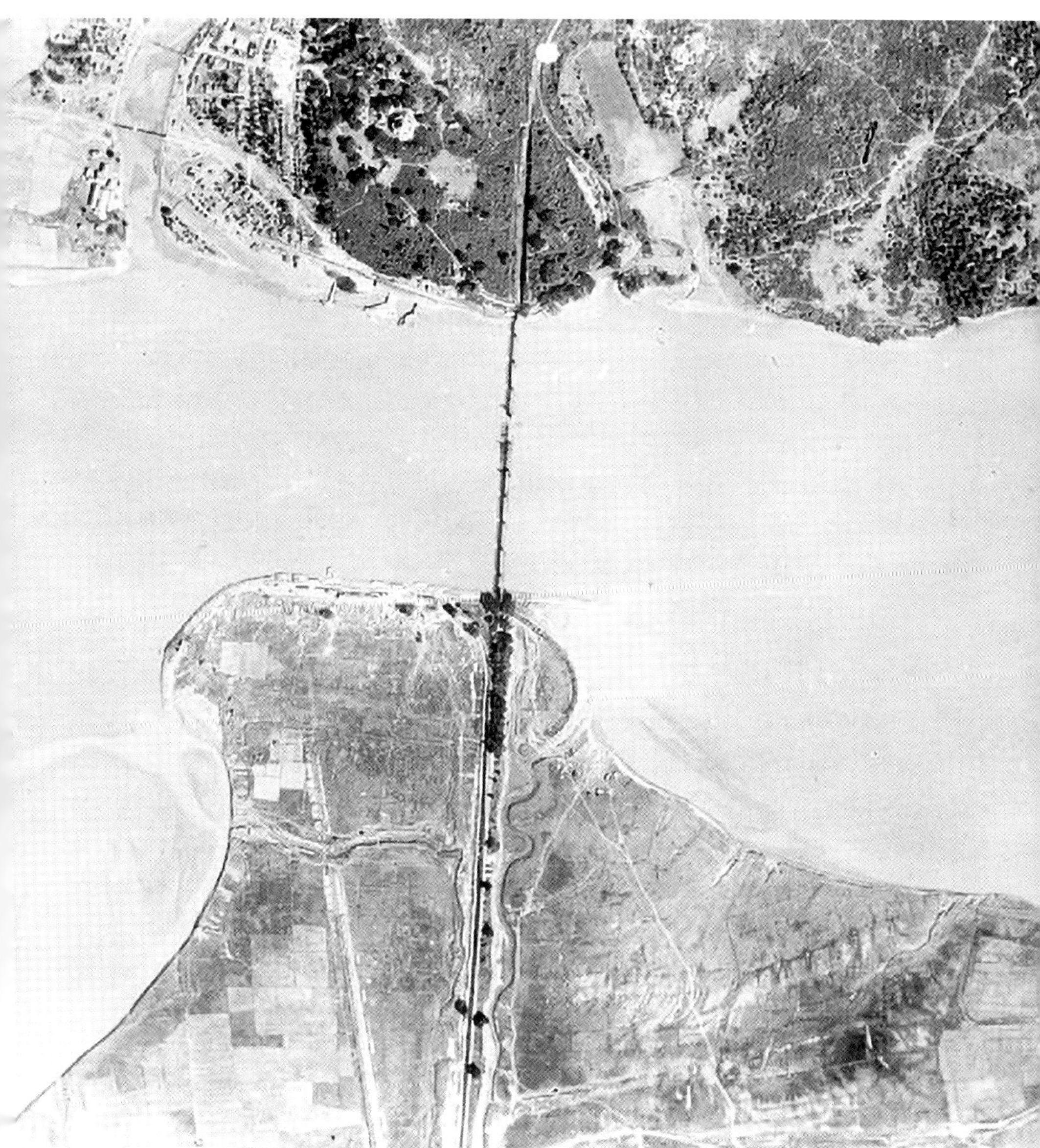

Ariel reconnaissance photograph of the bridge over the River Sittang. RAF Photographer. (*Wikimedia Commons*)

to handle the situation, as he knew best the condition of his troops. However, Smyth urged Hugh-Jones to try to get across the Thebyu Chaung before dark, if that were possible, as the situation was so fluid that the only safe place at the moment was Kyaikto.

Smyth promised to send a fleet of lorries to help Hugh-Jones, and it was not long before these arrived on the scene. The Brigadier wasted no time in hustling his tired men to the west bank of the Thebyu Chaung, demolishing the bridge after doing so. When he arrived at Kyaikto he was amazed to see that the rest of 17th Division were waiting for him, after they had cleverly disengaged during the hours of darkness and hiked the 17 miles to temporary safety. The security of the Sittang Bridge was now only 15 miles away.

The road beyond Kyaikto, already lacking the all-weather surface that had provided a reasonable line of communication so far, had been bombed and churned to an almost unrecognisable track by the traffic that had managed to attempt the retreat to the Sittang. Although he was all too aware of this, Smyth knew that he had to get the 17th out of Kyaikto as soon as possible, as the risks involved in delay were far too great. Towards mid-afternoon, he gave the order, and the division began to drag itself along the track towards the Boyagyi Rubber Estate, which was the last reasonably cultivated area before the dense jungle that stretched all the way to Mokpalin. A rail track ran between the rough road and the paddy fields that thrived on the verges of the Sittang, and the few infantrymen who began arriving on foot, ahead of the 17th Division, were told to step along its sleepers, all the way to the bridge. As they approached the crossing, they could see that it was partly obscured by a significant area of high ground, which they named "Bungalow Hill," and they were obliged to follow the rail track in a wide arc around it. Drawing closer, they realised that they were passing through a small valley between "Bungalow Hill" and another, which they referred to as "Buddha." The track then turned sharply to the left, where it crossed the bridge in the shadow of yet another hill that, because of the structure built on top of it, was called "Pagoda."

The bridge was a disappointment. Even now, the few lorries that had arrived on the scene were filing into position to negotiate the narrow decking, and the queue was growing longer by the minute. The surface had been constructed to take both rail and road traffic, but not together, and as the lorry drivers inched across, their eyes glued to the narrow strip of wood along which their tyres had to roll, the infantrymen stumbled along between them, always aware of the possibility of being crushed. The agonisingly slow crossing passed over eleven spans that were each 150 feet wide and towered above the boats of a ferry service that struggled to deal with a strong tidal bore in the widening river.

Smyth gazed down at the pitifully small force that had been allocated to the defence of the bridge and he knew that one company of the Duke of Wellington's Regiment, and the surviving 250 members of 3rd Burma Rifles, could not possibly stand up to a heavy attack. He knew that if the crossing was this tortuous when only a handful of vehicles and men were trying to negotiate it, the problems involved in getting the whole of the 17th Division to the other side of the river might well be insurmountable, especially under fire and with only a tiny group of battered, badly equipped soldiers to hold back the enemy.

The leading brigades of the 17th Division were still in the area of the rubber plantation, and the entire division was exhausted by its four-day battling withdrawal. The air was almost entirely dominated by the Japanese fighters that regularly patrolled above the pathways through the forest and ruled out any daytime attempt to use motor transport. All the time, the forward units of Japanese infantry were moving around the division's northern flank and pushing up the rail track that led to Sittang. The 15 miles to the bridge would be full of danger.

Early on the 21st Smyth ordered the Malerkotla Field Company and 4/12th Frontier Force Regiment up to the bridge, where they were to complete preparations for demolition and strengthen its defences. He was informed that 17th Division Headquarters was to lead the main withdrawal, followed by 48th and 16th Brigades, with 46th Brigade acting as rearguard, and he hoped that they would arrive in a steady stream, although he knew this to be very unlikely.

The Malerkotla Field Company and 4/12th Frontier Force Regiment moved off early in the morning and were followed by Divisional Headquarters at 10 am. 48th Brigade was supposed to cover the rear of the HQ force, but in the event, was not able to move off until very late in the morning. The blazing sun beat down on the hard-baked road as the convoy threw up a cloud of thick red dust that choked and blinded the men and mules, as they were repeatedly bombed and strafed. The mules carrying the wireless sets broke free and galloped off into the jungle.

That morning, British air reconnaissance had reported an enemy column of three hundred vehicles moving through Kyaikto to Kinmun, and all available aircraft at Rangoon were scrambled for an attack. Unfortunately, they were mistakenly directed to the Kyaikto-Mokpalin Road, and the attack ripped into 17th Division as they tried to take cover in the roadside jungle. The mounting casualties brought the march to a halt, and as the stifling day ended, the Malerkotla Field Company and 4/12th FF Regiment arrived at the bridge to find that very little had been done to prime it for demolition.

That night, Divisional HQ, 7/10th Baluch, and 1/4th Gurkhas camped at the quarries just outside Mokpalin, and 2/5th and 1/3rd Gurkhas halted on the rail track. The 2nd KOYLI, with the rest of 16th Brigade, were in the rubber plantation, with 46th Brigade still holding the rearguard position west of Kyaikto. The Frontier Force unit sent to guard the flank of the column had been attacked by a strong Japanese force at 2pm but had been unable to get news of this to HQ until evening, after falling back along jungle tracks to a position near Sittang.

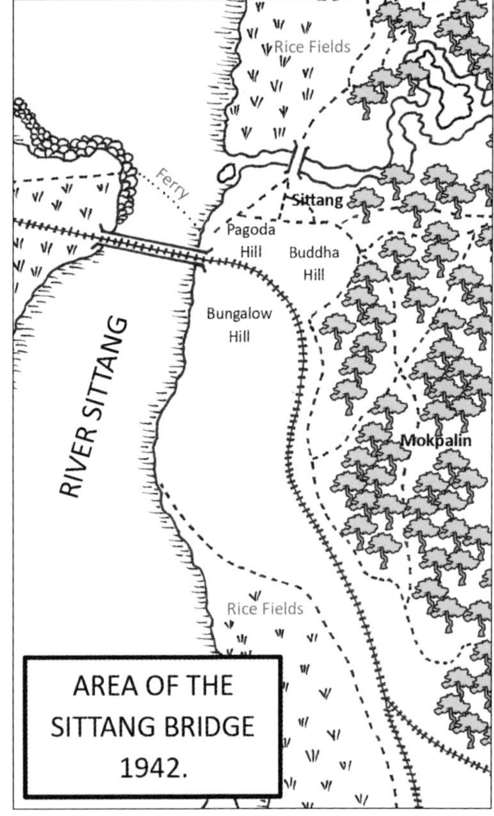

For most of the day, Divisional HQ was unable to make radio contact with either Rangoon, 16th, or 46th Brigades, and it was midnight before they received a message telling them of the possibility of a Japanese parachute landing at the bridge. Smyth immediately ordered 1/4th Gurkhas to move up to the bridge, cross it, take the company of the Duke of Wellington's Regiment under command, and watch for an attack by paratroops at first light. At 1 am he advised 16th and 46th Brigades that, as a strong Japanese force was probably moving around the division's flank, they should begin their move to the bridge as soon as possible. Six hours before this message was received, Brigadier Ekin of 46th Brigade had reported to "Jonah" Jones of the 16th that his rearguard units had encountered enemy patrols. He was convinced that the Japanese were trying to outflank the division from the north.

The two brigadiers realised that the track ahead would be blocked by 48th Brigade, which would have to set off before they could move towards the bridge, so they decided to wait a while before moving off in stages: 16th Brigade would be the first to go at 6 am, with the rearguard 46th immediately behind. 4th Burma Rifles would withdraw along the rail track. Smyth's message at 1 am did nothing to change their plans, as it would take several hours to get 48th Brigade out of the way.

At 4 am, Divisional HQ moved towards the bridge, preceded by their transport. They stood back as the lorries started to cross, and watched in horror as one of the first in the convoy ran off the decking and fell into the supporting girders. It took two hours before the bridge was cleared and the crossing could begin again; a delay that caused a massive tailback, made worse as the transport of 48th, 16th and 46th Brigades began to arrive. By 8.30 am, only a small portion of the division had managed to cross when the column was hit by a barrage of gunfire from the northeast of the bridgehead, as Japanese soldiers swarmed out of the jungle and overran the detachment of 3rd Burma Rifles that was holding this area. An immediate counterattack drove the enemy back, and at 10 am, Smyth ordered Hugh-Jones of the 48th to take command of all the troops holding the bridgehead. 24th Field Company was ordered to destroy all the power-driven boats at the ferry dock which could not be manned. The ferry itself was destroyed in a Japanese bombardment later in the day.

Meanwhile, the Japanese were attacking the jam of transport vehicles on the Kyaikto Road, and 2/5th Gurkhas, the next battalion in the line of march, was quickly ordered to clear the high ground on the eastern side of the road. They were to keep the enemy back until all the transport had crossed the bridge. In view of the fact that the mules had stampeded with all the mortars, they had to do this without any form of artillery support, and they were shelled all the way to the railway station at Mokalpin, where they set up their HQ. The next battalion in line was 1/3rd Gurkhas, and as the commanders of the two trailing battalions had not been informed of the exact situation at the bridge, they decided that it would be prudent to assume that both Pagoda and Buddha Hills were now in enemy hands. Their plan was to send 1/3rd Gurkhas to take back the hills, under cover of the artillery that was now beginning to arrive, as 2/5th continued to hold on to the high ground to the east of Mokpalin. The artillery bombardment started at 2 pm and the Gurkhas charged up both Pagoda and Buddha Hills, driving the shocked Japanese troops from the heights in a chaotic scramble such as they had not experienced in the whole of the campaign so far. The bridgehead forces were now able to attack the disorganised enemy who had just arrived on Bungalow Hill, before moving to relieve the Gurkhas on Pagoda. As they did this, the Japanese gathered themselves together and were bolstered by reinforcements to stage a counterattack. When it went in, the 1/3rd Gurkhas were able to fall back to Buddha Hill, as the bridge force defended Pagoda Hill, but these actions had now created a gap between them and 2/5th Gurkhas at Mokpalin.

Further south, 46th Brigade had halted to allow the rearguard to catch up, but they failed to notify 16th Brigade ahead of them. The 16th continued to march north, creating a 1-mile gap between the two forces., and the Japanese happened to arrive just as this gap had opened. The enemy commander quickly realised the situation and ordered his men to build a roadblock, using the plentiful trees at the roadside. When they arrived, the leading battalion of 46th Brigade, 3/7th Gurkhas, charged forward in an attempt to clear the blockage, but behind them, the rest of the brigade was suddenly attacked by an overwhelming Japanese force that sent in a deluge of machine gun and mortar fire, before surging out of the trees to engage in a confused, hand-to-hand fight. Although the Japanese were driven back, Ekin decided to lead a party of 500 men through the dense jungle, to keep them at bay until the main force had passed through, and although 200 of his group were lost, this action allowed 3/7th Gurkhas to clear the roadblock with the help of the remnants of the Duke of Wellington's Regiment.

As darkness fell, Ekin's group encountered a party of Japanese coming up the rail track, and the fight that followed caused them to fall further behind the main force, which had arrived at Mokalpin to meet 4th Burma Rifles and a scene of total confusion. When 16th Brigade arrived, Brigadier Jones took command and quickly organised a perimeter defence around the village. Two companies of 2nd KOYLI took up position in line with the expected spearhead of the Japanese advance, but no sooner had the perimeter been set up, the Japanese attacked it from three sides and the artillery batteries were forced to fire over open sights, at an enemy who flitted in and out of the shafts of moonlight that filtered through the thick forest canopy. The defence held firm, but that night, when Jones tried to get through to Smyth by radio, the atmospheric conditions interfered with the signal, and he realised he was on his own. The path to the bridge was dominated by the Buddha and Pagoda Hills, and as Jones was also forced to presume these to be in the hands of the Japanese, he determined to attack them at dawn.

At the bridgehead, the three central spans had been wired for demolition, but the cables were too short to allow the firing point to be located clear of the bridge. Hugh-Jones was still unable to contact 16th and 46th Brigades, but from the reports of the few men who began to arrive at the bridgehead, it seemed that the Japanese attacks had shattered the column and wrecked their transport. The bridge itself was now coming under fire and Hugh-Jones asked the officer in charge of the demolition team if he could guarantee its destruction if he delayed the order until the following morning. The officer confirmed that, due to the exposed position of the demolition firing point, the men sent out on the bridge to blow it would be easy targets for the Japanese snipers in daylight conditions. He could give no guarantee, and after a meeting with his battalion leaders, Hugh-Jones decided that it was too dangerous to delay the demolition and so leave the road to Rangoon open to the enemy. His Staff Officer had been able to make telephone contact with Brigadier Cowan at divisional HQ in Abya, and over an extremely bad line, he said that it was unlikely that the bridge could be held for more than an hour if the Japanese attacked. Cowan asked if "Jonah Jones" had made it across, and the Staff Officer stated that he had. In fact, "Jonah" Jones was still in the jungle on the eastern bank, along with 2nd KOYLI and the rest of his 16th Brigade. It is possible that the Staff Officer only heard the word "Jones" and thought that Cowan was asking about Hugh-Jones. As a result of this, when Cowan relayed the conversation to Smyth it seemed clear that the main body of the division had crossed the river, and the Brigadier consequently relayed Smyth's authority for Hugh-Jones to blow the bridge as soon as he saw fit. The decision was made at 5.30 am, and when all the covering troops were across, the demolition charges sent two spans of the bridge crashing down into the water below.

The sound of the explosion drowned out the rattle of machine gun fire and sent thousands of birds screeching into the air above the jungle, signalling to the survivors of 16th and 46th Brigades that their only route of escape had now been slammed shut. "Jonah" Jones was not ready to give in yet. He immediately cancelled his planned counterattack and gave orders that a detail of his exhausted men should begin to make rafts, as the remainder dug in to protect their position. When night fell, they were going to thin out as they withdrew to the water's edge, climbed aboard the rafts, and set off for the safety of the western bank.

All through that morning, the Japanese, supported by artillery and mortar fire, tried to break into the Mokpalin position, but the defence held firm. Just after 11 am, the enemy aircraft came in and some of their bombs exploded amongst a few boxes of ammunition, causing the surrounding jungle to burst into flames. Jones could wait no longer: he ordered a general withdrawal at 2 pm.

The 2nd KOYLI had been divided along the defensive perimeter, and now the companies that were holding the more northerly of those positions were ordered to retreat. They withdrew to the river in good order, as they tried to stick together as a unit, but then it was a case of each man finding a suitable place to enter the water. Even then, they tried to stick together, as the swimmers dragged the non-swimmers through the dark river, towards the safety of the far bank. Some men swam back across, some several times, to bring across the wounded, yet many were drowned in the swirling, mile-wide torrent. A few men decided to take their chances in the jungle, working their way north, where they managed to cross at a narrower point in the river. Some even reached the bridge itself and constructed a lifeline. Although the Japanese snipers picked off many of these men, as they dangled in the air, more than 300 of the rearguard managed to escape in this way.

The troops still holding the southern sector of the Mokpalin perimeter were 8th Burma Rifles, two companies of 2nd KOYLI, the HQ Company of 3/7th Gurkhas, and the remnants of 5/17th Dogras. They had not received the order to retreat and continued to hold up the Japanese force that was attempting to join in the attack on the riverbank. They realised that the situation was now desperate, as the glowing tracer bullets were arcing out of the black jungle, on all sides. At about 7.30 pm, they started to withdraw in small groups, and as individual soldiers. Some began to crawl through the deep undergrowth, within feet of the Japanese gun positions, and this game of cat-and-mouse continued until all were either captured or had managed to get to the river and swim to safety. The majority were destined for over three years in the appalling conditions of a Japanese prisoner-of-war camp.

As a fighting force, 17th Division had almost ceased to exist, but the eighty officers and 3,404 shattered, wounded, and disorientated men who remained, made their weary way to the Pegu area and a short period of rest, leaving behind most of their guns, transport, and equipment. They included 206 KOYLI.

3.5 Retreat from Rangoon

General Iida now ordered 33rd and 55th Divisions to cross the Sittang and capture Rangoon by a rapid advance.

On 5th March, there seemed only two courses of action open to the allies: to close the gap between 1st Burma and 17th Divisions, or to accept defeat and leave Rangoon. Abandoning the people of the city to the tender mercies of the Japanese was unthinkable, and Hutton therefore instructed the remnants of 17th Division, reinforced by 63rd Brigade, and 7th Armoured Brigade, to take the offensive in the Waw area, as 1st Burma Division advanced south from Nyaunglebin.

At Waw, 7th Armoured found the Japanese in full control and impossible to move. On the second day, a scout patrol encountered Japanese on the main road south of Pyinbon, and at Kyaikhla, where once again the enemy refused to be driven back. The village of Payagyi was overrun in a night attack before patrols discovered more Japanese west of the River Pegu, well north of Pegu itself. This was the expected outflanking movement, and soon the road south of Pegu had been cut, as an armoured unit was reported to have passed through Paunggyi, making for the Prome Road.

Having been informed of developments in Burma, Prime Minister Winston Churchill sent General Harold Alexander to Rangoon, with instructions to take control of the situation. On his arrival, Alexander learnt that, although reinforcements were now being concentrated 12 miles north of Rangoon, 7th Armoured and 48th Brigade were in the vicinity of Pegu, where they

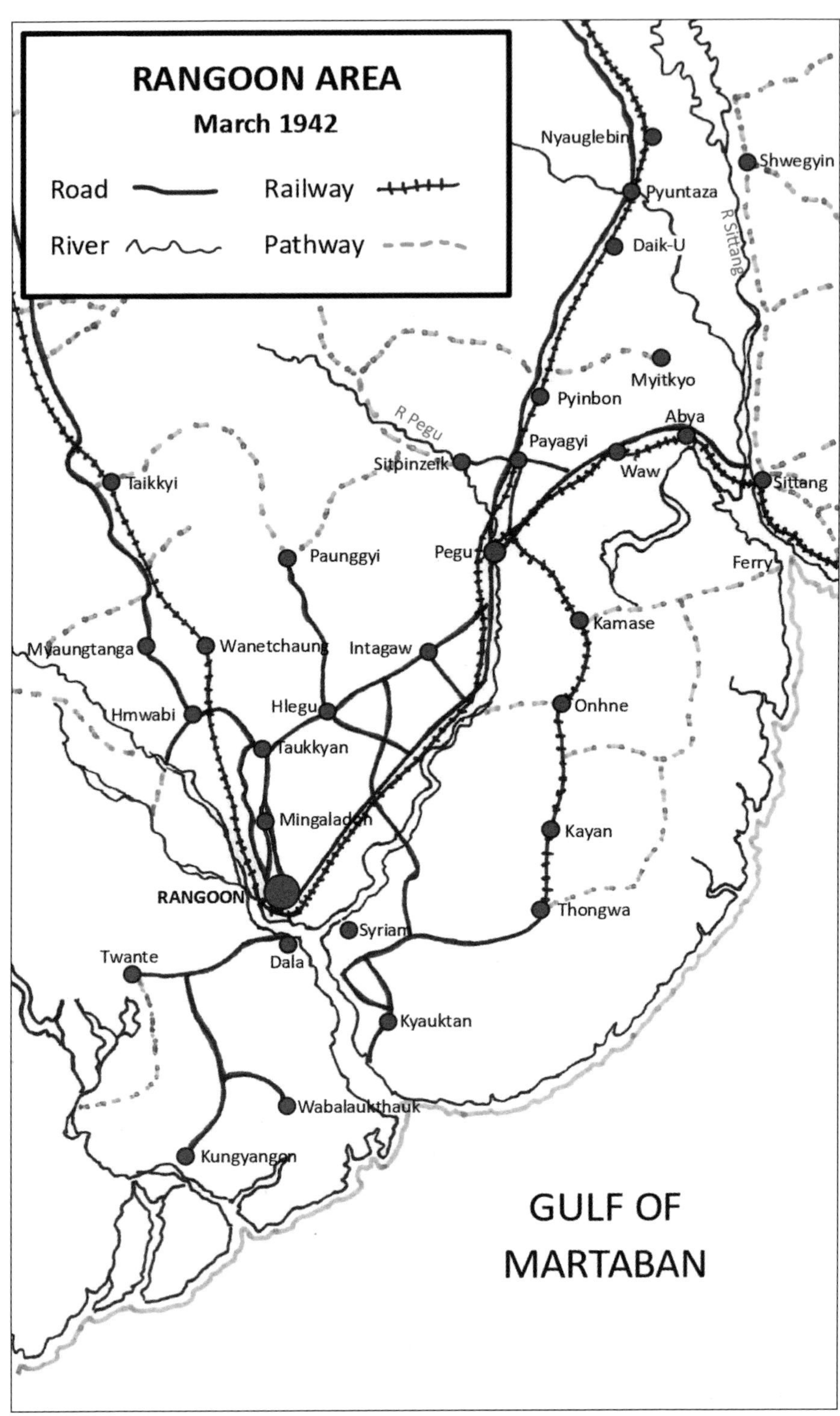
RANGOON AREA
March 1942
Road
Railway
River
Pathway
Nyauglebin
Shwegyin
Pyuntaza
R Sittang
Daik-U
Myitkyo
Pyinbon
R Pegu
Abya
Payagyi
Waw
Sitpinzeik
Sittang
Taikkyi
Paunggyi
Pegu
Ferry
Kamase
Myaungtanga
Wanetchaung
Intagaw
Hmwabi
Hlegu
Onhne
Taukkyan
Mingaladon
Kayan
RANGOON
Thongwa
Syriam
Twante
Dala
Kyauktan
Wabalaukthauk
Kungyangon
GULF OF
MARTABAN

were engaged in a deadly fight to prevent the Japanese splitting 17th and 1st Burma Divisions. As they were doing this, more enemy units were pushing towards the Rangoon-Prome Road, with the obvious intention of cutting it.

Although the defending forces battled hard to save Rangoon, by 6th March it was obvious that the situation was beyond rescue, and on that day, Alexander made his decision to evacuate the city. Its garrison was to move up the Prome Road to Tharrawaddy, covered by an advanced guard of 7th Hussars, a battery of 1st Indian Field Regiment, and two companies of 2nd KOYLI. The 17th Division, with 7th Armoured Brigade, was ordered to hold the town of Hlegu until the retreating column had passed Taukkyan, at which time they were to form up as the rearguard. As the garrison reached Taukkyan they learnt that the Japanese had established a roadblock a few miles up the road, and an attack was quickly organised. It failed. A second attack was launched at dusk, and it too was driven back.

Meanwhile, 17th Division was also being forced back to Taukkyan, and soon the crossroads there were jammed with men and vehicles. The southern skyline was thick with black smoke from the burning oil refinery at Rangoon, and when the advanced guard, with 2nd KOYLI, arrived at Tharrawaddy soon after midday, they were told of the roadblock that was holding up the retreating column. There was nothing for it except go back to help, but as they began to arrive on the scene they were met by a barrage of British shells: the overshoots from the forces still trying to destroy the roadblock from the south. Their radio was out of commission, and they had no alternative but to go back to Tharrawaddy, leaving a detachment at Wanetchaung.

Eventually the Japanese manning the roadblock were driven off, and at 10 am on the 8th, the Rangoon garrison, followed by 17th Division, with 16th Brigade as rearguard, was able to recommence the withdrawal. They were almost totally cut off from help, relying on a few air drops for supply, and facing the prospect of a long retreat to India, through the trackless jungle.

It was simply a question of how long the small British force, aided by 5th and 6th Chinese Armies, could hold central and upper Burma. General Iida was very aware of the opportunity that beckoned him, and by 7th March he had already directed 15th Army to seek out and destroy allied forces wherever they were encountered. He was planning on a decisive battle near Mandalay that would wipe out the entire allied force in Burma by the end of May. Indeed, Iida had every cause to be confident. To meet the Japanese offensive, Alexander had two weak divisions, an armoured brigade, and two Chinese armies, each of which was the equivalent of a division. Air support totalled 150 aircraft. Three-quarters of this force was needed to defend the vital oilfields at Yenangyaung and the new base area near Mandalay. The 6th Chinese Army was in the Shan States, protecting the right flank and guarding against any Japanese advance northwards from Indochina, so it could take no part in the upcoming battle for central Burma which, as Alexander knew, could only be another case of holding on for as long as possible. To achieve this, he decided to concentrate the British forces in the Irrawaddy Valley, where they could also protect the oilfields, and keep 5th Chinese Army in the Sittang Valley to cover the direct road and railway leading to Mandalay. Unfortunately, the Chinese commanders were reluctant to move their forces south of Toungoo, so the British units in the Irrawaddy Valley had to be pulled back to the Prome area. These were 1st Burma Division, currently in the Sittang Valley, and 17th Division, which was reforming at Tharrawaddy.

Wavell dismissed Major General Smyth on the spot, blaming the loss of Rangoon on his premature decision to blow the Sittang Bridge.

3.6 Burcorps

Lieutenant General William Slim arrived at Magwe on 19th March and assumed command of "Burcorps": the new designation for the combined force of 1st Burma Division, 17th Indian Division, and 7th Armoured Brigade. The decimated 2nd KOYLI were now combined with 2nd Battalion the Duke of Wellington's Regiment, which had also lost many men, to form "A" Battalion, nicknamed "The King's Own Dukes", and remained assigned to 16th Infantry Brigade.

William Slim. Commander of "Burcorps." No 9 Army Film & Photographic Unit. (*Wikimedia Commons*)

On 12th March, Alexander had ordered 17th Division to withdraw to Okpo, as 1st Burma Division moved back through the Chinese forces, to be transported by rail to

Taungdwingyi. The 17th Division reached Okpo with little opposition. From there, they carried out a series of raids behind Japanese lines, during which they drove the enemy out of Letpadan. The 1st Burma Division was forced to fight all the way to Yedashe and the train for Taungdwingyi.

By 17th March, 17th Division and 7th Armoured Brigade had been concentrated in the Prome area. 2nd KOYLI, with the rest of 16th Brigade, were stationed between Sinmizwe and Prome.

The Chinese forces had been defeated at Toungoo, by the time Alexander met Slim on 1st April, and they agreed that it would be suicide to leave 17th Division where it was. 16th Brigade was holding the Paukkaung Road, just east of Prome, and at midnight they were suddenly confronted by a Japanese motorised column. The enemy troops poured out of the lorries and the battered remnants of 2nd KOYLI joined their comrades in trying to hold back the tide. As some of the enemy engaged the defenders, the majority of 215th Regiment swept past them towards the town, threatening to overwhelm the forces stationed there. At the same time, 214th Regiment made an attack on the town of Hmawza, and even though they were driven back, it became obvious that the only option available to the two brigades stationed there, was a night retreat through the screen provided by 16th Brigade, to take up a position further along the road.

On the morning of 2nd April, news came through of another Japanese column approaching Duyingabo, in a move that seemed certain to cut 17th Division's only escape route. Brigadier Cowan, who had replaced Smyth as commander of 17th Division, radioed Slim and informed him of the situation, whereupon he was given clearance to march for Duyingabo, as soon as possible.

In Burma, the month of April usually sees temperatures soar. The 17th were marching into the most arid part of the country, where waterholes were few and far between. As the infantry dragged themselves through the seemingly endless jungle, the Japanese Air Force appeared through the choking cloud of dust that rose from the hard-baked road into the clear sky. Time and again, the fighter bombers flew down the avenues between the trees, strafing and bombing the troops as they dived for cover. When darkness fell, the survivors were able to complete their march to Duyingabo. Next day, they set off again as the sun began to rise, and the Japanese aircraft rose with it, attacking the desperate column all the way to Allanmyo, where it passed through the outlying units of 1st Burma Brigade. 2nd KOYLI were amongst the last to make it to safety, and their former brigade gave them a warm welcome, before they collapsed into an exhausted sleep.

Alexander was acutely aware that the lack of allied aircraft had allowed the Japanese Air Force complete freedom to attack ground troops whenever they pleased. He was concerned about the condition of all the forces under his command, and on the 5th, he cabled Wavell to share these thoughts, asking that fighters be made available, along with more transport aircraft to fly in reinforcements. The 17th Division was, he said, tired and dispirited, which was the main reason for the defeat at Prome. Unit commanders were complaining that they had been fighting for over three months without a break, and until reinforcements were made available, their units would get progressively weaker.

This was the situation as the stage was set for the main battle for central Burma. The Japanese Army was well-trained, experienced, and organised. Their Air Force had total superiority, and sea communications were secure, so that reinforcements could be easily transported through the newly captured port at Rangoon. The future looked bleak for the few who were to stand in their way.

3.7 The Battle for Central Burma

The Japanese victory over the Chinese forces at Toungoo had opened the road through the Keren Hills, into the Shan States. On 2nd April, General Iida arrived there and set up his HQ for the next stage of his plan to conquer Burma. A top-secret document had been found amongst the detritus left by the defeated Chinese, which clearly indicated that most of their remaining forces were already south of Mandalay, and Iida now planned to create a start line that ran from Loikaw, through Yamethin, to Yenangyaung. The Burma Road was a vital supply link to China, and now the Japanese planned to cut it in the vicinity of Lashio, before turning to trap all the allied forces in a pocket, with their backs to the mighty River Irrawaddy.

56th Division was to move from their position at Bawlake, through Loikaw and Hsipaw, to Lashio, and they were to be provided with lorries, a regiment of tanks, and two artillery battalions, to help them deliver a quick and decisive blow. Meanwhile, 18th and 55th Divisions were to follow the main road and rail link, all the way to Mandalay. As the 18th cut the Burma Road to the east of the town, the 55th would push the retreating allies up against the river. In the meantime, 33rd Division was to outflank the retreating allies by striking out for Myingyan, to the west of Mandalay, and to cross the river to Shwebo, if necessary. General Alexander had decided to make a stand on the line between Minhla, Taungdwingyi, Pyinmana, and Loikaw. As can be seen from a brief look at a map, Iida was several steps ahead of him.

By 6th April, General Slim had allocated 16th and 63rd Brigades to defend the extreme left of his new line, from Migyaungye to Satthwa, a few miles south of Taungdwingi. His plan was to send scouting parties along the available tracks to watch for any enemy columns moving north towards Taungdwingyi. Any such move could then be attacked in its flank. The area now covered by Burcorps was sparsely populated. Streams cut into the hills, but apart from the offshoots of the Irrawaddy, these were dry at this time of year; something that Slim had been forced to consider, as water supply by road would be both difficult and hazardous.

General Iida had refined his plans for the last stage of his invasion of Burma. The flank of the assault on Yenangyaung was to be protected by 215th Regiment, as 213th Regiment advanced to capture Magwe, and 214th Regiment moved to seize the ferry over the river north of Yenangyaung. Both attacks were to be supported by 33rd Mountain Artillery Regiment and would, if successful, effectively cut off the British line of retreat.

The first clashes occurred on the evening of the 9th April and seemed to indicate that the Japanese were advancing towards Migyaungye. 1st Burma brigade was sent forward to hit the enemy flank as they approached 13th Brigade's area. The fighting went on for three days as the Japanese probed both sides of 13th Brigade's position in the line, but finally, the allies had to fall back when it was discovered that the enemy had occupied a village just to the south of Migyaungye and were moving north in strength. When a battalion was sent to secure Migyaungye, they discovered that it had already been taken and the defending company destroyed. Attempts to retake it failed, and 1st Burma Brigade were ordered to withdraw, as they were in danger of being surrounded. Slim was not prepared to withdraw from the road, as he knew that this would seriously threaten the line, and indeed the whole defence of the country. 2nd Burma Brigade were ordered to send 5/1st Punjab and 7th Burma Rifles across the river to Magwe, whilst 2nd

Japanese troops advance on a Burmese oilfield, 1942. Unknown. (*Online Collection | National Army Museum, London* (*nam.ac.uk*))

KOYLI were sent to Myingun, as 13th Brigade went to help 1st Burma Brigade to disengage. Both brigades were then to withdraw to the line of the Yin Chaung, a stream that ran into the Irrawaddy at a point on the east bank, just north of Minhla. As the next source of water was forty miles to the north, abandoning this line of defence would be a serious matter indeed, and Slim attempted to bolster it by sending 2nd Royal Tank Regiment to guard the ford where the road crossed the stream. They were to carry 2nd KOYLI with them, as far as Myingun.

In the early hours of 14th April, the KOYLI were surrounded and steadily withdrew to a tight defensive perimeter around Myingun. 1st Burma Division was also forced back to a position between the riverbank and the road. A reserve, codenamed Magforce, was hurriedly formed in Magwe, as 2nd Burma Brigade withdrew to Minbu. By the end of the day, the KOYLI had been reduced to 150 men. These few broke out of Myingun, and in a dawn charge that took them across the Yin Chaung, they managed to join up with Magforce before taking up a covering position at the road junction 7 miles northeast of Magwe, so that the rest of the 1st Burma Division could begin to fall back across country at 9.30 am. During the day, Burcorps ordered 2nd Burma Brigade to withdraw from Minbu to Saku.

To the north, the 1st Burma Division's transport and supply column, which had been ordered to be the first to withdraw, had just passed through the blazing town of Yenangyaung when they were halted by an enemy roadblock. In their rear, the ford over the Pin Chaung, which joined the Irrawaddy just north of Yenangyaung, was seized by the Japanese, who immediately attacked the town from that direction, effectively cutting off 1st Burma Division's line of retreat and separating it from its supply column.

3.8 The Battle of Yenangyaung

The allies had to stay close to their only water supply, and the Japanese knew it, but the leading units of 38th Chinese Division were now beginning to arrive from the north, and during the day, Slim arranged that two Chinese regiments, supported by the elements of 7th Armoured Brigade north of the Pin Chaung, should attack at dawn on the 18th to clear the ford, as the forces in Yenangyaung broke out. After breaking the roadblock to the north of the town, the next objective of the division would be Twingon.

The sun glared down on the barren landscape around Yenangyaung, drying out the web of steep-sided streams, as black smoke from the burning town and the surrounding oilfields, choked and blinded the retreating allies. For two days they fought it out with the exultant Japanese forces. The shortage of ammunition meant that only one artillery piece was available to support

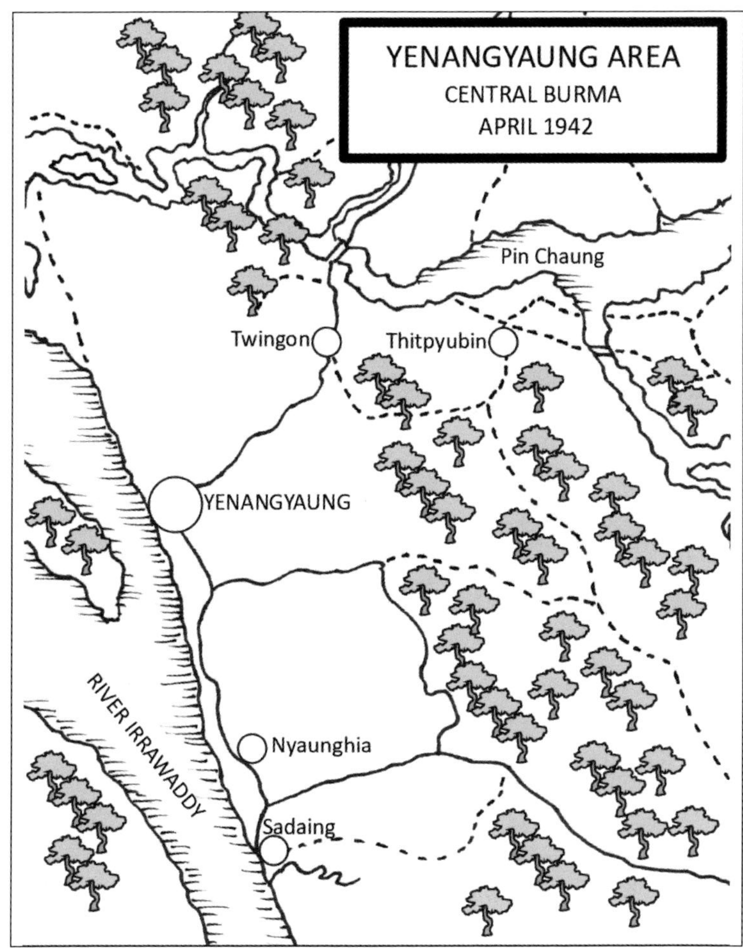

the infantry, who tried in vain to hold onto the riverbank as the Japanese moved south along it. The forces sent towards Twingon were faced with the task of clearing the enemy from the two ridges that looked down on the town. Having worked their way around the outskirts, two companies of the 1st Royal Inniskilling Fusiliers were delighted to be met by a unit of Chinese soldiers. In fact, they were Japanese, and the Inniskillings were quickly taken prisoner.

During the afternoon, the divisional transport had been able to press forward again, and as daylight faded, the whole division had been able to concentrate south of Twingon. Major General Scott believed 1st Burma Division should abandon its transport so that it could move across country and escape encirclement, but Slim still hoped that the intervention of the

Chinese would swing the balance, and he ordered Scott to hold fast in anticipation of a Chinese attack on the next morning. Scott had no choice but to order his exhausted men, who had been fighting all day, without water, and in the baking sun, to set up a defensive perimeter. Sure enough, just before dawn the next day, the Japanese began to close in from the north, west, and south. As 13th Brigade fought off an attack from the direction of Twingon, the enemy mortars and heavy machine guns began to take their toll in the growing light, and 2nd KOYLI, together with 2/7th Rajputs, began to circle around to attack the Japanese positions from behind, but aware that Chinese forces were in the area, and with the recent case of misidentification in mind, Burcorps recalled them before they could make contact.

At noon, a company of 1st West Yorkshire Regiment, supported by tanks, had forced a crossing of the Pin Chaung, well east of the ford, and had made contact with 2nd KOYLI. The opportunity to open the road for the division seemed within grasp. However, a report then came into Burcorps HQ that the Japanese were in Kyaukpadaung, and all troops that had crossed the Pin Chaung were recalled, to join in the defence of the vital road junction at Chauk. When the advance force arrived at Kyaukpadaung, they quickly realised that the soldiers occupying the town were Chinese, not Japanese, and with this final mistake, the last chance to open the road for 1st Burma Division was lost.

Although the Japanese had been deprived of their vital oilfields, the allied forces had suffered badly in the fighting around Yenangyaung. They had lost a fifth of their strength, together with most of their transport and equipment, including four 3.7-inch howitzers, four 25-pounders, and almost all their Bofors guns and mortars.

They were drawing ever closer to the Indian frontier, and Alexander's plan was still in place. If Mandalay was lost, 1st Burma Division was to protect the road that ran through Kalewa to the border crossing at Rikhawdar. 17th Division, less one brigade, was to retreat along the line, Mandalay-Shwebo-Katha, to cover the escape route from Ledo, through the Hukawng Valley. 7th Armoured Brigade, accompanied by an infantry brigade from 17th Division, was to take the Burma Road through to China, as were those Chinese forces west of the Salween; and members of the 6th Chinese Army who were still east of the Salween would reach home through Keng Tung.

3.9 The Final Retreat

So, Burcorps began the final leg of the retreat on the night of 25th April. By the last day of the month, the allies were across the Irrawaddy and were ordered to hold the line of the river until the rearguard units had caught up, after which the corps would march up the River Chindwin, towards Imphal.

As part of 16th Brigade, 2nd KOYLI were at Ondaw, preparing to move on Myinmu, and the Japanese attempt to trap the allies in the loop of the Irrawaddy had failed. General Iida had been frustrated yet again, and in a final attempt to crush the forces that had slipped through his fingers so many times, he unleashed all four of his divisions in a furious charge that cut wide and deep into the new lines of retreat. 56th and 18th Divisions were launched towards Lashio and the Salween, as 55th Division cleared out the Mandalay area, and 33rd Division pushed north towards Shwebo, sending part of its force to cut the line of retreat that ran through the Katha-Bhamo area. The attack on Lashio was completed more quickly

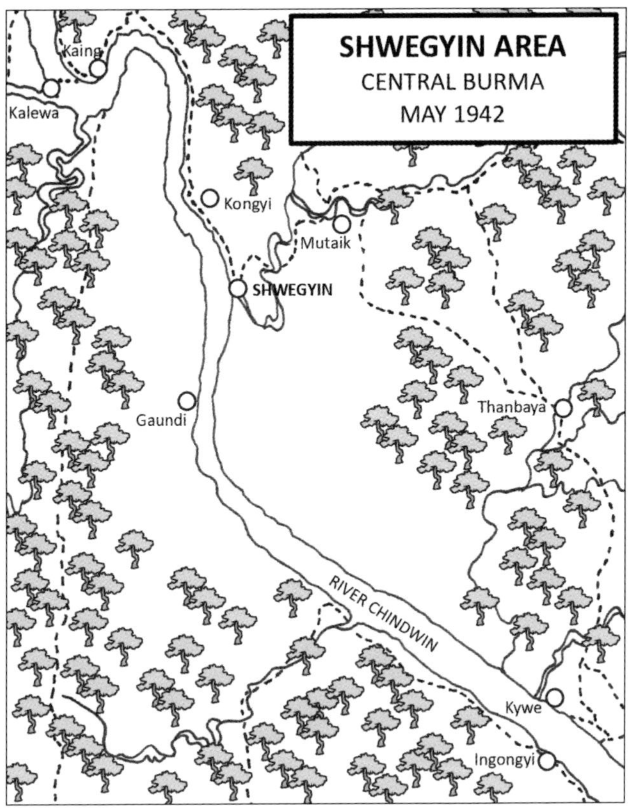

than had been anticipated, allowing Iida to swing 56th Division towards Bhamo and Myitkyina. On the 26th, the advance forces of 33rd Division began their approach to Myingyan, just after 2nd KOYLI had left the village of Ondaw, a few miles to the west. The Japanese momentum was now unstoppable, and by nightfall on the 30th, the first troops of 215th Regiment found themselves looking across at the town of Monywa, from the west bank of the Chindwin.

The allied forces in Monywa were in the process of evacuating the civilian administration staff and their families, who had been sent from army HQ at Shwebo during the previous day. Most were now waiting for further transport at Alon, just north of Monywa, when the Japanese suddenly appeared on the opposite bank, sending artillery, mortar, and machine gun fire into the terrified crowds. Upon hearing the commotion, Slim believed that the town was being assaulted, although the Japanese had made no attempt to cross the river. The loss of Monywa would also mean the loss of the last remaining escape route, and so Slim ordered 1st Burma Division to move on the town immediately. 48th and 63rd Brigades were to join them, as was 16th Brigade. 2nd KOYLI found themselves covering the southern approaches to the town, as Japanese reinforcements began to arrive. 1st Burma Divisional HQ was forced to fight its way out of the trap, and by dawn, the Japanese had crossed the river and captured the empty town.

Slim's worst nightmare had now come true, and the only option was to get away from the Irrawaddy line as soon as possible. By the night of 2nd May, the 2nd KOYLI were at Ye-U with the rest of 16th Brigade, whilst 7th Armoured Brigade had joined 1st Burma Division at Alon. All were aware that the Japanese still controlled the direct route up the Chindwin to the vital crossing from Shwegyin to Kalewa, and 16th Brigade was sent forward to secure the area before the enemy arrived. This achieved, the whole British force began to move towards and through Ye-U, and on to the gateway at Shwegyin. They were placed on half rations as they tried to help the column of refugees that struggled along the track, in a race against the gathering monsoon clouds. Air and train evacuations had ended when the arrival of Japanese bombers had made them too dangerous to contemplate, so now the rapidly diminishing fuel situation meant that only a few lorries could be used to transport the mounting casualties and exhausted refugees. Nevertheless, no one was left behind.

When the pitiful column reached Shwegyin, those on foot set out on the path through the hills, to the crossing itself. All transport and guns had to be ferried across the river, and the six steamers available were insufficient to carry anything but those lorries packed with the wounded, vital supplies, and ammunition. Nevertheless, by the morning of the 10th, the column, and most of the troops following up, were over the Chindwin, as the Japanese advance moved inexorably towards them. The forces in the rearguard, battled against daunting odds to hold the enemy at bay, all the while falling back ever closer to the embarkation beach at Shwegyin. They took up position on the high ground, around the crossing point, and fought on, until at 7.55 pm on the 10th, they were ordered to leave their positions under cover of all the remaining artillery.

On the 17th, the main body of 17th Division reached Tamu. The 63rd Brigade were last to arrive, two days later.

The retreat from Burma was the longest in the history of the British Army: 1000 miles had been covered, under almost constant attack, and the casualties had totalled 13,463. When it reached the town of Imphal, in India, 2nd KOYLI numbered eighty men. They were reinforced and stationed on the Burmese border until December 1943, when they moved to Delhi to undergo training for the upcoming invasion of Malaya.

Chapter 4

North Africa 1940–3

4.1 Syria and Palestine

At the outbreak of war, in September 1939, the men who were to become 9th Battalion KOYLI were members of another proud Yorkshire regiment: The Queen's Own Yorkshire Dragoons.

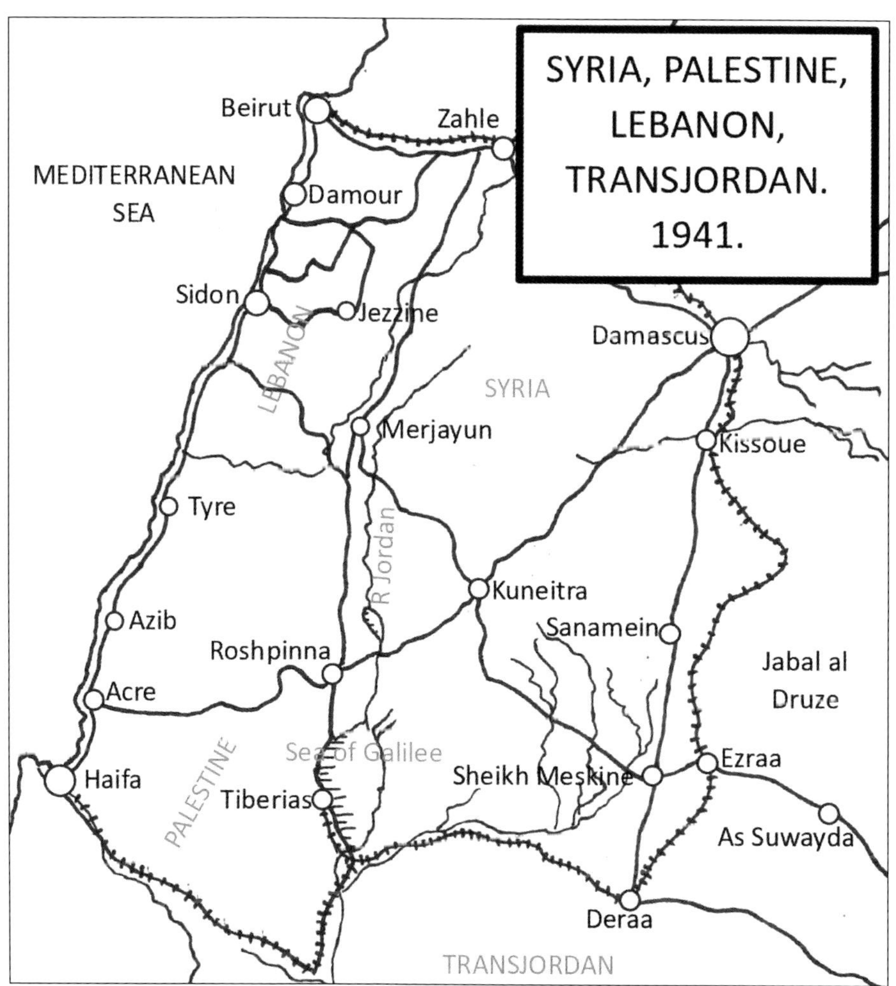

British infantry advances into Syria, 13th June 1941. Jarché. (*Wikimedia Commons*)

The Yorkshire Dragoons, together with the Yorkshire Hussars and Sherwood Rangers, were part of the 5th Cavalry Brigade, in 1st Cavalry Division, and were quickly brought up to war strength, before taking part in three months of training, around the fields of Lincolnshire. The regiment left its HQ in Doncaster on 1st January 1940, bound for France.

The long troop trains set off from Dieppe and Cherbourg, bound for Marseilles, where the men and horses embarked for the stormy voyage to Haifa. It was two months before the horses were in good condition again, and the regiment could begin the task of providing a mounted police force for the country, which was always liable to erupt into internecine fighting between the Arab and Jewish populations. In June, Italy declared war, and suddenly the threat of bombing raids on Palestine, carried out from Italian bases in the Dodecanese, became real. The possibility of air landings was also considered, and the Dragoons were moved to the Plain of Esdraelon, to protect the vital oil pipeline that ran through the area. Sure enough, Haifa was bombed shortly after the Italian declaration of war, and the Dragoons found themselves moved from camp to camp, all along the length of the oil pipeline. They were at Rosh Pinna, on the Syrian border, when the threat of an Axis takeover became severe enough to warrant an armed intervention in Syria and Lebanon, and in late June 1941, the regiment crossed the frontier and occupied Kuneitra, to protect the left flank of the lines of communication to Damascus. In July, they moved to Ezraa, to counter the threat from the pro-Nazi Vichy forces garrisoned in the Jabel Druze mountains. Here they fought a mounted skirmish with Vichy Jabel Druze cavalry, which was almost certainly the last mounted engagement ever undertaken by the British Army. The patrol involved was led by Lieutenant Bruce Hobbs, who was the youngest rider ever to have won The Grand National. In 1938, only

Cavalry patrol at Merjayun in Syria, 16th June 1941. Keating G (Capt), No 1 Army Film & Photographic Unit. (*Wikipedia*)

17 years old, he had guided "Battleship" to victory; a horse no bigger than a modern polo pony.

The campaign was soon over, and the Yorkshire Dragoons led the triumphal march into As Suwayda, the capital of the Jabal al-Druze, on 28th July. After this, they garrisoned the Jabal al-Druze, and kept up a series of regular scouting missions, in an area that was very open to an Axis attack from the Caucasus; something that could have threatened the vital Suez Canal. If such an invasion had happened, 5th Cavalry Brigade would have been part of the final defensive line.

In December, the regiment moved to Azib in Northern Palestine. The move was made entirely on horseback and involved a ride of 124 miles in four and a half days, over the mountains and valleys that formed the spine of Palestine. The plan was for them to be trained in mounted mountain warfare but the developing situation in the Western Desert led to a sudden drastic change for the men of the Yorkshire Dragoons. In February 1942, they were told that all the horses were to go, and they were to be moved to Egypt. The last mounted parade was held at the end of that month, and the Yorkshire Dragoons thus became the last active horsed cavalry regiment in the British Army, by a margin of a few days. They were told that they were to become an armoured regiment.

4.2 Egypt

In early March they moved to within sight of the Pyramids. At Mena, they were told that they were to become part of the secret "A" Force: a unit set up to try to hide the weakness of the 8th Army by camouflage and deception. The horsemen became drivers, signallers, and all the other specialists that are needed by an armoured unit. The urgency of the situation meant that training was cursory, and they were sent into the Western Desert in May, driving canvas tanks that were meant to represent an armoured brigade. Other duties involved the supply of food, water and petrol to the many units that had been thinly spread out to face the coming onslaught by the newly arrived German Afrika Korps.

4.2.1 The Battle of Gazala

In early 1941, General Erwin Rommel arrived on the scene in the North African desert, having distinguished himself in the German "Blitzkrieg" armoured offensive during the battle for France. He had immediately set about attacking the 8th Army in its positions towards the eastern part of Libya, and his success had been stunning. In two months, he had driven the British back across the Egyptian border but had been unable to break the siege of Tobruk, which was a vital supply port, and this had led to a setback, when the British had finally pulled themselves together, to lift the siege, and to push the Germans back to the position from which they had started.

Rommel was both brilliant and impetuous. He was not the sort of general who waited for his opponents to dictate his actions, and almost immediately, he ordered his Panzerarmee Afrika back on the offensive. This time, the British retreat stopped just to the west of the town of Gazala, and both sides stared at each other over the vast, open desert, trying to predict the next move of their opponent.

In the front line of XXX Corps were the British 1st and 7th Armoured Divisions, and the newly motorised Yorkshire Dragoons had been placed under the command of 2nd Armoured Brigade Group, which was part of 1st Armoured Division. A total of 100,000 men and 1,000 tanks, stood in front of Rommel's army, along the line at Gazala. They had put down a carpet of mines that provided a frontal defence for a distance of over 40 miles, and in that minefield, they had built a series of "boxes," that could each provide a defensive position for an entire brigade group and delay any German offensive until armoured support arrived. At least, that was the plan. But, once again, they had planned without the genius of the "Desert Fox," as the British soldiers had now Christened Rommel. With his air reconnaissance having an almost free hand in the skies above the prospective battlefield, he had been provided with a detailed plan of the position and nature of the British "boxes," and when his attack began, it was to come in the form of an arc that would sweep around the southern end of the line, and so take most of those positions out of the fight, in one swoop.

The forces available to the Desert Fox, comprised two divisions each, from XX, X, and XXI Italian Corps, two light infantry regiments from 90th Light Division, 15th and 31st Panzer Divisions, and three reconnaissance battalions.

The battle began on 26th May, when the Axis forces swept forward, their tanks simply outgunning the British armour that stood in their way. One of these units was pushed back towards a box that had been named "Knightsbridge," by the homesick British, but as they drew close to the position, the enemy tanks were attacked from the east, by the units of 2nd Armoured Brigade, which included part of the Yorkshire Dragoons.

In the sweltering heat of the desert, and the billowing dust, the German tanks appeared out of the haze, like some giant prehistoric creatures that threatened to crush the men of 2nd Armoured Brigade's motorised infantry, who were battling to stop the onslaught. From hastily dug holes, they struggled to set up light anti-tank guns that blasted away at the monsters bearing down on them. Almost incredibly, the enemy armour veered away, and for a while, the British thought they had won a victory. In a way, they had, but it was only a temporary one, as the tanks of 15th Panzer had decided to push to the east of the Knightsbridge Box, in order to take Bir Lefa by a less well-defended route.

This was happening all along the line, as one box after another was isolated and left behind the battlefront. On 11th June, Rommel launched his reserves into an assault that ripped into the British forces positioned to both the north and the south. The next day, the evacuation of the Knightsbridge Box was authorised, and the Yorkshire Dragoons set off to fight through the enemy forces that now blocked the way back to their own lines. They

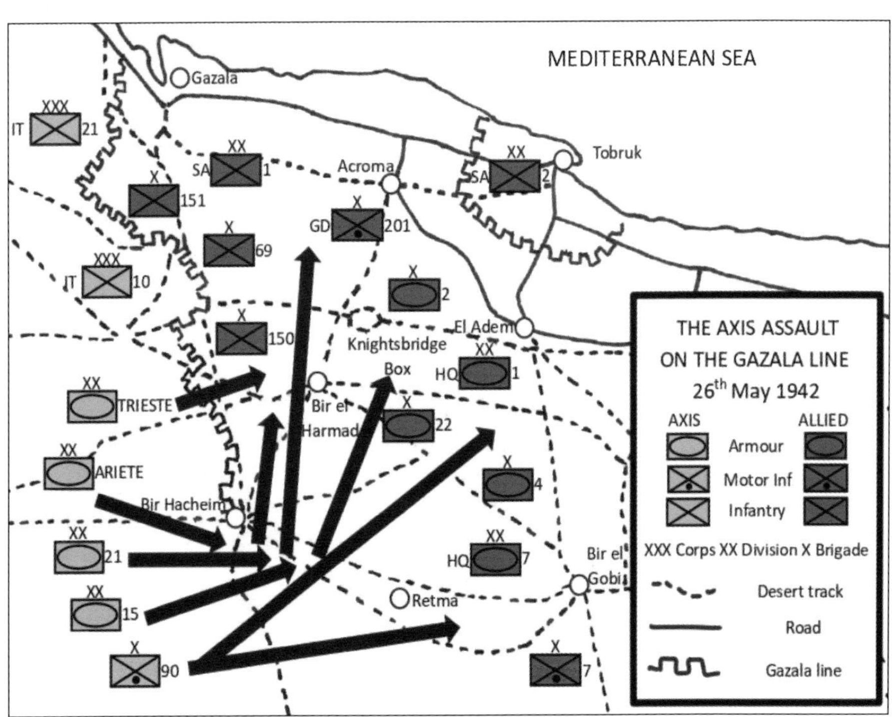

were followed on the 14th, by the survivors of the entire Gazala Line, and together, they smashed a way through the jubilant enemy forces, to begin what the allied soldiers sarcastically called, "The Gazala Gallop," a frantic retreat into Egypt, hotly pursued by the rampant Panzerarmee Afrika.

4.2.2 The Battle of El Alamein

The way to the oilfields of the Middle East seemed open, and the dizzying prospect of wiping out the allied forces in North Africa now appeared to be very real to the newly promoted Feldmarschall Rommel, and his Fuehrer in Berlin, as the 8th Army halted at the railway station of El Alamein, to make a final stand against the Panzerarmee Afrika. The Yorkshire Dragoons were part of "Delta Force": a last line of defence should the Alamein line be broken, but in August they were temporarily moved out of the Nile Delta, to Sidi Bishr, near Alexandria, to protect the Fleet Air Arm base at Dekheila aerodrome. Any remaining hopes of becoming an armoured regiment, as had been promised, were dashed when it was announced that the scale of tank losses in the recent desert battles, meant that there were insufficient vehicles to equip them. Instead, they were to become a motorised battalion under the command of the 2nd Armoured Brigade of 1st Armoured Division. They had seven weeks to train for this role before they were thrust back into action in the Second Battle of El Alamein, Rommel's first attack having been driven off. The training had been carried out under an entirely new commander, as Lieutenant Colonel Stephenson had been badly injured in a training accident and had been replaced by Lieutenant Colonel Chapman of the 60th Rifles.

Brigadier Fisher, in command of 2nd Armoured Brigade, decided to divide the Yorkshire Dragoon Squadrons amongst the armoured regiments under his control. "A" Squadron was assigned to the Queen's Bays, "B" Squadron to the 9th Lancers, and "C" Squadron to the 10th Hussars. The specialist, anti-tank "D" Squadron was retained under brigade control.

The battle that British Prime Minister Churchill later called "the end of the beginning," began on the night of 23rd October. The air was still, yet filled with tension, as a full moon shone down from the clear sky. Just after 9.30 pm, the horizon erupted, as 1,000 artillery pieces fired as one. The noise was increased when the ships that had approached the shore after nightfall, began to bombard the enemy positions with their heavy shells, and the ground shook for miles around. After the opening salvo, the artillery guns fired at will, each one adding a bright flash to the staccato lightning all along the eastern horizon. Eventually, they had to stop firing as the gun barrels were given time to cool down, and fire coordinators got to work, pushing forward the curtain of death, step by step, as the advance began.

The men of each squadron of Yorkshire Dragoons stared at the blanket of tracer shells that whined over their heads and lit up the anxious faces of their comrades. As the tanks rumbled forward, the Dragoons moved with them, along the cleared lines that had been laid into the minefield, by the sappers. They tried to talk to each other, but it was pointless, as ear drums became numbed by the cacophony of war. Goggles were pulled into place, as the desert sand, whipped into fury by the tracks of an endless column of

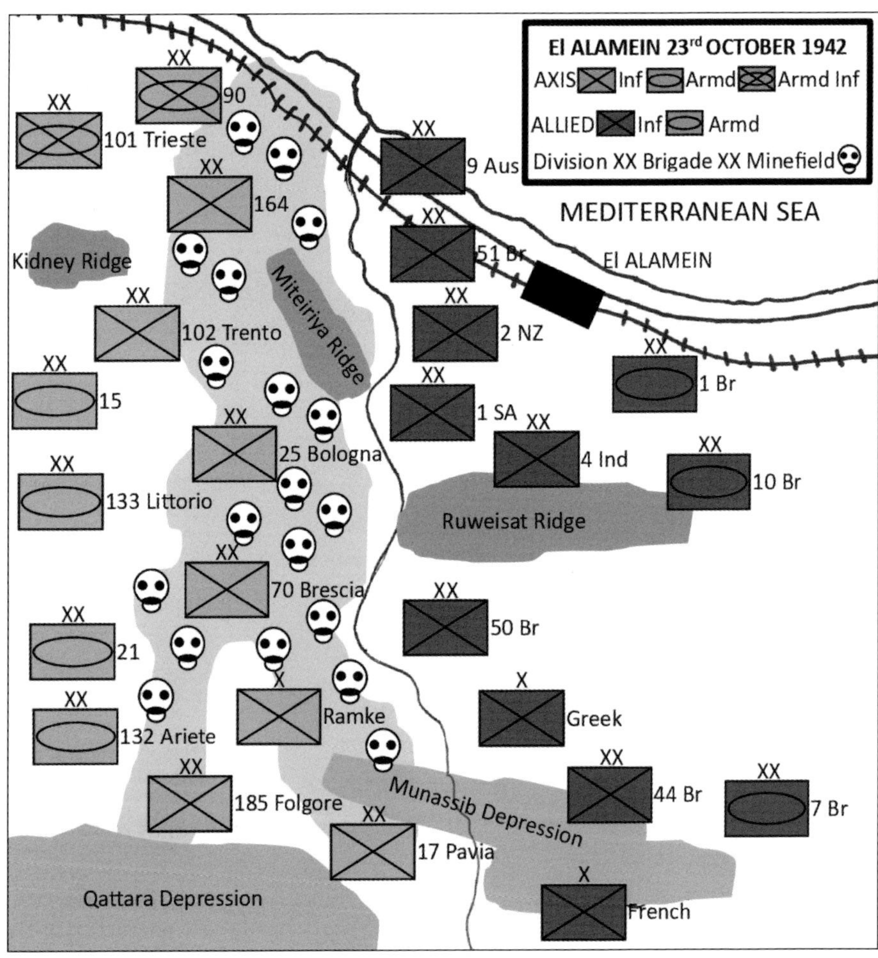

tanks and lorries, hammered into faces already sore from exposure to the merciless Saharan sun.

As an anti-tank unit, "D" Squadron had been equipped with 6-pounder anti-tank guns, tracked universal carriers, Bren machine guns and 3-inch mortars. They were soon to be called upon to put their new training into practice.

The barrage went on through the night, never stopping, never allowing the enemy to leave the positions that they had carved out of the sand and rock. But the allied advance was not going according to plan, and both infantry and armoured units found themselves bogged down in a minefield that had been expertly laid, and which was much deeper than had been expected. As daylight began to creep across the landscape, the artillery bombardment slowed, and the attacking forces were hit by a crossfire that came from the guns of the massed divisions of the Panzerarmee Afrika.

The infantry began to dig in, as the tanks fired back at the enemy guns, trying desperately to avoid being hit in that bare, desolate plain. Many failed, and the carcasses of burnt-out vehicles studded a landscape that now resembled an elephant's graveyard.

One of the main tasks of each motor squadron within the tank regiments of 2nd Armoured Brigade was to take over sections of the front line at night, to relieve the tank crews and to protect their vehicles, but the men of the Yorkshire Dragoons found themselves called upon to do much more than that. Their 6-pounder guns, 3-inch mortars, and Vickers machine guns were constantly in use, as they tried to provide a response to the enemy anti-tank fire that was decimating their tanks. They also took part in infantry clearing operations, as the first enemy positions started to be overrun. During these unheralded episodes in the Alamein "dogfight," the Dragoons suffered many casualties, and for their bravery, Troopers Gallop, Leach and Linley, were awarded the Military Medal.

By the 25th, the advance had torn a six-mile-deep and five-mile-wide gap in the minefield, yet still, the attackers were stuck fast in the grip of death. That morning, General Montgomery, now commanding 8th Army, decided to change the direction of the armoured thrust, and the Yorkshire Dragoons found themselves up in support of the tanks of 1st Armoured Division, as it swung to the northwest, towards the high ground that, because of its shape, had been dubbed "Kidney Ridge."

The ridge was the only outcrop on an otherwise featureless area of desert. About one mile to the northwest of it was an Axis defensive strongpoint that had been codenamed "Woodcock," and about one mile to the southeast was another, named "Snipe." The Yorkshire Dragoons were to take part in the fighting around "Woodcock."

The attack began at 11 pm on 26th October, as 2nd King's Royal Rifle Corps (KRRC) attacked into the darkness and dust, created by shell impacts and tank tracks. By dawn, they found themselves out in the open desert and exposed to enemy fire, having missed "Woodcock" in the chaos of the night. They had no alternative but to dig in.

As planned, the three regiments of 2nd Armoured Brigade, with their Yorkshire Dragoon Squadrons, went forward as the sun rose behind them, their aim being to swing around to the north of "Woodcock." Because the KRRC had failed to neutralise the Axis guns, the armour came under intense fire, and by midday, they had been driven to the east of the point where the rifles were now entrenched.

Rommel now decided to do some attacking of his own, and sent forward both 90th Light, and 21st Panzer Divisions, to bolster the units of 15th Panzer, and 164th Infantry Divisions, who had been assigned to the task of pushing the allies back from the 6-mile front that they had established. At 4 pm on the afternoon of the 27th, a 5-minute artillery bombardment heralded the German charge towards the exposed forces around "Woodcock." Stuka and Junkers 88 dive bombers came roaring over the horizon, strafing and bombing the infantry as they dived for cover. Above them were the curling white vapour trails, left in the clear blue sky by the fighters that twisted and turned in a dance of death, as the Spitfires, Hurricanes and Kittyhawks, tried desperately to get at the bombers that were creating havoc below.

The Yorkshire Dragoons ran to set up their 6-pounder guns, in an attempt to halt the onrushing tanks and their supporting infantry. After 4 hours of intensive action, the Germans were stopped, and Rommel ordered them to dig in. Behind their guns, the Dragoons watched the Germans through the quivering heat that rose from a desert surface littered with burning tanks, lorries, guns, and Bren carriers. The ever-present flies now swarmed over the bodies of those who had not survived the battle at "Woodcock," and tormented the sweat-streaked faces of those who had. The fighting for "Snipe" had been at least as brutal and devastating, but there too, the Germans had failed to break the will of the defenders.

By dawn, 2nd Armoured Brigade was moving forward again, swinging along the northern flank of the battlefield, and by 29th October, Rommel was seriously considering a withdrawal along the whole front, even though the allied forces at "Woodcock," and "Snipe," had been ordered to take up a defensive posture. The main issue that prevented this, was the lack of fuel needed to extricate all his units. So, the fighting went on.

On 1st November, 9th Armoured Brigade launched an attack that was the first stage of Montgomery's new plan, "Operation Supercharge," the aim of which was to force the Germans to fight in the open; something that Rommel was determined to avoid, due to his disastrous fuel situation. Montgomery knew that, by drawing the enemy into a flowing battle, they would most certainly lose enough tanks to put their entire North African expedition in real jeopardy, and if the allies could capture the main Axis base at Tel el Aqqaqir, then they would have little alternative but to take flight.

Just before dawn, on 2nd November, 9th Armoured Brigade made an almost suicidal attack on the Axis line, which some of those observing compared to the charge of the Light Brigade at Balaclava during the Crimean War. But this charge was the result of cool planning, not incompetence. The losses that threatened to be incurred, which some of those in command estimated might amount to 100% of the tanks involved, would, it was reasoned, be justified in that the enemy would be bled dry of both fuel and armour in bringing them about. Another result would be the creation of a gap in the enemy line that could be exploited by the full might of 1st Armoured Division. In the event, no such gap was made, but the damage inflicted upon Rommel's army was such that he was forced to appraise Hitler of the situation, which was that the enemy could not be stopped. Hitler's lack of strategic understanding is evident from his reply, which Rommel received on 3rd November:

> "It is with trusting confidence in your leadership and the courage of the German-Italian troops under your command, that the German people and I, are following the heroic struggle in Egypt. In the situation which you find yourself, there can be no other thought but to stand fast, yield not a yard of ground, and throw every gun and every man into the battle. Considerable airforce reinforcements are being sent to C-in-C South.

> The Duce, and the Comando Supremo, are also making the utmost efforts to send you the means to continue the fight. Your enemy, despite his superiority, must also be at the end of his strength. It would not be the first time in history that a strong will has triumphed over the bigger battalions. As to your troops, you can show them no other road than that to victory or death. Adolf Hitler."

The Rahman track ran from Sidi el Rahman to the rim of the vast and impassable Qattara Depression, which formed the southern edge of the battlefield. It passed directly in front of Tel el Aqqaqir, and Montgomery now saw the opportunity to use it as the start line for his final breakout. His idea was that, once the infantry had neutralised the enemy artillery along the track, 2nd and 8th Armoured Brigades would push through to the open desert and lead the way to a decisive victory in North Africa.

In the minefield. Second Battle of El Alamein. Mapham, J (Sgt), No 1 Army Film & Photographic Unit. (*Wikimedia Commons*)

The infantry attack failed, and 2nd Armoured was forced to go to the support of 2nd KRRC. They were met by a few German, and many Italian tanks, as Rommel tried to obey the command of his Fuehrer, and the men of the Yorkshire Dragoons once again joined in the destruction of, what were now, some of the last tanks in the Panzerarmee Afrika. That is, the last that were not part of the Afrika Korps: Rommel had already ordered his German units to withdraw for a distance of 6 miles, taking with them all the fuel supplies they could lay their hands on, and leaving their Italian allies to their fate.

On the night of the 3rd November, Montgomery sent his reserves to the edge of the Rahman track, but by the time they arrived at Tel el Aqqaqir, the Germans had gone, and the pursuit could begin.

2nd Armoured Brigade was at the head of the chase, and passing the port of Tobruk, which was soon back in allied hands, the units to which the Yorkshire Dragoons were attached, managed a further ninety miles before running out of fuel and supplies, the supply vehicles having become bogged down in the quagmire caused by a torrential storm.

4.3 Libya and the Mareth Line

The Dragoons stayed at Tmimi over Christmas, to be refitted and reinforced. Those who had been less severely wounded in the battle returned, but the losses had been great: fifty-two killed or missing, and thirty-seven wounded. During the stay at Tmimi, the entire corps transport was engaged in ferrying supplies to the front line around Benghazi, in an effort to keep the advance moving, because the plan to carry out the supply by sea had been scuppered by a tremendous storm that had destroyed Benghazi harbour. By the end of January, the Yorkshire Dragoons were off in pursuit again. They were at Medenine, where the Axis armour tried to hold up the allied advance with a forceful counterattack that broke against the stubborn resistance of the allied defence.

The enemy retreated behind the Mareth Line, which was a series of strong emplacements strung out along the steep sides of the Wadi Zigzaou, and a frontal attack that had been ordered by General Montgomery was flung back with heavy casualties. The general decided to change tactics and planned a “left hook” around the Mareth Line, through the gap between Djebel Tebaga and Djebel Melab.

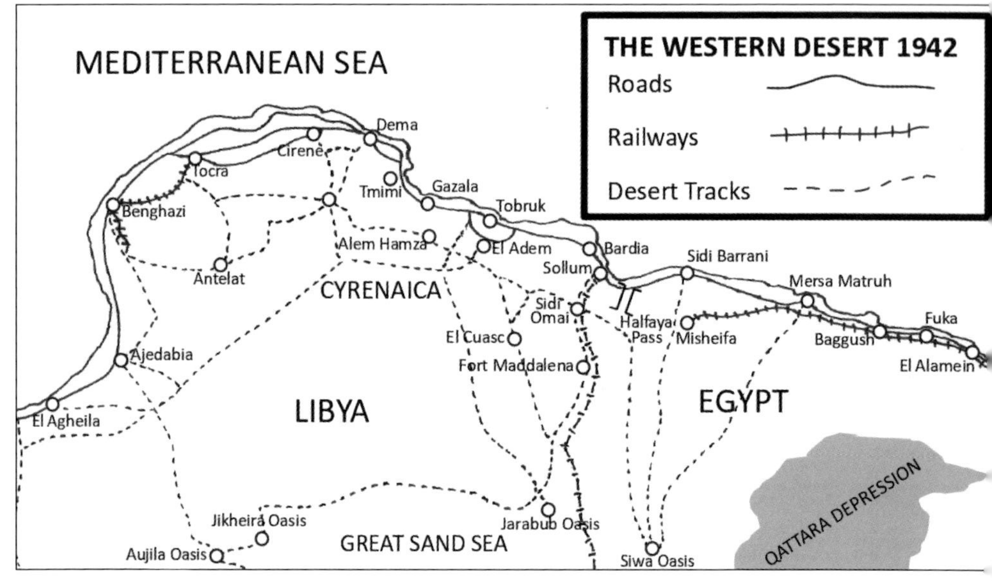

On the night of 25th March 1943, the Yorkshire Dragoons, as part of 1st Armoured Division, were forming up with units of the New Zealand Corps and 8th Armoured Brigade when they were hit by a fierce sandstorm, known as a "khamsin". Both friend and foe were forced to seek cover, as the wind whipped the ground into a driving, cutting, piercing blanket of grit and rock. Still, they endured, and as dawn broke, they were ready to attack. The 8th Armoured Brigade, together with the New Zealanders, cleared the gap between the two areas of high ground, and 1st Armoured Division, with 2nd Armoured Brigade and the Yorkshire Dragoons in the lead, swept through. Brigadier Fisher drove them on: "speed up, straight through, no halting!" The brigade smashed into the enemy line and by 7.30 pm, they had reached the proposed forward staging area, which they held as the rest of the division began to arrive.

Just after 11 pm, the moon began to rise but was almost hidden in cloud. Although visibility was poor, at midnight, General Briggs, commanding 1st Armoured Division, ordered the advance to El Hamma and one minute later 2nd Armoured Brigade was off. The Axis forces were in full retreat towards the southwest of El Hamma, and in the darkness, they clashed with the men of 2nd Armoured Brigade. 15th Panzer Division tried to attack the rear of 1st Armoured Division's column but was driven off. Nevertheless, the rest of the Axis forces had managed to put together an effective anti-tank screen,

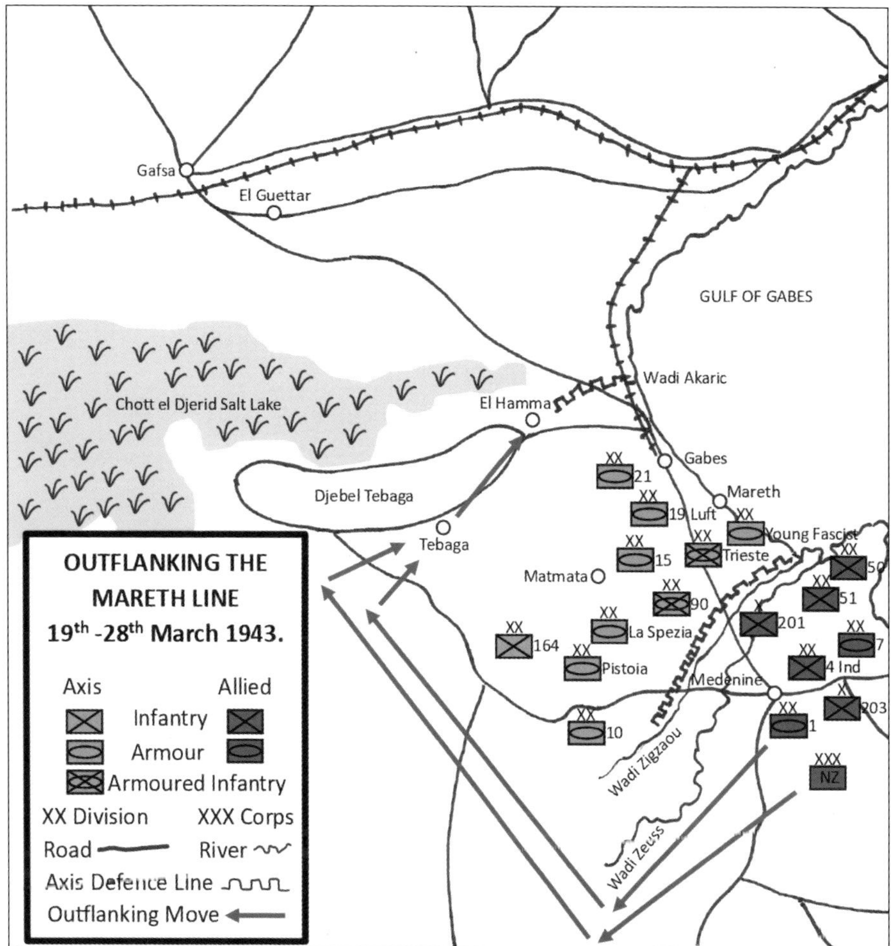

and 2nd Armoured Brigade was unable to break it. They tried an outflanking move, but the position had been cleverly sited between two hills, and they found it impossible to find a way around them.

Despite this, the Dragoons knew they had been a major factor in the victory at the Mareth Line. As a result of their exploits in the Tebaga Gap and beyond, they had captured four 88mm guns and two hundred prisoners. Two days later El Hamma fell, and the 8th Army moved up to Wadi Akarit. Captain Pettifer of the Yorkshire Dragoons was awarded the Military Cross.

On 29th March, 1st Armoured Division, with the Yorkshire Dragoons once again in the thick of it, began to probe the enemy defences at Wadi Akarit, to determine whether, with the support of the rest of X Corps, they could force the position without heavy loss. Lieutenant General Horrocks,

Crusader tanks in El Hamma, 29th March 1943. Silverside (Sgt) No 2 Army Film and photography unit. (*Wikipedia*)

commanding X Corps, sent a warning to General Montgomery, based upon their findings. He explained that, although a lightning attack might prove successful, the losses involved would be heavy, and Montgomery, as usual, opted for a more cautious approach until the build-up of forces could guarantee success. He told Horrocks to continue probing for another 24 hours, by which time it should have become clear if a full-frontal attack would get through, or not. If the situation then warranted it, XXX Corps would be brought forward before the assault continued. Horrocks did as he was told, but the next day, he was forced to concede that X Corps alone, could not force the positions around Akarit.

The Wadi Akarit was the last natural barrier, before the coastal plain of Tunisia. It was very narrow, with the eastern flank being up against the sea, and the western flank against the great salt marshes. To the east, a bare ridge ran parallel to the sea: 500 feet high, and so steep as to be impassable to vehicles. To the west was a maze of rocky hills, gullies and escarpments, the approaches to which were across open country. The metalled road between Gabes, El Guettar, and Gafsa, was dominated by high ground and there was no room for manoeuvre. In the fight that finally allowed 1st Armoured Division to push through the barrier at Wadi Akarit, the 8th Army suffered 1,289 casualties and lost 32 tanks.

Chapter 5

Tunisia 1942–3

5.1 The Battle of the Goubellat Road

As 1st Armoured Division continued to chase the Axis forces into southern Tunisia, they were told of allied landings in Morocco and Algeria. In a meeting at Klessheim Castle, Hitler had told Mussolini that Tunisia must be held at all costs, but in saying this, he chose to ignore the fact that the jaws of the allies were now closing on the Axis forces in North Africa.

British infantry in Tunisia, 1943. Wackett, Frederick (Sergeant) No. 2 Army Film and Photographic Unit. (*Wikipedia*)

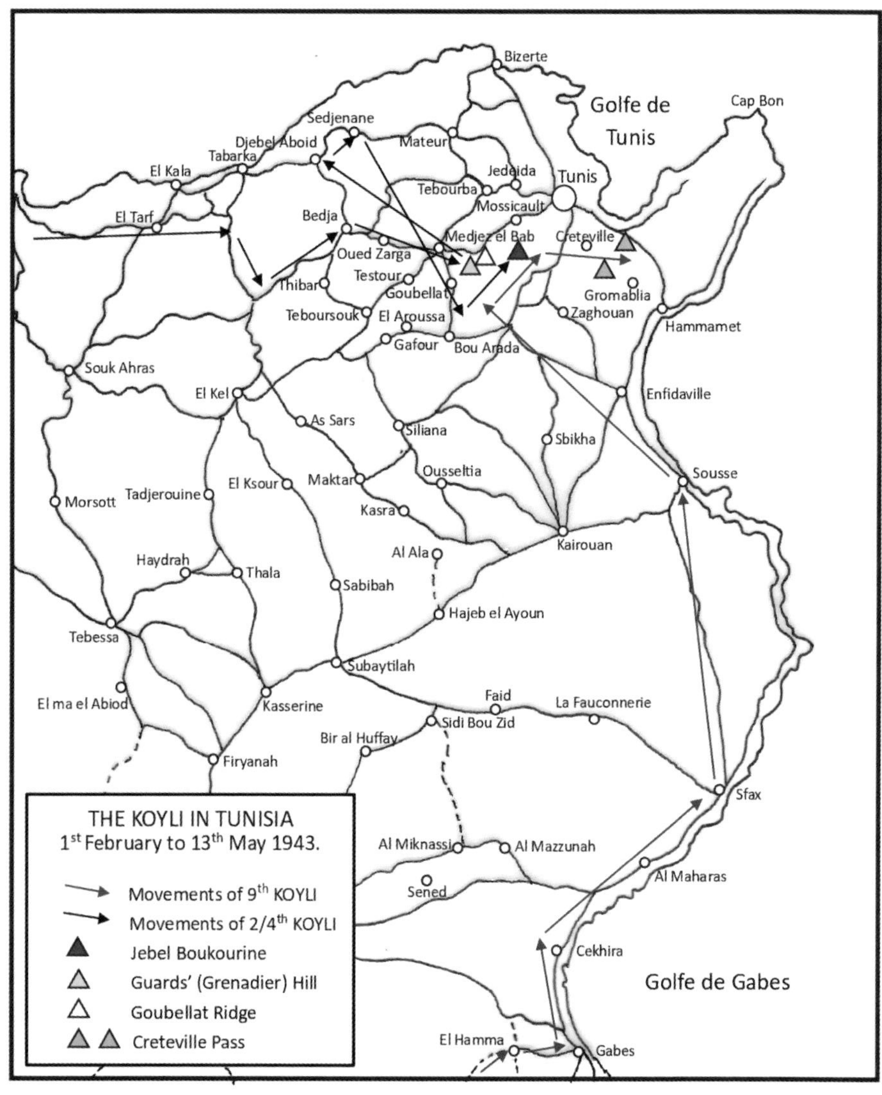

Following the allied landings, codenamed "Operation Torch," the Axis forces found themselves trapped between the British 8th Army, advancing from Libya, and the newly landed forces to the west. They reached Tunisia and had no alternative but to make a stand there, in a defensive position that Hitler believed could be held "indefinitely." 46th Infantry Division was to reinforce the Torch landings and help defeat the Axis forces in North Africa for the last time.

2/4th KOYLI arrived at Algiers on 17th January, and by 1st February they, together with the rest of 138th Brigade, had crossed the border into

Tunisia to take up position on the Bedja – Oued Zarga road, to the west of the city of Tunis. They found themselves in a range of mountains that stretched all the way from the Sahara to the Cape Bon Peninsular. North of their position were a succession of rolling hills and open plains, and to the east was the Mediterranean Sea, and a wide plain that stretched along the entire coastline. To the south, it was mostly desert. From their position, they could see the daily flights that brought enemy reinforcements into Tunis airport, building up the Axis force that already numbered 40,000 infantry, along with 300 tanks, and 150 fighter aircraft. 138th spread out to cover the Medjez-el-Bab sector along the valley, where the main road from Bedja ran east, to Tebourba and Tunis. East of the town of Medjez-el-Bab lay the ridges where the Guards had battled on Christmas Day, and to the south, another ridge covered the main road. 2/4th KOYLI were on the Guards' Hill, with outposts as far as the so called Goubellat Ridge.

On 22nd February they were part of a composite unit called "Burrforce," when an Axis force attacked towards Bedja. The British were very thinly spread, and took shelter in the widespread Berber villages, as the Medjez-el-Bab sector was turned into a salient. Supplies had to make a 70 mile detour through Teboursouk, but it was not until 1st March that the enemy pushed the 2/4th KOYLI positions back, and they were withdrawn from the ridge, to be followed by the whole of Burrforce on the following day.

2/4th attempted to retake the Goubellat Ridge but were driven back. Even so, the position was stabilised, and they settled down to withstand regular shelling and dive-bombing raids. The defensive operations had stretched resources to breaking point, as the losses mounted on isolated hills that were regularly overrun. 139th Brigade had suffered during a 20-day retreat to the north, and 138th took over the Djebel Abiod front on 20th March, after the enemy advance had finally been stopped. Many prisoners had been taken, but several important areas of high ground had been lost, along with the important road from Bedja to Medjez-el-Bab. Despite the losses, 46th Division was ordered to recapture the town of Sedjenane.

5.2 The Battle of Sedjenane

Sedjenane occupied an important strategic position on the railway line between Mateur, and the port of Bizerte. Following the "Torch" landings, the allied "run for Tunis" had been stopped in its tracks by German paratroops, in the hills to the east of the town, where they had ambushed the British advance on 29th November 1942. All through December, January, February, and March, the Germans held on to the three dominant hills, known to the allies as "Green Hill," "Baldy," and "Sugarloaf." The town had fallen to the Germans and Italians on 4th March, after much vicious fighting, and 139th Brigade had been pushed back towards Djebel Aboid, where they had been withdrawn due to terrible losses. On 28th March, eight days after arriving in the area, 138th Brigade, with 128th Brigade in reserve, and reinforced by 36th Infantry Brigade, 1st Parachute Brigade and several French units, attacked under the cover of the artillery of two divisions. The mountains in that region were strewn with boulders and covered with a dense scrub that was, in some places, eight feet high. 2/4th KOYLI had to hack their way through the vicious undergrowth, using axes and knives, as the torrential rain poured down. Despite this, they reached their first objective, taking prisoners as they went, before being involved in a double-

Vickers machine gun crew in the Tunisian hills, April 1943. Stubbs (Sgt) No 2 Army Film and Photographic Unit. (*Wikimedia Commons*)

flanking movement that took the enemy positions around Sedjenane from the rear, and regained the town on 30th March. The hills to the north and south were taken the following day in an action that required the use of pack mules, and an advance of 18 miles had been achieved in just four days. Almost 1,000 prisoners had been taken.

By early April, Sfax had fallen, and 1st Army, moving down from the north, was able to join up with 8th Army. On the 11th, General Alexander signalled Montgomery and set out what he expected from his subordinate. "Monty" was told that, despite any objections he might raise, the next phase of operations would be undertaken by 1st, not 8th Army, and that planning was well underway for the attack to begin on 22nd April. It is not too difficult to imagine the chagrin of the man who now saw himself as the best of the allied generals, when he was then instructed to hand over his famed, 1st Armoured Division, to the "latecomers." If that were not enough to drive the 8th Army commander into a fit of rage, Alexander ended by urging him to fight hard against the Enfidaville position, at a time judged to fit in with the needs of 1st Army.

So, 1st Armoured Division was placed under command of 1st Army, and along with the New Zealand Divisions, they now took the inland path, where the desert dissolved into a plain dotted with small white villages, olive groves, and areas of cultivation. The Yorkshire Dragoons were with them when they attacked across the Goubellat Plain, on 23rd April. On the second day of the advance, they ran into determined anti-tank fire and armoured counterattacks, as they struggled through a vast cornfield that was strewn with mines. They were ordered to hold tight, and during this time, the Dragoons carried out raids against the enemy positions, as well as day and night patrols. For their bravery in these raids, Lieutenants Hobbs and Hershman were awarded the Military Cross, and Sergeants Middleton and Harrhy, the Military Medal.

5.3 The Battle of Tunis

The advance on Tunis by 46th Division had been scheduled to begin on the 22nd at 2 am, but on the day before this, 2/4th KOYLI had reported that they were under attack from considerable enemy forces. These were from the elite Hermann Goering Division, which was largely made up of fanatical Nazis, who hurled themselves forward, to disrupt the impending advance of the 46th Division. Out in the most advanced positions, 2/4th KOYLI were hampered by the fact that they had been forbidden to use radio transmissions, and a company that had been sent to counter the attack had been insufficient in the face of the overwhelming enemy numbers. It was only at 1 pm, that the Germans were driven back by the combined force of 2/4th KOYLI and a fully supported tank attack. The KOYLI lost several officers.

Already exhausted by the time the advance began, 2/4th set out on 8 days of fierce fighting, their delayed attack having to be made in daylight. On a misty morning, they approached an apparently abandoned farm, only to find that it had been turned into an enemy strongpoint, and a fierce battle took place before it could be subdued. Eventually, they crossed open cornfields towards the distant heights, and on 26th April set off with the rest of 138th Brigade towards the Djebel Boukornine, an awkward hill that they referred to as "the twin tits". The Germans emplaced there, were able to hold up the advance of the armour, but the 46th pushed ahead into the Medjez-el-Bab sector, and the 138th were left behind to fight it out, as the rest of the division began its triumphal descent into Tunis.

On 8th May, Tunis fell, and the Axis forces retreated into the Cape Bon Peninsular, which was a position of great strength. The 1st Armoured Division was ordered to force its way into the peninsular through the Creteville Pass, which meant crossing a flat plain, under intense fire, before fighting through the narrow pass by taking the high ground to right and left. The Dragoons took the hill on the left, where they took part in a grim battle with the infantry attached to 10th Panzer Division, who had been inspired by Hitler's order to fight to the last round. Although they obeyed their Fuehrer, the infantry action on both sides of the pass allowed the tanks to race through, and as the British infantry disengaged, the Germans were left behind, to be mopped up later. On 12th May, came the final surrender of the Axis forces in North Africa. Since the Battle of Medenine, the Yorkshire Dragoons had lost 78 men killed, or wounded. The survivors were given the break they needed and spent the following nine months in a North Africa that was now at peace. It was during this time that they were told of the new decree, that motor battalions should in future, be made up of men from two regiments only: the 60th Rifles, and the Rifle Brigade. The Yorkshire Dragoons were to become a lorried infantry battalion in the 18th Lorried Infantry Brigade of the 1st Armoured Division. In this way, they became 9th Battalion, KOYLI.

British infantry advances near Medjez-el-Bab, April 1943. Unknown. (*National Army Museum Study Collection*)

2/4th KOYLI had been involved in clearing up operations around Djebel Boukornine, The enemy began to surrender, but the Nazis amongst them were still convinced that they would soon be freed by a triumphant German Army. As they guarded the tens of thousands of prisoners, the men of 2/4th KOYLI began to look ahead to the next step in the war against the dictators and to wonder what else was in store for them. Both of the KOYLI battalions who now began to recuperate on the beaches of Tunisia, knew that the next ones they encountered would almost certainly be Italian.

Chapter 6

Sicily 1943

6.1 The Plan

The first stage of the Italian campaign was to be the capture of Sicily. It was codenamed "Operation Husky." Facing the attacking forces were almost 10,000 square miles of rocky mountains and hills, narrow valleys, and dry watercourses, where, apart from a few roads, movement was restricted to cross-country tracks. Most of the men had fought only in the deserts of North Africa, yet here was the prospect of having to fight mountain warfare, in an average daytime temperature of 24 degrees Celsius, with very little rain to cool the rock and reduce the dust. The hot scirocco wind swept up from the African desert, the rivers were dry, and the only sheltering trees were up in the highlands that each fully loaded infantryman could only reach after an exhausting climb over terraced slopes and steep jagged ridges. The few main roads were blocked with hundreds of tonnes of rock that would have to be dealt with, under a hail of shells, mortar bombs, and machine gun fire, which usually meant having to try to drive vehicles up steep boulder-strewn slopes, across stone walls, and along narrow sunken ravines: all this under the threatening shadow of the 10,740 ft volcano, Mount Etna.

It was decided that, to avoid this landscape, the British forces should take to the coastal plain between Syracuse and Catania, which is twenty miles long and eight miles wide, and forms the flood plain of the Rivers Simeto, Dittaino, and Gornalunga.

German opposition in Tunisia had been incredibly strong, and it was feared that this would now be matched by the Italians, as they would be defending their own soil. So, the decision was made to concentrate all forces on the southeastern shore. As part of 5th Infantry Division, 1st KOYLI was to land at Cassibile, to the south of Syracuse, and establish a local bridgehead before moving on to capture Syracuse itself, and later Augusta and Catania in conjunction with 1st Airlanding Brigade. The landings were to be "shore-to-shore," which meant that 5th Division was to be transported from North

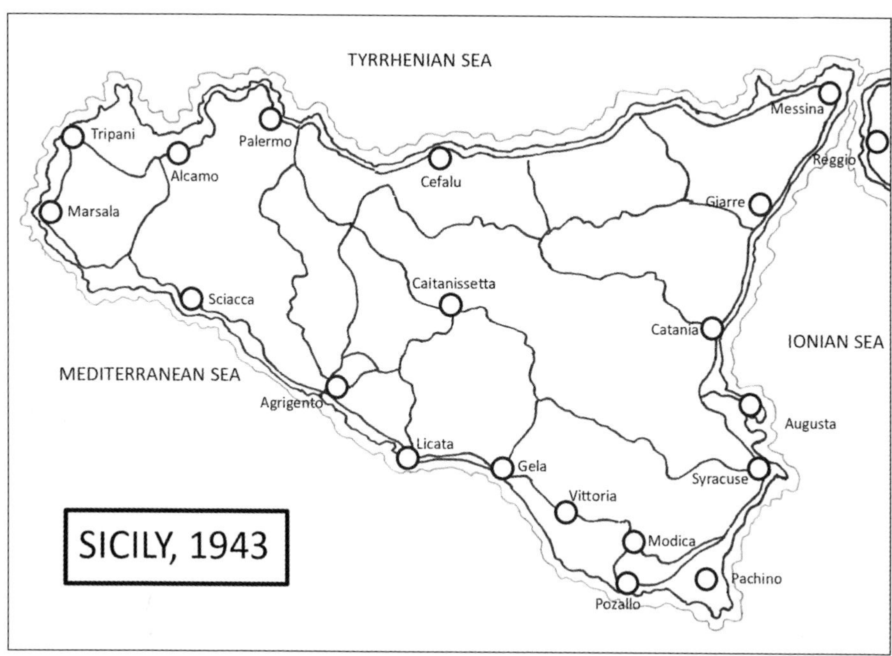

Africa by ship and then transferred to landing craft when in sight of the beaches. Many of the techniques used in amphibious operations were tested for the first time in the Italian campaign, and the experience gained probably saved thousands of lives when the time came for the D-Day landings in Normandy, the following year. As would be the case in Normandy, the weather situation in the landing areas proved to be problematic. In June 1944, the landings only took place when the allied meteorologists could predict a short period of calmer seas. In Sicily, the assault went ahead in a 40 miles per hour gale that tossed the ships and landing craft around and drove the airborne landings off course.

At the time of the landings, the Axis forces in Sicily amounted to 250,000. The morale and equipment of the Italian army had suffered badly during the final part of the North African campaign, and they now became fully aware of the suffering that the war had inflicted upon their own people. The cause for which they were fighting had become a chimera that seemed destined to destroy their country, and forever link it to the wrongdoings of Nazi Germany.

Such were the feelings of the men in 206th Coastal Division, as they sat behind the guns that were soon to be directed towards the beaches where

1st KOYLI were to land. On the other hand, the German units in the area were made up of experienced fighters, whose morale had probably been strengthened by the fact that they were now fighting on European soil. During their time in Africa, they had been able to find consolation in defeat, by listening to the daily bulletins put out by Propaganda Minister Goebbels, who told them that the homeland was inviolable. Now, there was no expanse of sea between the horrors of war and their own families, and there seemed no option other than to stop the allies in the toe of Italy.

The Hermann Goering Panzer Division was made up of such men, as were the 15th Panzer Grenadiers. Between them, they could muster 160 tanks, including the formidable Tigers, 140 artillery pieces, thirty-six batteries of rocket launchers, several batteries of assault guns, and many anti-aircraft batteries. The main fixed defences had expertly emplaced gun positions, connected by a sophisticated fire control system behind an inland main defence line. All roads were blocked, and the land between each roadblock had been covered in anti-personnel mines and barbed wire.

6.2 Operation Husky

On 9th July 1943, the British convoys from the United Kingdom and the Middle East made their rendezvous south of Malta. 1st KOYLI had sailed from Suez. The task force of which they were a part, had 182 ships and 126 landing craft, and as they approached Sicily the wind increased to such a degree that the landing craft were tossed about and driven off target. The troops they carried were sea-sick, cramped, cold and wet, for at least 12 hours, as the speed was reduced, but eventually, guided by the lights of beacon submarines, the landing craft approached the beaches, and the men of 1st KOYLI could gaze up to see the aircraft and towed gliders of 1st Airlanding Brigade, flying at 500 feet. This was the first wave, and the KOYLI could only hope that the enemy would be sheltering inside their bunkers, convinced that no assault could be made in such weather.

The plan was that two companies of 1st KOYLI were to be the first troops ashore on 46 beach, at 2.45 am. Two further companies would follow them at 3.30 am. 5th Infantry Division would have the help of seven supporting landing craft, one cruiser, five destroyers, a monitor, and a gunboat because artillery was not included in the first wave. Overhead would be fighters

Unloading stores from tank landing craft. Sicily,10th July 1943. Parnall, C H (Lt); Royal Navy Official Photographer. (*Wikipedia*)

from Malta, Gozo, and Pantelleria: the Maltese garrison at last being able to aid the invasion of the land that had been the Luftwaffe base during the long and terrible air offensive against the Island Fortress. Now the pilots watched the landing craft as they approached the beach, like huge black whales, spewing out seven hundred infantrymen per hour in the first invasion of occupied Europe. In the event, the 1st KOYLI assault troops were landed far from their correct position on Beach 46, and almost an hour late. The follow-up companies landed as the assault companies were still battling to neutralise the Italian guns, and a destroyer was called upon to provide the necessary artillery support, but by 10 am, 15th Brigade had established a bridgehead in the area around Cassibile. The build-up on the beaches could now begin.

The invasion of Sicily was the largest amphibious operation of the war, as 2,700 ships and landing craft, unloaded over 180,000 men, and hundreds of vehicles, along a 105-mile stretch of coastline, between the Gulf of Gela and the Gulf of Noto. Some, of course, did not make it that far, as several

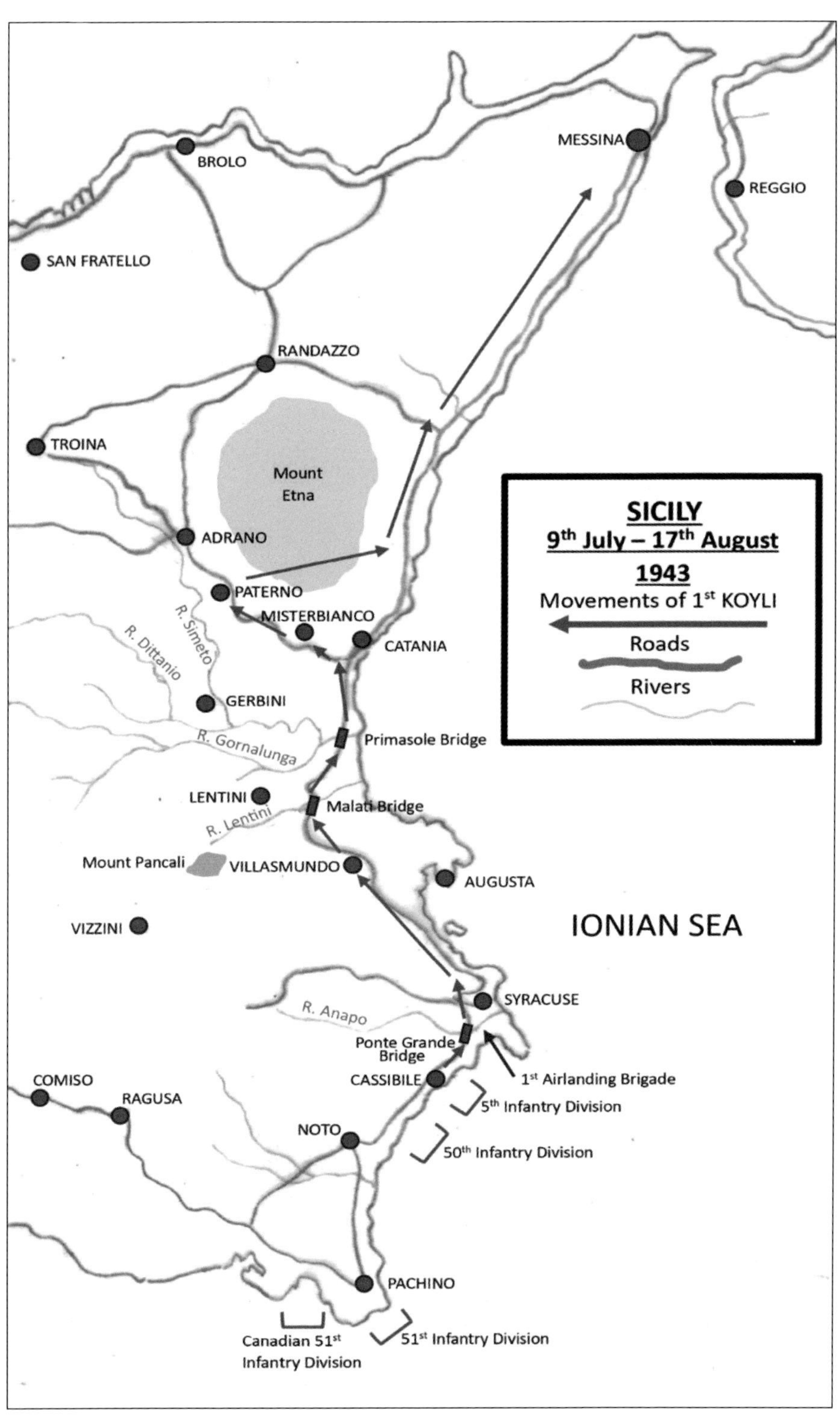
MESSINA
REGGIO
BROLO
SAN FRATELLO
RANDAZZO
TROINA
Mount Etna
ADRANO
PATERNO
MISTERBIANCO
CATANIA
R. Simeto
R. Dittanio
GERBINI
R. Gornalunga
Primasole Bridge
LENTINI
Malati Bridge
R. Lentini
Mount Pancali
VILLASMUNDO
AUGUSTA
VIZZINI
IONIAN SEA
SYRACUSE
R. Anapo
Ponte Grande Bridge
1st Airlanding Brigade
CASSIBILE
5th Infantry Division
COMISO
RAGUSA
NOTO
50th Infantry Division
PACHINO
Canadian 51st Infantry Division
51st Infantry Division
SICILY
9th July – 17th August
1943
Movements of 1st KOYLI
Roads
Rivers

troopships were torpedoed as they made their way across the Mediterranean. The Normandy landings involved only 156,000 men and a 50-mile stretch of coastline.

General Alexander's plan involved pushing his two armies up both coasts until they reached a line between Catania and Licata, when they would move inland, to clear the island. For the British forces, the capture of Syracuse, and Pachino airfield, was to be the first step, before a move to take the ports of Augusta and Catania and the airfields of Gerbini. It was vital that the ports be taken so that re-supply did not solely depend upon the beaches. 5th Infantry Division was to push north, along the coast road, and relieve 1st Airlanding Brigade, who had flown over their heads as they had landed on the beaches. The objective of the airborne troops had been to take and hold the Ponte Grande Bridge over the River Anapo, which was two miles south of Syracuse, so that 5th Division could cross it into the city before pressing on to Augusta.

The high winds, lack of landmarks, and heavy anti-aircraft fire resulted in most of the gliders being carried well off target. Some crash-landed, and some disappeared into the sea, but nevertheless, the few men who managed to reach the bridge, took it at 6.30 am on 10th July and held on, waiting for the arrival of reinforcements. At the same time, 1st KOYLI were holding on in the vital bridgehead.

Eventually, 17th Brigade reached Ponte Grande and pushed back the enemy forces that had been attacking the remnants of 1st Airlanding Brigade, before taking the city of Syracuse. When they entered Augusta, in the early hours of 13th July, it was time for 15th Brigade to take up the running and push westwards, towards Villasmundo.

The next task in the overall plan for XIII Corps, of which 5th Infantry Division now formed a part, was to secure a bridgehead across the River Simeto, seven miles south of Catania. To achieve this, 5th Division was to push up the main coast road, whilst 50th Division moved along a parallel road further inland. The bridges at Malati, on the River Lentini, and Primosole on the Simeto, were to be seized by a sea landing from 3rd Commando, and an air landing by 1st Parachute Brigade. It was expected that 5th and 50th Divisions would relieve them within a few hours. 15th Brigade was the first to move, at 5 am on the 13th July, and three hours later, 6 miles from Villasmundo, they ran into two battalions of the enemy's 3rd Parachute

Stretcher-bearers bringing in a wounded British soldier. Sicily, 1943. Stubbs (Sgt) No 2 Army Film & Photographic Unit. (*National Army Museum Study Collection*)

Regiment, and part of 115th Panzer Grenadier Regiment, who had dug in along a wooded ravine that was almost impossible to outflank. 1st KOYLI joined in the battle that, even with artillery support, could not be won by a frontal assault. In fact, it became a series of raids by small units, sent into the trees, to find and wipe out enemy positions. This process took eleven hours, and it was a punch-drunk KOYLI that set out on the next stage of their task: to take the town of Villasmundo.

Inland, 69th Brigade were attacked from a bare ridge south of Mount Pancali, and it was not until 10 am on the 14th that they managed to push the enemy off the mountaintop. As they approached Lentini they were again met by a German force that fought an expertly planned delaying action, destroying the town bridge before withdrawing, and so preventing the northward movement of tanks.

The men of 3rd Commando were now in serious difficulties after their initial success in driving the Italian defenders out of Angone and over the Malati Bridge. A much larger Italian unit had been sent against them, and with no relieving force in sight, they were pushed back, drawing their exultant enemy behind them. The bridge was therefore left unguarded, as another, at Primosole, was captured by fifty men of 1st Parachute Brigade, which had lost 115 men out of 292. General Alexander banned any more airborne operations until better training techniques had been developed.

5th Division was now given the job of taking the town of Misterbianco, by crossing the River Gornalunga, at a point three miles west of the Primosole Bridge. 1st KOYLI were not in the first wave of the assault, but at 1.30 am on the 20th, they, along with the 1st Green Howards and the 1st York and Lancs, attacked through the small bridgehead that had been created. Once onto the open plain that immediately spread out before them, they were met by mortar and machine gun fire from the men of the Hermann Goering Division, who had taken up position in a mesh of ditches that cut the ground into squares. It was very dark, and calling for a creeping artillery barrage was out of the question, as they would have no way of knowing where to drop their shells without risking their own troops. 15th Brigade had advanced over 3,000 yards before they were pinned down. 5th Division tried to send in a back-up force, but troops assigned to this were decimated by a German artillery bombardment as they were assembling. All they could do was sit tight, as the 15th did the same in their waterlogged trenches.

Nevertheless, the Germans were withdrawing in the face of the American advance in the west. They seemed to have recognised that their only hope was to hold on to the northeastern sector of the island. Elements of 16th Panzer Division began to explore the rising ground in the foothills of Mount

British infantry scramble over rubble in a devastated street in Catania, 5th August 1943. Silverside (Sgt) No 2 Army Film and Photographic Unit. (*Wikipedia*)

Etna. The Germans were now looking to find a point from which they could cover an evacuation from the port of Messina.

On 3rd August, XIII Corps began to advance on Catania, and at last, the stalemate outside Misterbianco was broken, when the Germans withdrew from the open plain as night fell, hotly pursued by 15th Brigade and the rest of 5th Division. Two days later, Catania, Misterbianco, and Paterno were taken. East of Mount Etna, the country became a tangle of obstacles as the thickly populated, narrow strip of land, turned into a patchwork of cultivated areas surrounded by stone walls that made ideal defensive positions. 1st KOYLI slogged their way through this obstacle course, towards the heavily defended Messina, until General Montgomery, determined to preserve the

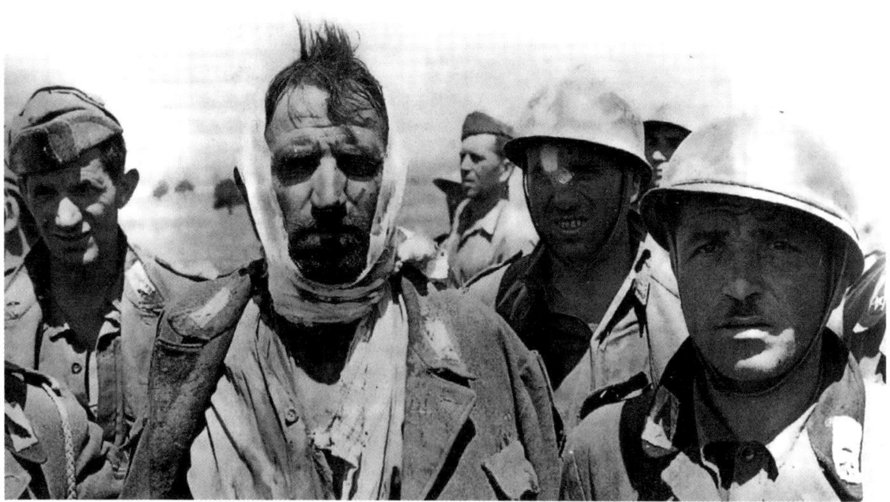

Italian soldiers of the 206th Coastal Division taken prisoner by British forces after the landing in Sicily. Unknown. (*Wikipedia*)

nucleus of a force to attack the Italian mainland, pulled 5th Division out of the fight, along with the Canadian Division. They had done enough for now.

Just before dawn, on the 17th August, the German commander, General Hube, sailed from a beach north of Messina in the last boat evacuating German troops from Sicily, having obeyed Hitler's order to fight to the last round. Operation Husky had been completed in thirty-eight days.

Chapter 7

Italy 1943–5

7.1 Operation Baytown

The first stage of the invasion of the Italian mainland was to involve the landing of 8th Army's XIII Corps in Calabria, across the Straits of Messina, and of 5th US Army's VI Corps with the British X Corps at Salerno.

With XIII Corps, was 5th Infantry Division and 15th Brigade, which included 1st KOYLI, and with X Corps was 2/4th KOYLI as part of 138th Brigade, in 46th Infantry Division. The Calabria landings were given the codename "Baytown," whilst those at Salerno were called "Avalanche."

In relation to "Baytown," Alexander told Montgomery that he was to secure a bridgehead that would allow naval forces to operate in the Straits of Messina. If the enemy withdrew from the "toe," he was to be pursued with all the forces available to XIII Corps, so that, and this must have seemed like another slight to the importance of 8th Army, pressure would be taken off the Salerno landings.

Probably the biggest issue involved in operational planning for the invasion was the availability of landing craft. Both landings would need more than was available at the time, and there was a great deal of wrangling between the operational planners, concerning which should have priority. In addition, until 16th August, the plan had been for three landing sites: Salerno, across the Straits of Messina, and the Gulf of Gioia. It was eventually recognised that such a wide spread of landing zones would require far more landing craft than was possible, and even when reduced to two landings it would be a close-run thing to get men and supplies ashore, within the time that was estimated would be available before strong enemy counterattacks. In the end, agreement was reached, and plans finalised. The assault for "Baytown" was to take place on two beaches north of Reggio. 15th Brigade, with 1st KOYLI, was to be in the second wave, which was to go in as soon as the landing craft could be turned around.

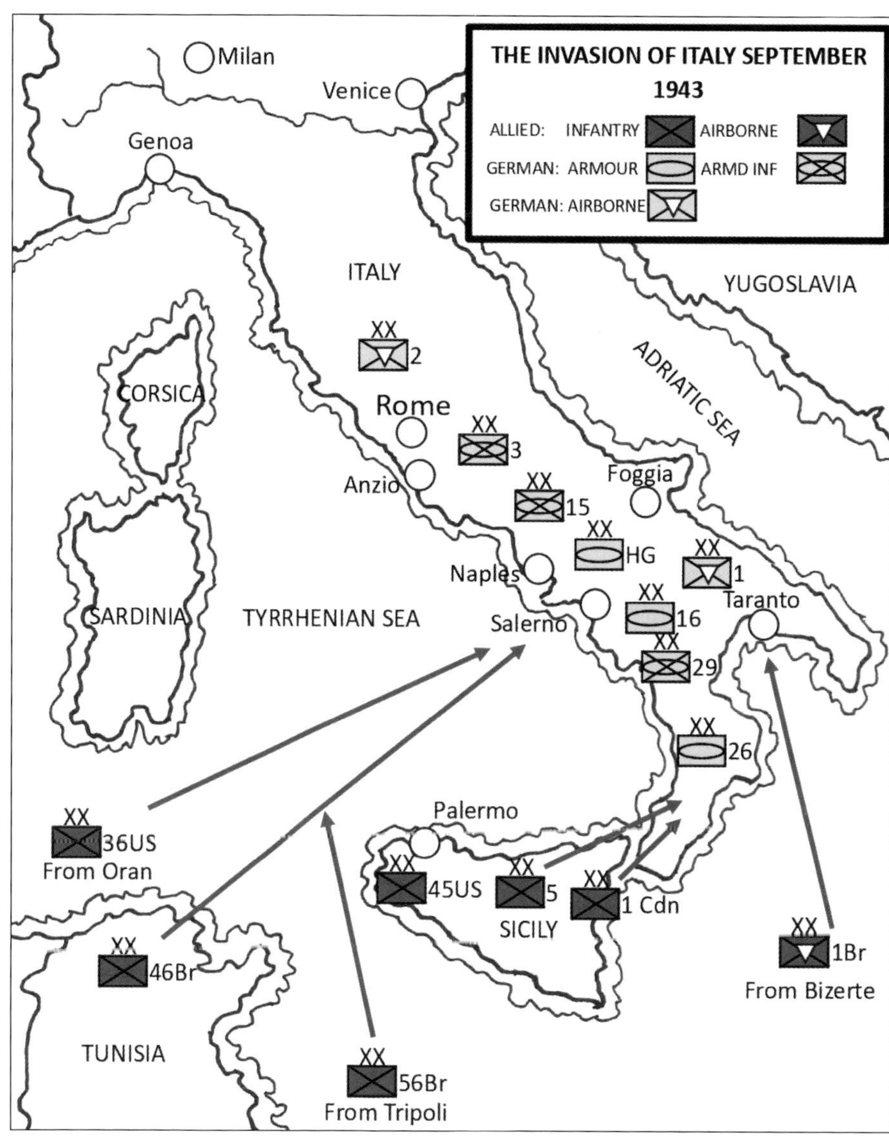

In the very toe of Calabria, stood the vast bulk of the Aspromonte Plateau, which rose to a 6,400 ft peak, called Montalto. All the roads twisted and turned, around and through the Aspromonte, and the viaducts, bridges and tunnels were ideal targets for enemy demolition units. However, by 2nd September, General Montgomery's Chief of Staff, Freddie de Guingand, was able to remark upon the lack of activity on the other side of the straits, as the mass of the allied invasion force swarmed onto the beaches below him. Was this going to be easier than had been expected?

British infantry come ashore at Reggio. Drennan (Sgt). No 2 Army Film & Photographic Unit. (*Wikimedia Commons*)

At 3 am on 3rd September, the artillery barrage began. 29,000 shells rained down onto the landing grounds before the assault troops were ferried ashore with almost no opposition. The only major problems were due to the strong tide and the thick smoke of the artillery hits, which caused some of the landings to be made in the wrong place. Reggio was occupied before midday, and at the start of the following day, 1st KOYLI were advancing along the western coast road, along with the rest of 15th Brigade.

The 15th Panzer Grenadier Regiment had withdrawn from the Reggio area to prepared positions at Bagnara, 25 miles away, and so, at first, the only real difficulties facing 15th Brigade were the roadblocks, demolitions and mines that the retreating Germans had left behind.

General Montgomery salutes his troops in the streets of Reggio, 3rd September 1943. Keating (Maj), No 2 Army Film & Photographic Unit. (*Wikimedia Commons*)

5th Division continued its advance along the coast road, each brigade taking it in turns to provide the spearhead of the advance. They made contact with 1st Special Reconnaissance Squadron, who had landed at Bagnara in a seaborne raid that sent the defenders into a panicky retreat. On the 7th, they clashed with a German rearguard at the River Mesima, north of Roscano, before linking up with 231st Brigade, which had landed near Pizzo in another one of those dynamic seaborne attacks. Together, they pressed on towards Nicastro.

On 9th September, General Montgomery messaged Alexander. He pointed out that his forces were now spread over a very large area. They must, he insisted, be rested for two days, as they were reorganised and regrouped.

He informed his commanding officer that he would be halting his forces on a line between Catanzaro, and Nicastro, from where they would carry out a thorough reconnaissance of the territory in front of them, all the way to the line: Crotone- Rossano- Spezzano -Belvedere. He had decided that, because the build-up of his forces across the Straits of Messina had been so pitifully slow, due no doubt, to the incompetence of the Navy, he would begin his advance to the Spezzano-Belvedere neck, on 13th or 14th September.

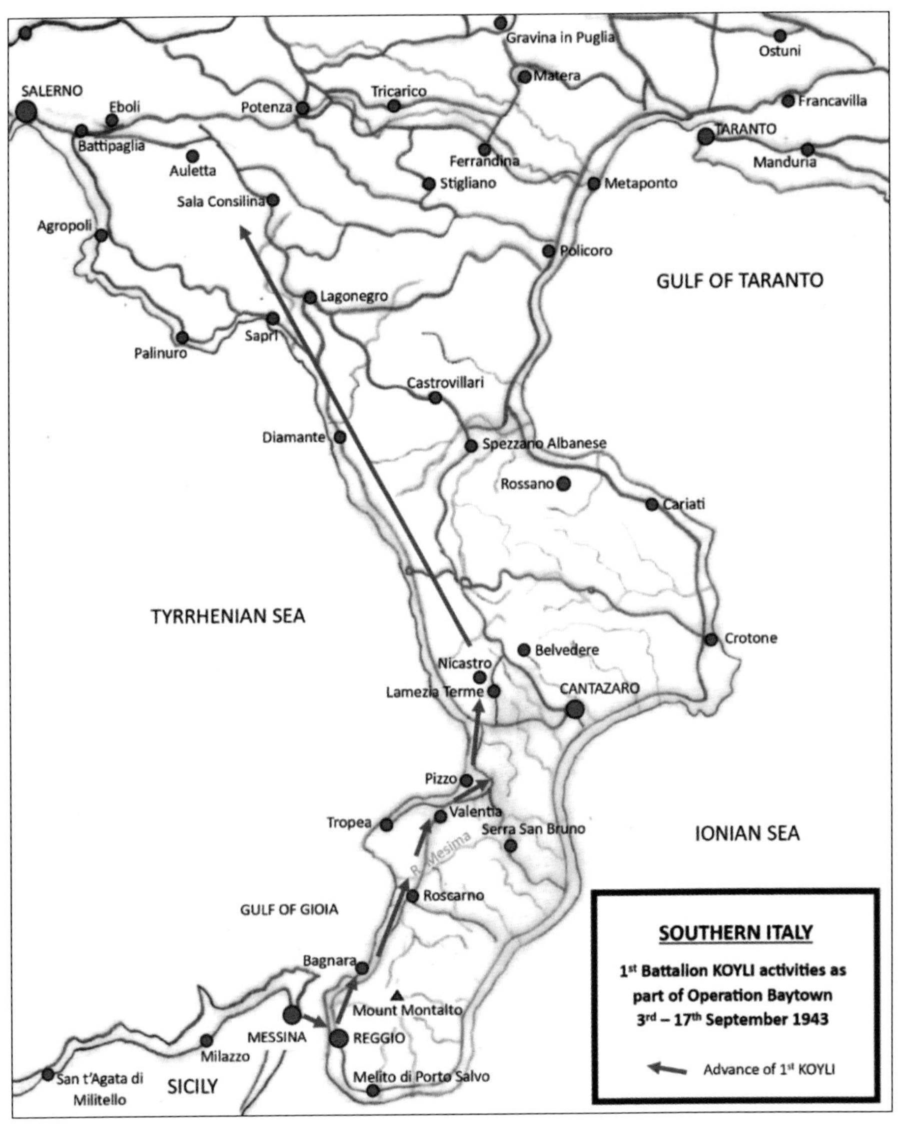

Alexander held his temper. After again emphasising the vital importance of keeping the enemy distracted from the Salerno landings, he tried to encourage his surly subordinate by telling him that more forces were soon going to be available to him. 1st British Airborne Division, he reminded Monty, had already been sent to Taranto, and would be followed by port construction units, V Corps HQ, and 8th Indian Division, on about 25th September. If he needed them, the 2nd New Zealand Division would also be sent to help. Monty seemed to be pacified.

On the day that 1st KOYLI had landed, they had heard the news that a new Italian government had finally signed an armistice with the allies. As they marched towards Lamezia Terme, on 8th September, they had no idea that any hopes they might have had, about the possible easing of their task, were sadly misplaced.

After the arrest of Mussolini, Hitler had ordered preparations for the total German takeover of Italy. The plan, codenamed "Operation Achse" ("Axis") was to free Mussolini, arrest the conspirators, invade the Vatican, and seize The Pope. Five days after Mussolini's fall, a panzer division was in place north of Rome, and in the next two weeks, eight more divisions had arrived, as Rommel's Army Group B occupied the north of the country. In the south, the German 10th Army had disarmed the eight Italian divisions there and confiscated fuel and supplies. A half-hearted, disillusioned opponent had been replaced by a battle-hardened army of warriors, who knew they had no option but to fight to the end, if the total and unconditional surrender of Germany was to be avoided.

7.2 Operation Avalanche

As part of 138th Infantry Brigade, of 46th Infantry Division, 2/4th KOYLI was destined to be part of Lieutenant General Mark Clark's US 5th Army, to which the British X Corps had been attached. The plan for 5th Army was to land in the Bay of Salerno, capture the port of Naples and cut off the Germans retreating from the forces that had landed from the Straits of Messina.

South of Salerno, the Sele Plain was a wedge-shaped area of open flat land that stretched down to the beach. At the water's edge, it was twenty miles wide, and it narrowed as it stretched inland for about twelve miles.

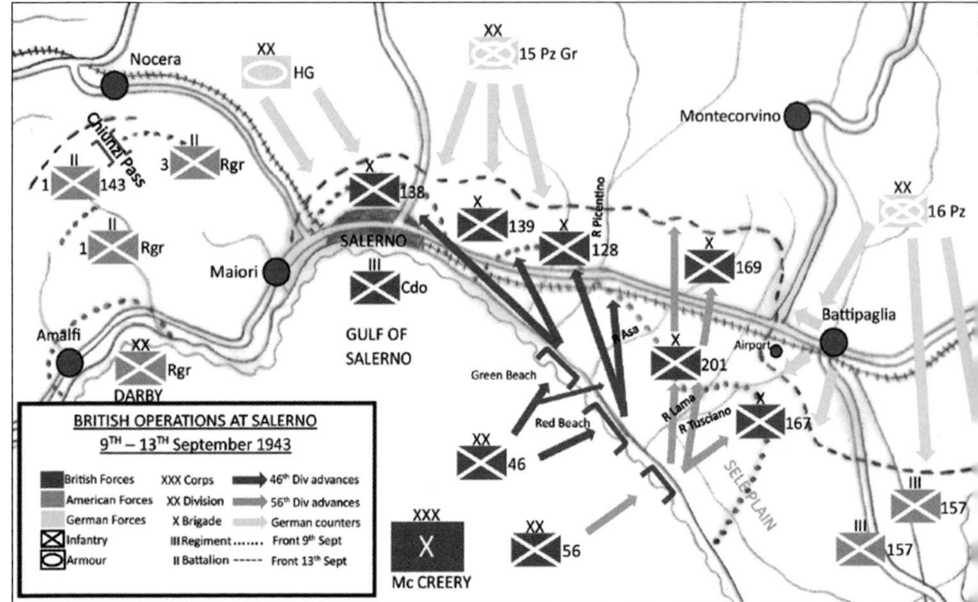

On each side, the cliffs rose up to meet the mountains of the Sorrento Peninsular to the north, and the Punta Licosa to the south, which meant that the entire landing area would be under direct observation and crossfire from any German positions there. Through the hills to the north ran two ravines which were the only available routes to Naples.

General McCreery, commanding the British X Corps, set out a plan of attack that would involve 7th Armoured Division racing towards Naples, through the beachhead that had first been established by 56th and 46th Infantry Divisions, around Salerno, and the hills that ran south to Battipaglia and the River Sele. The British would take the left flank of the landings.

46th Division would assault the area between the Rivers Picentino and Asa, which was a front of just over a mile, before moving on to secure the vital passes to the north, through Cava and San Severino. The initial landings were to take place on two beaches, codenamed "Red," and "Green." 128th Brigade was to take the enemy beach defences and the hills overlooking the Salerno Road, whilst 138th Brigade was to capture Salerno and link up with 2nd Commando, who would have been landed at Vietri.

In the early hours of 9th September 1943, Operation Avalanche began. The men of 2/4th KOYLI were crammed into landing craft which then crashed through the waves and the surf, towards Green Beach. The rocket

Salerno, 9th September 1943 (Operation Avalanche). British troops and vehicles from 128 Brigade, 46th Division are unloaded from LST 383 onto the beaches. Gee, Richard (Sergeant) No. 2 Army Film and Photo Section, Army Film and Photographic Unit. (*Wikipedia*)

ship assigned to their beach had spewed its projectiles half a mile to the south, and some of the landing craft found themselves on the wrong side of the River Asa. The undamaged gun posts around the warehouse to the right edge of the beach raked the sand with machine gun fire as the first wave charged ashore, and it took 50 minutes to subdue them. On Red Beach the assault forces had to navigate a minefield, although there was only light opposition, and on both beaches the landing craft continued to disgorge their human and vehicular cargoes. When dawn came, the air was full of smoke, and the crash of shellfire from the ships standing offshore competed with the roar of aircraft that swooped down to attack the enemy positions. On Red Beach, the 1/4th Hampshires forced their way through thick vines and trees, where snipers and German half-tracks hid. They crossed the road and took up their assigned positions on the small hills beyond. On Green Beach, the Beachmaster had called for reinforcements as the enemy gunfire continued to pour down from the hills above. 2/4th KOYLI set off for the shore, along with the 6th Lincolnshires, but the air had cleared with the rising sun and the German gun emplacements scored hit-after-hit on the LSTs as they were unloaded. The beach became a deadly scrapyard of blazing vehicles and stranded landing craft, and it was decided to stop any further landings there until the enemy gunfire had been neutralised.

Elements of 2nd and 5th Hampshires had managed to cross the River Asa and drive inland for a distance of half a mile. They had lost touch with one company which had veered off to the right to deal with some enemy positions, before advancing inland without crossing the river. This company managed to reach the airfield south of Pontecagnano, whilst the rest of 2nd Hampshires advanced to Pontecagnano itself.

2/4th KOYLI were preparing to advance with 6th Lincolnshires when the Germans suddenly counter attacked, and they dived to take up position in the dunes that lined the beach within a hundred yards of the sea. The panzers came rumbling down a narrow track that was bordered by dry stone walls and drove the attackers back. Fifty men took up position in a warehouse, as the rest dispersed into small, isolated groups, hiding amongst the dunes.

The main body of 2/4th KOYLI was on their own too. In the muddle of the landings, their HQ and one company had landed on Red Beach, from which there was only one exit, down a narrow road flanked with ditches that were starting to fill up with the detritus of war, as vehicles were hit and abandoned. But on Green Beach, the main priority was to bring together all the dispersed units to create a coordinated, purposeful force. To achieve this, the entire right wing of the attack was put under the command of Brigadier James of 128th Brigade, and immediately this scratch force of companies from 2/4th KOYLI, 6th Lincolnshires, 2/5th Leicestershires, and the remnants of two Hampshire battalions, were pulled together to stem the attack of enemy tanks and self-propelled guns. As night fell, they had fought the enemy to a standstill, and the Germans then began to pull back under the cover of darkness.

By that time, the Commandos and US Rangers were hanging on to Vietri and Maiori to the north of Salerno, whilst the 1/4th Hampshires

A 3-inch mortar in action at Salerno, 15th September 1943. Gade (Lt), No 2 Army Film & Photographic Unit. (*Wikimedia Commons*)

were in the low hills overlooking the main Salerno Road. When Brigadier Harding arrived with 138th Brigade HQ, to take control of the situation, the 6th York and Lancs were still on Red Beach, along with B Squadron 46th Reconnaissance Regiment, 232nd Anti-Tank Battery, and parts of both 71st Field Regiment and 271st Field Company. Harding immediately ordered the 46th Reconnaissance, along with the field engineers, to drive up the Salerno Road and make contact with the commandos. This done, the engineers were to set about clearing the dock areas as the rest pushed on up the Vietri pass. The York and Lancs were to advance to block the Sanseverino road. Back on Green Beach, the KOYLIs and the Lincolns were still fighting their own battle in a series of isolated actions. There was no plan, no aim other than to fight for their lives, and HQ had no idea what was happening in this sector of vicious close-contact encounters. However, slowly but surely, the men of these two battalions fought their way forward, along the beach tracks that led to Pontecagnano. One company of the KOYLIs arrived in time to surprise and capture an enemy convoy. 139th Brigade landed towards evening and had to settle for a night on the beach, as their proposed concentration area was impassable to their vehicles, but the bridgehead had been secured. By the end of the first day, 2/4th KOYLI's division had suffered 449 battle casualties.

On day two, all was confusion. The fighting between small, isolated units in difficult terrain, continued in a series of short, sharp, and vicious encounters, as the commanders struggled to work out just what was happening on this constantly moving battlefield. The beachhead seemed to have been secured by the sheer guts and tenacity of individual soldiers, but it was recognised that the enemy had not yet brought up its reinforcements. When they did, it was vitally important that the allies were in possession of the high ground behind the beaches, so that they could either cover the intended breakout or hit the Germans as they assembled for a counterattack.

On the German side of the peninsular to the north of Salerno was the hastily organised Battle Group Doernemann, together with 2nd Battalion of 1st Panzer Grenadier Regiment Hermann Goering, at Cava di Terreni on the Vietri sul Mare-Nocera road. The Hermann Goering Reconnaissance Battalion were at the Chiunzi Pass on the Maiori road. These forces were hurled against 2nd and 41st Commando at Cava di Terreni, but the arrival of 6th Lincolns balanced the scales, and the result was a stalemate.

The German build-up of forces continued, and immediately available to 10th Army commander, Generaloberst von Vietinghoff, were 15th Panzer Grenadier Division, the Hermann Goering Division, 29th Panzer Grenadier Division, and 26th Panzer Division. The Wehrmacht Commander in Chief, South, Feldmarschall Kesselring, ordered units of 3rd Panzer Grenadier Division to the Salerno area, from their positions north of Rome.

On the morning of 13th September, von Vietinghoff was told of a 7-mile gap that had opened between the British and US sectors around Salerno. He gave orders to drive the enemy back into the sea, and the resultant fighting developed into a mincing machine that drew more and more allied troops into its jaws. There seemed no possibility of a breakout in the near future, and plans were made for the evacuation of the forces trapped there.

The future of the entire Italian campaign, now depended almost entirely upon the determination, skill, and bravery of individual soldiers on both sides of the line, fighting on a series of rocky steep hills, or on a vast expanse of open plain that separated units and cut communications. Small German units would appear out of nowhere, send a withering burst of machine gun fire into an equally small and isolated unit, then withdraw behind the rocky outcrops and obstructions that littered the hills and the plain. No one knew from which direction the next attack would come, and even as they sheltered in some crevice in the hillside, or behind a smoking wreck, the British soldiers were still vulnerable to sniper fire from the high ground in front of them. Hour after hour they battled away in this game of nerves, and those nerves were beginning to fray. Between 9th and 18th September, X Corps alone had almost 3,000 battle casualties at Salerno.

British infantrymen take cover behind a burning German tank. Salerno 22nd September 1943. Lambert (Sgt), No 2 Army Film & Photographic Unit. (*Wikimedia Commons*)

138th Brigade, British 46th Infantry Division, enter Salerno, 10th September 1943. Bowman (Sgt), No 2 Army Film & Photographic Unit. (*Wikipedia*)

On 14th September, the main German pressure was against 46th Division, now dug in on the hills around Salerno. Once again, the fighting was intense, but the dogged determination of 2/4th KOYLI and their comrades forced the Germans to shift their attack to the area around Battipaglia, and 56th Division. As both British divisions stood their ground, von Vietinghoff began to see his hopes starting to disappear. In a last-gasp attempt to throw the enemy back into the Mediterranean, he ordered the 26th Panzer, and Hermann Goering Panzer Divisions into the fight.

2/4th KOYLI again faced the spearhead of the German attack, and again they held it at bay. In another hand-to-hand battle, they absorbed the impact of these fresh enemy troops and restricted them to an advance of only 200 yards. The Germans recoiled, before trying their luck further along the allied front line, but again they met with determined resistance.

The whole perimeter of the beachhead held throughout the night, and when the exhausted 2/4th KOYLI began to advance through the trees, towards the vital high ground, the Panzer Grenadiers fell back. Through a hail of withering fire, the KOYLI drove on, to take their objective, and to hold it.

This had been a tough soldier's battle, on a snarled-up beach, where small groups fought their way across exposed areas, to dive into a shell-crater, or behind a smouldering wreck, and to hold on. The reserves had all been thrown into the fight, so the possibility of trying any flanking moves did not exist. For seven days, all that the exhausted infantryman could do, was to keep on fighting, until the other side broke under the relentless pressure.

After taking their objective, 2/4th KOYLI were withdrawn from the hills surrounding Salerno, to the city itself. There, they evacuated the patients in the hospital, to a safer place, before taking down the red crosses and setting themselves up in a new defensive position.

7.3 The Advance to The Winter Line

By 17th September, the Germans had withdrawn to a new defensive line between Manfredonia, to the north of Bari on the Adriatic coast, and the Sorrento Peninsular, in the Bay of Naples. The British 8th Army had managed to drive a path up the Castrovillari Isthmus and were now in the process of pushing northwards, towards Auletta, and Potenza.

When Churchill had referred to Italy as "the soft underbelly of Europe," he had not taken into account the enormous difficulties presented by the terrain, and by the weather. Only now were the allied commanders becoming aware of the full extent of the task confronting them. Indeed, General Clark was later to refer to Italy as "a tough old gut." So far, the campaign had been based upon guesswork, and the ability to react quickly to changing situations and unexpected challenges. This not only applied to the men in high command but also to the individual soldiers who, confronted by a kind of fighting never before witnessed in the entire history of warfare, were developing the techniques and finding the answers as they went along.

The need for a secure and capable supply network was now obvious to both those at the top and those on the front line. Airfields, ports, and railheads needed to be taken in one piece, or repaired within days of capture, if the advance was to be maintained. Two separate armies needed to be organised and reorganised in order to carry out the tasks of what was now recognised would be a long-drawn-out campaign, over the entire length of the country. Although they learnt through their experiences, the ever-changing landscape, climatic conditions, and tactical challenges would ensure that they would be kept guessing, right until the end.

On 17th September, the "best guess" seemed to be that an advance to the line of Highway 7 would be the most effective way for 5th Army to secure its base, before attempting to take the city of Naples. Accordingly, orders were given for an advance to the northeast, in order to secure the highway between Teora and Avellino, before swinging southwest to Castellammare, on the Bay of Naples. In the meantime, 8th Army was to take the area around Potenza, to the southeast of Teora, before there would be a pause to allow the build-up of forces and equipment for a push on to Naples by the 5th Army, and to Foggia, by the 8th Army. Once again, the "guesswork" was to be tested out by the men on the ground.

On the 21st, Alexander called for the seizing of all-weather airfields, ports, and centres of road communications. This would, he said, be followed by the regrouping and reorganisation of both armies before the full weight of the allied advance could be brought to bear. In the meantime, the enemy would be kept busy by the constant activities of light mobile forces, as each new supply base was targeted. This armed reconnaissance might also help to gain intelligence that would lessen the degree of guesswork needed from now on.

Alexander then elaborated upon his plants for the upcoming operations. The first phase was to reinforce the line between Salerno and Bari. The second was to take Naples and the airfields around Foggia. The third would be the capture of Rome and its airfields, together with the communications centre of Terni. The fourth was to be the capture of the port at Leghorn, together with Florence and Arezzo. The extent of the conjecture involved in making these forecasts must have been evident to Alexander at the time that he made them, but the eventual course of the campaign proved just how accurate they were. At that time, Alexander had no reason to suspect that the Germans would drastically change their views on how their campaign would be conducted.

The Allied Chiefs of Staff had a clear view of the purpose and direction of the Italian campaign. In a communique dated 17th August, they described these as:

1. The elimination of Italy as a belligerent, and the establishment of air bases in the Rome area and if feasible, further north.
2. Seizure of Sardinia and Corsica.
3. The maintenance of unremitting pressure on German forces in Northern Italy, and the creation of the conditions required for "Overlord," (the codename for the Normandy invasion).

The Germans were well aware that the next move of the allies would be to continue the advance north, but Kesselring also appreciated that there

British troops in open country around Barletta during the 8th Army's advance towards Foggia, September 1943. Unknown. (*National Army Miuseum Study Collection*)

might be further landings on either coast. His strategy was to employ a scorched-earth policy in the path of the allies, through the destruction of any resources that might prove useful to them, and through the transfer of Italians to Germany as slave labourers.

The line between Salerno and Manfredonia was to be held until at least 30th September, before a staged withdrawal to the Rivers Volturno and Biferno. This line would be held until 15th October. After that, it was planned to withdraw to the strongest defensive position, which ran from the western coast at Mondragone, through the Abruzzi Apennine Mountains, and along the River Sangro, to Ortona, on the opposite coast.

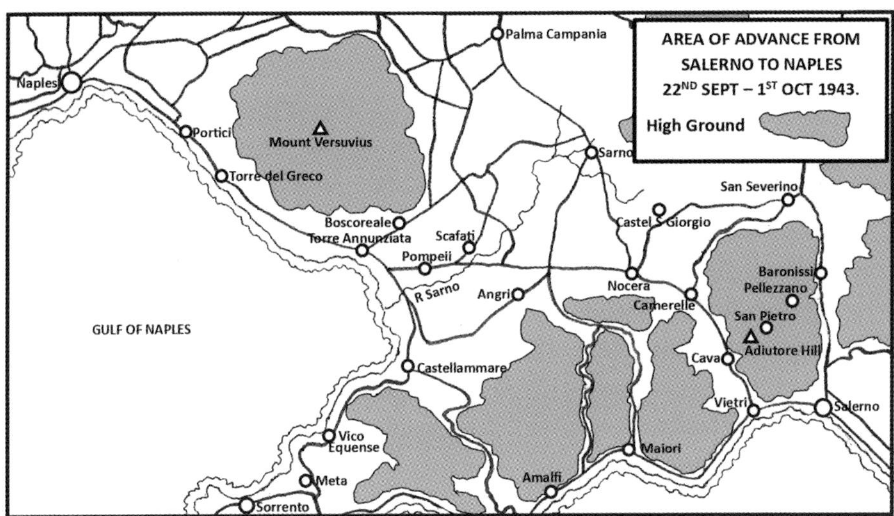

British X Corps now set about the task of securing the high ground above Nocera, before crossing the great plain outside Naples along the roads from Salerno to Baronissi, and from Vietri to Nocera. 2/4th KOYLI were at Vietri when the attack began on the night of 22nd September, and they joined in the assault on the area around Camerelle. This was a vital task, and the Germans knew it. If the penetration was deep enough, it would take the crossing point on the River Sarno, near Scafati, and keep the road open for 7th Armoured Division to burst through and continue the advance. So, von Vietinghoff put in all available forces to prevent the Allies from reaching the Sarno Plain.

A series of valleys ran through the Lattari mountains, which were, in some places, over 3,000 ft high. Patches of deep forest stood out amongst

A Vickers machine gun team in action, Italy. Unknown (*National Army Museum Study Collection*)

the bare open outcrops of rock, which were scarred by deep gullies and cut by sheer cliffs. Even from such a distance, it was obvious to the men of 2/4th, that although climbing those mountains would be difficult in itself, the task getting supplies and ammunition to them might well prove impossible, especially with enemy guns emplaced on the peaks. They did not know that those positions would be manned by the men of 15th Panzer and 3rd Panzer Grenadier Divisions, who were some of the most seasoned fighters that the Germans could call upon.

When the attack began, the men of 139th Brigade went forward to secure a line across the Vietri road. The object was to open a path that could be exploited by 138th Brigade, but it failed to take the whole of its objective, in the face of a devastating crossfire that came from cleverly sited machine gun posts. Unaware of the extent of this opposition, in the early hours of the morning, 138th charged through the small gap that had been made, straight into the fire of 139th Brigade, who were still fighting to subdue the enemy gun positions, in the pitch darkness. 2/4th KOYLI were forced to look for cover, before they began an agonisingly slow crawl, towards the machine guns that were sweeping the ground, like a deadly giant broom.

After what seemed an eternity, they reached the first of the rocky outcrops that led into the mountains. Here, one company discovered an abandoned ladder, which they used to help them scramble up and down the steep crevices that crossed their path. The others were not so fortunate, as their fingers searched for a grip on the sharp rocks, in the total darkness of a moonless night. Several men fell into the invisible crevices, tearing flesh, and ripping away webbing as they tried to stop their fall. Up and down the survivors crept, slowly feeling their way towards the Adiutore Hill, near San Pietro. Finally, they reached their goal and looked across to their left, to see that 16th Durhams had taken another high spot that could be used by artillery observers. At least they were not alone.

By the evening of the 24th, the scattered forces of 138th Brigade had been gathered together, and a trickle of supplies had reached them. Through the night, 2/4th KOYLI attacked San Pietro and Adiutore Hill, and by dawn they had secured both objectives. As they settled down for a brew-up, they watched 128th Brigade begin to advance into yet another storm of murderous gunfire. It was obvious that the attack was floundering, but the KOYLI were horrified to see what appeared to be two more battalions thrown into the fray and brought to a standstill. Out of ammunition, and low on food and water, the advanced units were stranded out on the bare mountains for 24 hours, until a few lines of sweating, cursing men, managed to climb the impossibly steep rock faces, to bring some of the vital supplies. Many fell to their deaths when they slipped on the wet and jagged surfaces, to plunge onto the rocks below.

2/4th KOYLI had lost, in a single day, 116 men. As they ripped open their packages of food and ammunition, they knew that they could not absorb this sort of punishment for much longer. The future of the battalion was in the balance.

General Clark was acutely aware of the problems being experienced by the whole of X Corps. They were still faced by the Sarno Plain, which would have to be crossed if they were to reach Naples. The roads that ran across the plain could barely be called that: they were narrow, uneven tracks, which were guaranteed to produce huge traffic jams, the moment that X Corps began to move its vast supply of vehicles onto them. The Sorrento Peninsular was narrow, and there appeared to be no other way to reach the first objective, which was Castellammare. So, Clark ordered VI US Corps to secure the road from Nola to Avellino, in the hope that they would be able to apply pressure from another direction, on the German defenders around Naples.

Those defenders were composed of three battalions of the Hermann Goering Division, who were in position on the ground to the east of Mount Vesuvius, and 103rd Reconnaissance Detachment to its south. This was not the major opposition that Clark had expected, but then, he was not fully aware of just what was happening in the streets of Naples. The citizens had taken up arms against the German garrison, and the fighting in the streets was causing a major problem for Kesselring and his plans for the defence of central Italy. The possibility of having an armed, hostile population, behind his front-line troops was unthinkable to the Commander in Chief, who promptly withdrew all forces south of the city, during the night of 30th September.

The advance of both corps was relentless. In a series of brilliantly coordinated attacks, they drove the remaining Germans back towards Naples, and by 28th September, Castellammare had been taken, and the River Sarno was in sight. 46th Division had surged into the Camerelle gap, and this had enabled its lorried infantry to launch an attack on the bridge at Scafati, as had been planned. San Severino was overrun, along with the road west to Castel San Giorgio. Avellino and Teora were taken in a night attack on 29th September.

Again and again, the ragged survivors of the Hermann Goering Division and the 103rd Reconnaissance Detachment fell back towards Naples, and when Torre Annunziata, just north of Pompeii, was captured by the allies on 30th September, they finally ran back into the city where they believed that their comrades would be waiting. They were not.

At 9.30 am on the following day, allied units began to enter Naples, where they too, expected to be confronted by the German garrison. Instead, they found a city deserted, except for a civilian population that had been subjected to four days of street fighting against a fully armed and enraged army that had been given clear instructions concerning how to deal with "partizans." The results were shocking, and as the soldiers of the 1st King's Dragoon Guards drove through the desolate, corpse-strewn streets, they discovered that all public transport had been destroyed, along with the water

Daimler scout car of 1st King's Dragoon Guards at the town hall in Naples, 1st October 1943. Mott (Sgt), No 2 Army Film & Photographic Unit. (*Wikimedia Commons*)

and electricity systems. Food supplies were almost non-existent, and as the docks had been totally wrecked, it was obvious that re-supply by sea would be out of the question, until the transport craft and unloading facilities could be replaced. This was to be the next task of 5th Army.

In the southeast, XIII Corps had halted on a line running from Catanzaro to Nicastro, on 10th September. As we have seen, General Alexander had insisted that Montgomery must press on, in order to draw German forces away from the 5th Army. The Commander of 8th Army had probably taken some time to calm down, before sending a reply to his boss. On 13th September, he seemed to be in an ebullient mood, as he informed Alexander that the 8th Army would resume its advance on the following day. Of course, he implied, it was the fact that Alexander had heeded his advice concerning the need for increased supplies and men, through the port of Taranto, that had brought about this new, positive situation. He could see no reason now, why he would not be able to come to the rescue of 5th Army, by launching an all-out attack on the south flank of the German forces facing them. He also generously offered to take over the front, from Taranto to Brindisi, as his army swept north, along the whole width of the country.

So it was, that the advance began again on 14th September, and by the 16th, the 5th Division had reached Sapri, whilst 1st Canadian Division was at Spezzano, south of Castrovillari. Another Canadian patrol met one from 1st Airborne Division forty miles south of Taranto, and 5th Division's Reconnaissance Regiment met patrols from 36th US Division at Vallo, north of Sapri.

So far, Montgomery was well on target to keep his promises concerning coming to Clark's "rescue." Kesselring knew that the game at Salerno was up. It had sucked in all the available force, in his attempt to defeat 5th Army before the arrival of XIII Corps, and now there was no alternative but to withdraw from the sector. However, the battle had given him time to complete his next surprise for the allied armies, and if the men of 1st, and 2/4th KOYLI thought they had experienced the worst that the Italian campaign had to offer, they were to be sadly disillusioned, yet again.

7.4 The Winter Line

By 18th September, the 1st Canadian Division were just north of Policoro on the east coast of Calabria, whilst 5th British Division were at Sapri, on the west coast. Potenza was to be the next objective, and as the Canadians went for the town itself, 5th Division aimed to secure the area to its west, up to the town of Auletta. Despite the presence of several units of 76th Panzer Corps, Potenza was captured during the night of 19th September, and Auletta fell on the following day.

During the night of 26th September, the Germans withdrew to the north and west of Foggia, which allowed 4th Armoured Brigade to occupy that town on the 27th.

As Alexander set about developing the next stage of his plan for the capture of Rome: the move to a line between Isernia and Termoli, Kesselring was receiving his orders from the Fuehrer. As was increasingly becoming his habit, Hitler wanted to assume control over the smallest details of the war. To Kesselring's annoyance, on 30th September, the man who, after the disaster at Stalingrad that February, had been given the ironic title of "GROFAZ" (Größter Feldherr aller Zeiten: the greatest military leader of all time) by many German soldiers, sent orders for a series of delaying tactics as far as a line from Gaeta, north of Naples, to Ortona, south of Pescara, which would then be held. In fact, Kesselring had already been working on a similar plan, and the building activity involved was spotted by allied reconnaissance aircraft, in early October.

To General Eisenhower, the head of Supreme Headquarters, Allied Expeditionary Force, whose job it was to plan and carry out the invasion

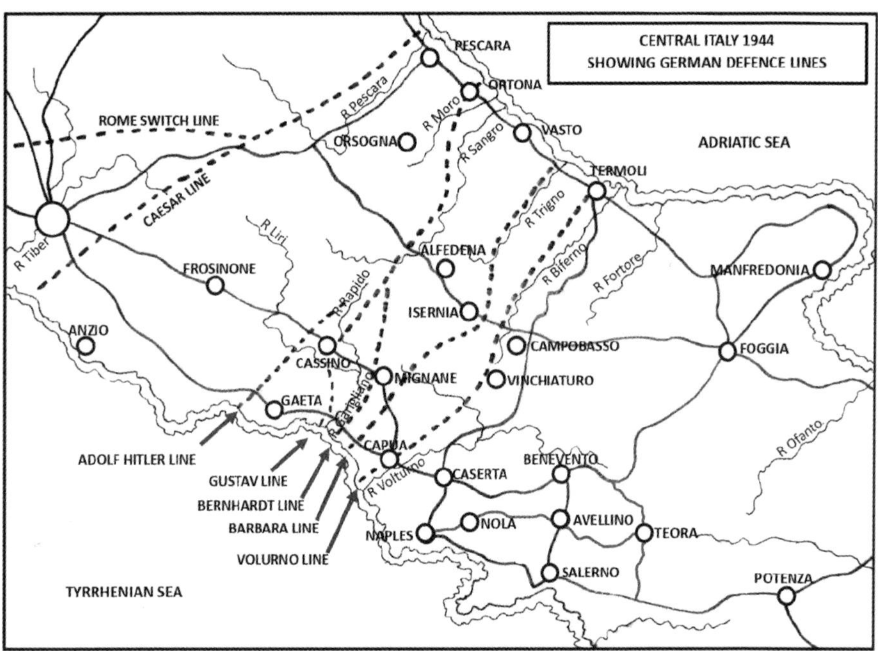

of northern France, Kesselring's ideas seemed to have a positive aspect, regarding the outcome of the whole war. As the D-Day landings drew ever closer, he was not alone amongst the allied High Command, in seeing the Italian campaign as a secondary theatre, whose main purpose was to soak up the Wehrmacht like a sponge. A war of attrition in Italy would save the lives of thousands on D-Day, and those who were to do the dying in the mountains now would probably make the difference between success and disaster, on the beaches of Normandy.

Such was the harsh reality of fighting a world war, and the soldiers in Italy were to experience it in all its fury. Until now, the allied forces had generally been able to rely upon modern motor transport, backed up by heavy weapons and tanks, but the mountains of central Italy were to prove an obstacle to any such tactics. Roads were few, generally poor and almost always susceptible to blockages and crossfire from the peaks. Only the Indian units and those from French North Africa had any experience of mountain conditions, being largely composed of men from hill country. The Germans were better organised for mountain fighting, having elements of specialist Gebirgsjäger mountain troops in their ranks, and they also had the advantage of being able to set up preferred defensive positions amid the jagged rocks and steep gullies. Although they had already gained some idea of just what mountain warfare could be like, the allied commanders still saw an advance up the spine of Italy as being the only way to break through the German defences, and as they began to formulate a series of strikes up the few passes that were navigable to their motorised and armoured units, they seemed not to have considered the possibility that the German commanders might have anticipated such a game plan. Even so, they must have been aware of the fact that any divergence from this strategy would take their troops into unchartered waters, for which they were ill-prepared, and perhaps this influenced their reluctance to consider what might in fact, turn out to be an inescapable outcome. Perhaps they were holding on to the comforting thought that both British and American soldiers had gained some experience of mountain fighting in Tunisia, and Sicily. Perhaps the learning curve might not be so formidable after all, but if this is indeed what they thought, they were deluded, and it was a delusion that would cost the lives of so many men in that cruel winter of 1943-1944, as they struggled to contend with atrocious conditions, in totally hostile and unfamiliar territory.

The men on the ground were the ones who would have to develop the tactics involved in fighting as small, isolated groups, out of contact with higher command. Where the ability to spot the best way up a mountain, to identify traps and hazards, and to stay connected through visual, line, or voice signals, were the basics of survival in this new warfare. The blatant neglect that Britain had shown to the physical welfare of her young men during the inter-war years, would now come back to haunt her, as the soldiers in Italy found themselves entirely unprepared for the physical nature of the

Monte Camino. The Winter Line, Italy, November 1943. Bowman (Sgt) No 2 Army Film & Photographic Unit. (*Wikipedia*)

fighting that they now encountered. Day after day, they would be forced to drag themselves up a steep slope, before plunging down into a crevice and dragging themselves out again, up slippery rock faces that continually ran with rainwater and rang with the ricochets of enemy gunfire. Facing them, was an army of men, who since the early 1930s, had been indoctrinated with the idea that physical fitness was the greatest of all human attributes. They had been fed on a diet of good food, and even better propaganda; raised in a national programme of both physical, and military training, and now they would be sitting in their mountain fortresses, waiting for the British to begin the climb towards them.

The front was just under one hundred miles long, and both German flanks were guarded by the sea. The Winter Line, as the Germans called it, had been constructed in depth, covering all the main mountain passes between the almost impregnable peaks. So, the allied commanders had to accept that the infantry would be the only force that could break it, even though their numbers were few and the area of operations so vast. They would have to learn from their experiences; how to use the craggy cover to infiltrate enemy positions, or to outflank them, and how to do it without accurate artillery support, as it blasted away blindly at hidden ridges and crests, where the enemy found so many places to take cover, and to maintain fire on the men dragging themselves upwards, through the storms of shrapnel and rain.

On 8th November, Alexander issued another directive. In it, he pointed out that the Germans seemed to be developing a stronger line of resistance than had previously been thought possible. To achieve this, he said, they were carrying out a scorched-earth policy that was devastating the country and destroying all installations and routes of communication. It would require a considerable engineering effort to fully restore the situation, but as it was vital that the capture of Rome be achieved as quickly as possible, only minimal repairs would be made in the short term. This would have to suffice.

Rome was to be the Holy Grail of the allied forces in Italy. Only after its capture, would it be possible to stop, and carry out the build-up of forces that would be needed to push on into the north of the country, and the Balkans.

As Alexander was expounding his thoughts for the future of the war in the "soft underbelly" and beyond, he was also issuing a new directive to Montgomery and Clark, regarding their next objectives. 8th Army was to take the road from Pescara to Avezzano, in order to attack the German lines of communications so that 5th Army could attack up the Liri and Sacco river valleys to reach Frosinone.

All this sounded straightforward on paper, but by the end of 1943, 8th Army was still well short of the Pescara to Avezzano road, and 5th Army was nowhere near Frosinone. The idea of landing a single division to the south of Rome had been broached earlier in the year, but this had been shelved. Now, as the situation in central Italy was developing an unexpected intensity, the necessity for such a seaborne landing was being reconsidered. By the end of the year, Prime Minister Churchill would have forced through his idea to send two divisions to Anzio, in an amphibious assault that would by-pass the German line of defence, and push on to Rome, as 5th Army continued to press towards Frosinone, and 8th Army fought it out with the forces to the east, so preventing them from counterattacking the Anzio invasion force.

But this was all in the future. The immediate task facing 1st and 2/4th KOYLI, as they lined up with the rest of 8th and 5th Armies, was the taking of the first layer of what Kesselring called "The Winter Line," and this was to prove more difficult than any of them could imagine.

In fact, the Winter line had been conceived by Kesselring as a series of lines, where his forces could make sure of the natural advantages that the terrain offered to defenders. The main barrier was to be the Gustav Line, which ran across the width of Italy, from the River Garigliano in the west, to the Sangro in the east. At the eastern end, Kesselring had built his main positions, with the west being protected by two additional shorter lines, designed to provide extra defensive depth on the road between Naples and Rome. The Bernhardt Line was constructed to the southeast of the Gustav Line, with the Adolf Hitler Line to the northwest. The two other coast-to-coast lines, called the Volturno and the Barbara Lines, were designed to delay the allied advance to the Gustav Line.

Four rivers flow into the Adriatic: the Fortore, Biferno, Trigno, and Sangro, all of which have their headwaters in the mountains on the eastern side of the country. To the west, the Volturno flows into the Tyrrhenian Sea at the Gulf of Gaeta, after starting its life in the narrow valleys of the mountains to the south of Alfedena and tumbling down through the lower mountains to the Campanian plain. The Winter Line took full advantage of the Rivers Volturno, Biferno, Trigno, Sangro, Garigliano, Rapido, and Liri.

The 8th Army was flanked by the Molise and Matese massifs, and after crossing the River Sangro it would be facing the Maiella mountains. The 5th Army was surrounded by Mounts Massico, San Croce, Maggiore, the western wall of the Matese massif, the Aurunci Mountains, Mounts Valle Martina, and Camino, and then heights overlooking Mignano, where one of the few valleys offered some hope. The others were at Cascano and the seashore.

7.4.1 The Volturno Line

As the first part of his Winter Line strategy, Kesselring had ordered that the Volturno Line be fiercely contested, so that time could be gained for the preparation of more defensive operations, and in response, General von Vietinghoff, in command of 10th Army, set about strengthening it with 26th Panzer, 29th Panzer Grenadier, 1st Parachute, Hermann Goering Panzer, 16th Panzer, and 15th Panzer Grenadier Divisions. Hitler once again interfered with the operational control of his front-line generals, by demanding that the Volturno be reinforced by two reserve divisions, and, reluctantly, Kesselring called for units of 3rd Panzer Grenadier Division from north of Rome. He ordered that only von Vietinghoff could authorise any withdrawal from the Volturno Line.

On the Adriatic coast, 8th Army had set about organising its forces for the advance on Termoli and Isernia. V Corps, with 5th Division, was to take the left flank of XIII Corps and protect the lines of communication as 8th Army pushed north. 5th Division, with 1st KOYLI, was sent to Foggia from their base at Potenza. On 1st October, the advance began along the coast road to Termoli and the rugged mountain road to Isernia. Many lesser roads ran north through the mountains, but these were unsuitable for anything more than small forces, especially as the weather was predicted to be heavy rainfall, followed by snow above 2,000 feet, as winter approached.

The Germans were well aware that the coastline offered many good defensive positions to the rear of the Volturno Line, and von Vietinghoff was

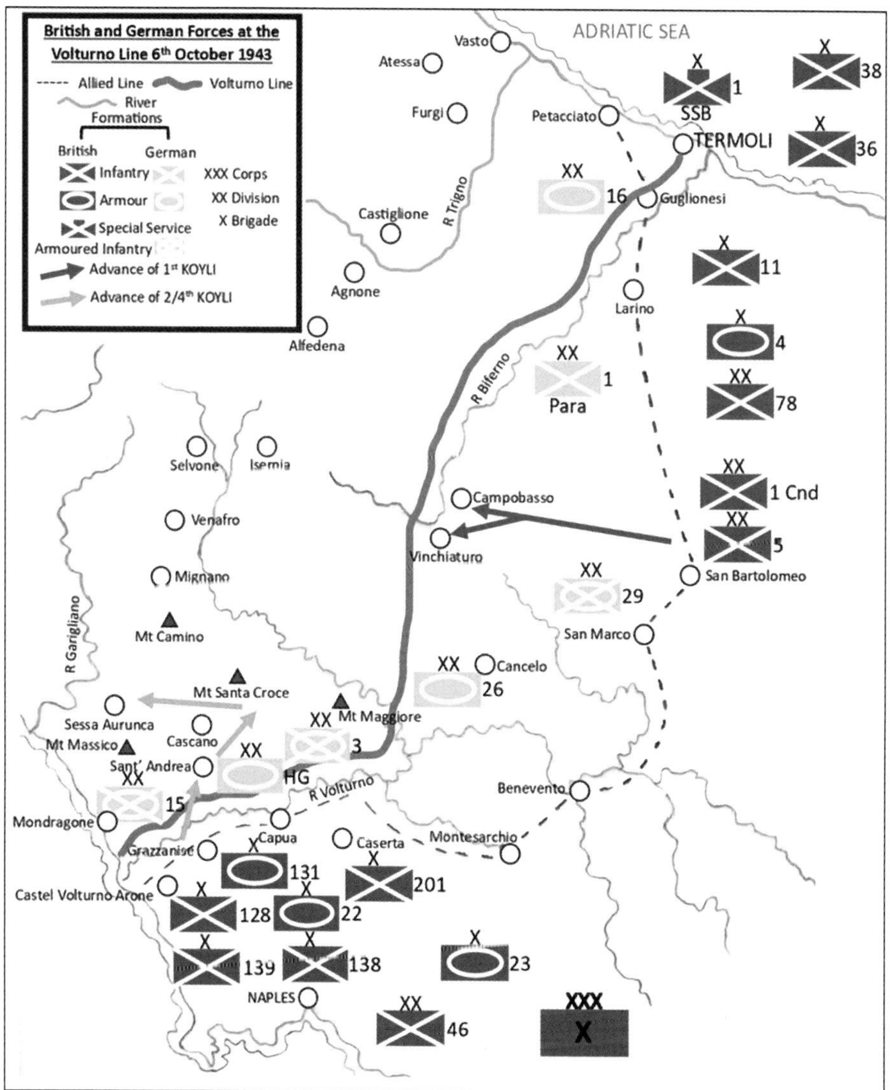

informed by intelligence that British XIII Corps consisted of no more than four newly reorganised divisions with very little naval support. Because of this, he believed that 1st Parachute Division would be sufficient to hold the line between the sea and the mountains, and after assigning a small, assorted battle group of about four hundred men to Termoli, he positioned the rest of the division to the southwest of the town. On 2nd October he was forced to react to a call for re-enforcements by sending 16th Panzer Division to the area.

The British plan involved 1st Canadians advancing up the main road to Campobasso as 1st Special Service Brigade seized Termoli, to be followed by further seaborne landings that would enable one brigade of infantry, and one of armour, to reach the town along the coast road. On 3rd October, the landings began before dawn, and the German battle group stationed in Termoli was swiftly overcome before the town was sealed off. The advance up the coast road had run into difficulties due to heavy rain, demolished bridges and some determined rearguard actions by the defenders. As a result, only infantry forces had managed to reach Termoli by the time 16th Panzer Division, which had passed through Campobasso on the previous day, began to arrive on the Coccia Ridge that overlooked Termoli.

Small groups from 11th Brigade of 78th Division, managed to forge a crossing of the River Biferno, south of Termoli, by wading across, or by using the boats of local fishermen. They were unaware of the approach of 16th Panzer and so they started up the Coccia Ridge, as others struggled across the stream to the northwest. The resulting fierce dogfight, ended in a stalemate that remained until 5th October, by which time the British had managed to construct a Bailey bridge for the first Sherman tanks to cross, having assumed that the approaching German forces would include armoured units. Indeed, a panzer regiment was approaching the Coccia Ridge, and the British forces there, found themselves hanging on with only a few anti-tank weapons at their disposal. When four Sherman tanks approached the ridge, they were destroyed by twenty Mark IV panzers that had managed to reach the battlefield, and the infantry slowly withdrew with heavy losses, back towards Termoli.

More British armour began to arrive and were quickly sent across the Bailey bridge in support of fresh infantry, as 16th Panzer at last began to wilt in the face of the determined defence that had been put up by the British infantry and the few tanks that had managed to get forward to support them. The attack had gained only 3,000 yards in two days, and as

British reinforcements began to arrive, the Germans were finally ordered to withdraw to the northwest.

Inland, the British 5th Division advanced alongside 1st Canadian Division through the Daunia mountains to take Campobasso on the 14th, and Vinchiaturo on 15th October, after they had first experienced the new German tactic of seeming to be determined to hold a particular defensive position by putting up fierce resistance, before suddenly disappearing. This had the effect of slowing the advance as the attacking forces probed what they thought were still heavily defended strongpoints.

As 1st Canadian and 5th British Divisions moved on Isernia from the east, General Clark ordered 5th Army to move north and east, across the lower Volturno to a line between Isernia and Sessa Aurunca, near Cascano, with VI US Corps on the right, and British X Corps on the left, closest to the Bay of Naples. The aim was to push through two gaps in the mountain range: at Mignano and Cascano, which would allow access to the Liri valley, and the Garigliano Plain, respectively. Facing the attackers would be, from west to east, 15th Panzer Grenadier, Hermann Goering Panzer, and 3rd Panzer Grenadier Divisions, together with the Viebig Battle Group from 26th Panzer Division of 76th Panzer Corps. The allied force consisted of:

British 46th Division: 128th and 139th Brigades at Castel Volturno Arnone.
138th Brigade with 2/4th KOYLI, to the north of Naples.
131st Lorried Infantry Brigade of 7th Armoured Division at Grazzanise.
201st Guards Brigade at Capua.
22nd Armoured Brigade to the south of Capua.
23rd Armoured Brigade in the rear.
3rd US Division north of Triflisco.
34th US Division from Limatola to Calore.
45th US Division from Telese to Pontelandolfo, through Benevento.
36th US Division in the Nola area.
82nd US Airborne at Naples.

A few remaining British support units were being held in reserve, and 56th Division was south of Capua, in the process of moving up to join the offensive.

The crossing of the Volturno began on the night of 12th October. The British force was positioned along a stretch where the river was a hundred yards wide and six feet deep. To the left of the American forces, it was possible to wade across, but the problem of getting vehicles down to the water was the same for everyone. As usual, the torrential rain had flooded the banks and turned the few tracks into a sea of mud. At Castel Volturno, Cancello, Grazzanise, and Capua, the bridges had been either destroyed or damaged, and the Germans had taken up positions that were perfect for decimating the engineer units that were sent to repair them.

2/4th KOYLI formed a line down the slippery riverbank and began to pass boxes of ammunition to the assault boats that bobbed about in the black water. Only 288 of such boats had been allocated to the entire front, and the men of the KOYLI watched, as other infantry units struggled to help the engineers manhandle the framework of the only available Bailey bridge. The whole party went down in a spray of mud and metal, as the bridge slid down the sloping bank, into the river.

The beaches on either side of the KOYLI's position had been mined, so it was imperative that they took a tight grip on the slippery mooring ropes and kept the boats within the marked lines of the cleared areas, as the men who were to form the first wave of the assault, struggled to climb aboard, with their loads of heavy equipment. The canvas boats shuddered and creaked as the inexperienced, non-sailors tried to keep them balanced, always conscious of the fact that the enemy must have seen the reconnaissance groups that had scouted the area for the best embarkation points.

The original plan had involved a far wider bridgehead that would have extended right up to the Regia Agnena Canal, three miles west of Volturno, and this was now resurrected, so that raft ferries could be built, out of the sight of enemy observation posts. This would, it was hoped, speed up the crossing of supplies and reinforcements

At 9 pm, the crossing began, when the assault battalion of 128th Brigade pushed their first two boats away from the bank. All was silent on the opposite side of the river. As more boats pushed off from their launching sites, they were caught by the swirling current and swept off course. Some were drifting out towards the sea, despite the frenzied paddling of those inside them. One was overturned, and its occupants were dragged beneath the surface by their heavy equipment. Still, there was no sound from the far bank.

Two hours later, the first troops clawed their way up the slimy bank and began to spread out amongst a maze of ditches and dykes. At last, the

Germans woke up to what was happening, and poured out of their foxholes to engage the isolated assault groups.

At this time, 2/4th KOYLI were engaged in getting supplies and ammunition across the river. The alerted enemy now began to find their range and pour a deluge of mortar and machine gun fire, onto the boat loading sites. Only two companies had managed to reach the Regia Agnena Canal, but another crossing had been made 5 miles upstream, to secure the right flank of the assault. Although under constant attack by both armour and infantry, the stranded companies held on, as the flank crossing was strengthened. During the afternoon, dive bombers and fighters appeared, spraying death and destruction along the length of the river, as men crawled on their bellies to probe the ground with twigs: the only way to locate the wooden box mines that the Germans had carefully buried along the shore.

Yet again, the weather broke, and the ground was turned into a torrent of mud. This brought about an unforeseen benefit in that the enemy tanks became stuck in the gluey morass, allowing the British infantry time to clear out the machine gun posts that littered the flat terrain of the far bank.

On 15th October, 138th Brigade was ordered to form a firm bridgehead around Cancello, which had been occupied on the previous night. They moved along the riverbank until they found a promising crossing place, and 2/4th KOYLI, together with 6th York and Lancs, clambered over a wrecked railway bridge, where on the previous day, one of their scouting patrols had been ambushed. Cancello had been reduced to a pile of rubble, alive with rats that swarmed all over the mass of putrefying bodies. Still there remained the danger of booby traps, and seven jeeps were destroyed by mines. Assault boats were used to keep the two battalions supplied, as the sappers who had been instructed to build a bridge at that point, were hurriedly sent to Capua, where the heavy equipment was now to cross. On 16th October, 2/4th KOYLI relieved the 2/5th Leicestershires, who had pushed along the hostile bank, and that night they advanced through ankle-deep mud and a storm of shells, to reach the vital canal at midnight. Making a rope out of rifle slings, they scrambled across the ruins of the demolished railway and road bridges. In the blackness, they ran into advance units of enemy infantry, and during the vicious hand-to-hand fighting that followed, they managed to take several prisoners before being forced to dig in. The casualties had been considerable, and that night, they were relieved by 6th Lincolnshires.

Allied transport crossing a pontoon bridge over the River Volturno, October 1943. Unknown. (*National Army Museum Study Collection*)

By this point, von Vietinghoff had decided to withdraw to the next defence line, and the Volturno Line was breached along its entire length on the 19th. On the following day, General Clark issued his revised aim for the next stage of 5th Army's advance, which was to be a line from Isernia to the mouth of the River Garigliano. 56th Division would be on the right of the British forces, with 7th Armoured Division in the centre. On the left, 46th Division was to cross the Volturno Plain and advance to Mount Massico.

The advance was heavy going. The soldiers of 56th Division were kept awake with Benzedrine tablets as they dragged themselves up mountain slopes and jagged hills. On the plain, 46th Division found itself entangled in another bridging operation, this time over a series of canals, as 7th Armoured Division struggled to push their tanks through ground that was boggier than had been anticipated. For this reason, they were switched to the firmer land on the left of the British advance, as 46th Division moved into the centre of the thrust. The boundary between the British and US forces had been defined by Clark, which meant that VI US Corps would take the road through the Mignano Gap and the area to its northeast, whereas British X Corps were assigned to take Mount Maggiore, Mount Camino, and the Cascano Gap.

46th Division moved to the northeast, through San Andrea, before swinging around to pass south of Mount Santa Croce, through the Cascano Gap. They reached Sessa Aurunca on 2nd November, and 2/4th KOYLI set up their HQ in the castle that had once been the HQ of Prince Umberto's army. It was a strong fortification and from its battlements they could see right across the plain and the river, towards the hills that spread out along the horizon. They were ordered to help the sappers in the repair of roads that had been expertly destroyed by the retreating enemy, and on 6th November, 138th Brigade took over the divisional front, sending out patrols into the

British infantry climb the heights of Calvi-Risorta, to the southeast of Isernia, 27th October 1943. Palmer (Sgt) No 2 Army Film & Photographic Unit. (*Wikimedia Commons*)

country between Sessa Aurunca and the River Garigliano. 56th Division was ordered to attack Mount Camino and its six-mile-wide series of rocky ridges and towering peaks. The assault was undertaken by four battalions, in a biting wind that drove rain and sleet into their faces, as units of 14th Panzer poured down fire from the crags and crevices 2,000 ft above their heads. The first battle for Mount Camino ended on 14th November, when the British were ordered back, having suffered enormous casualties. This was the date when British 5th, and Canadian 1st Divisions, captured Campobasso, after passing through the Daunia mountains to the east of 5th Army. On the 15th they took Vinchiaturo, to the southwest of Campobasso, before Montgomery ordered a halt for the regrouping of 8th Army. V Corps was now to be composed of 78th Division, 8th Indian Division, 4th Armoured

A Sherman tank being recovered from the River Biferno, near Campo-Marino, October 1943. Walker (Sgt) No 2 Army Film and Photographic Unit. (*Wikimedia Commons*)

Brigade, and 1st Army Group Royal Artillery. XIII Corps had 1st Canadian Division, 1st Canadian Tank Brigade, 6th Army Group Royal Artillery, and 5th Infantry Division, where 1st KOYLI was retained under 15th Brigade. V Corps took command of the sector between Vasto and Larino, where XIII Corps took over, up to the Matese mountain range, at Vinchiaturo. The aim was to cross the River Trigno before taking control of the main road from Vasto to Isernia and to enable this push, a railway supply depot for XIII Corps was set up at Barletta on the coast to the north of Bari, with another for V Corps at nearby Trani. The mountainous territory that faced them would mean that horse and mule transport would be vital, and five pack-transport companies were to be assigned for this purpose.

7.4.2 The Trigno and the Barbara Line

From 15th to 22nd October, V Corps approached the River Trigno, clearing out scattered opposition in a series of skirmishing attacks. Meanwhile, XIII Corps had pushed up to the Biferno, where they were ordered to carry out diversionary attacks between Vinchiaturo and Isernia until 29th October, so that V Corps could make the main effort against what was expected to be the greatest opposition, on the night of 29th October. Their objective was to be the River Sangro. Opposing the British forces were 16th Panzer Division, nearest to the coast, 1st Parachute Division in the centre, part of 3rd Parachute Division in the area around Tufillo, with the rest of 3rd Parachute Division occupying a reserve line in front of the Sangro. 26th Panzer Division was positioned to the southwest, in the area between Vinchiaturo and Isernia. The inexperienced 65th Infantry Division had been moved to the Chieti area from its security duties on the west coast, and now it was ordered to the coastal zone between Pescara and Ortona.

Once again, the forces of nature were stacked against 8th Army, as heavy rain turned the Trigno into a raging torrent that was six feet deep and 400 feet wide. As it approached the sea, the river skirted the 500 feet high. Cupello Ridge, before swirling its way across first a deep valley, and then a wide plain. Further west, were the rugged hills where the Trigno had its source, and these were accessible only by cart tracks, and poor, narrow roads. From Vinchiaturo to Isernia, the only main road ran alongside the sheer wall of the Matese, where 26th Panzer Division waited, having created roadblocks, not only on the highway but also in the mountain passes.

By 27th October, V Corps had crossed the Trigno, but an attempt to take San Salvo was driven off, and the state of the sodden roads meant that a one-way system had to be operated as a Bailey bridge was being built. The advance began again on 2nd November, but the never-ending rain swept away the road, and all attempts to re-surface it failed, under a torrent of

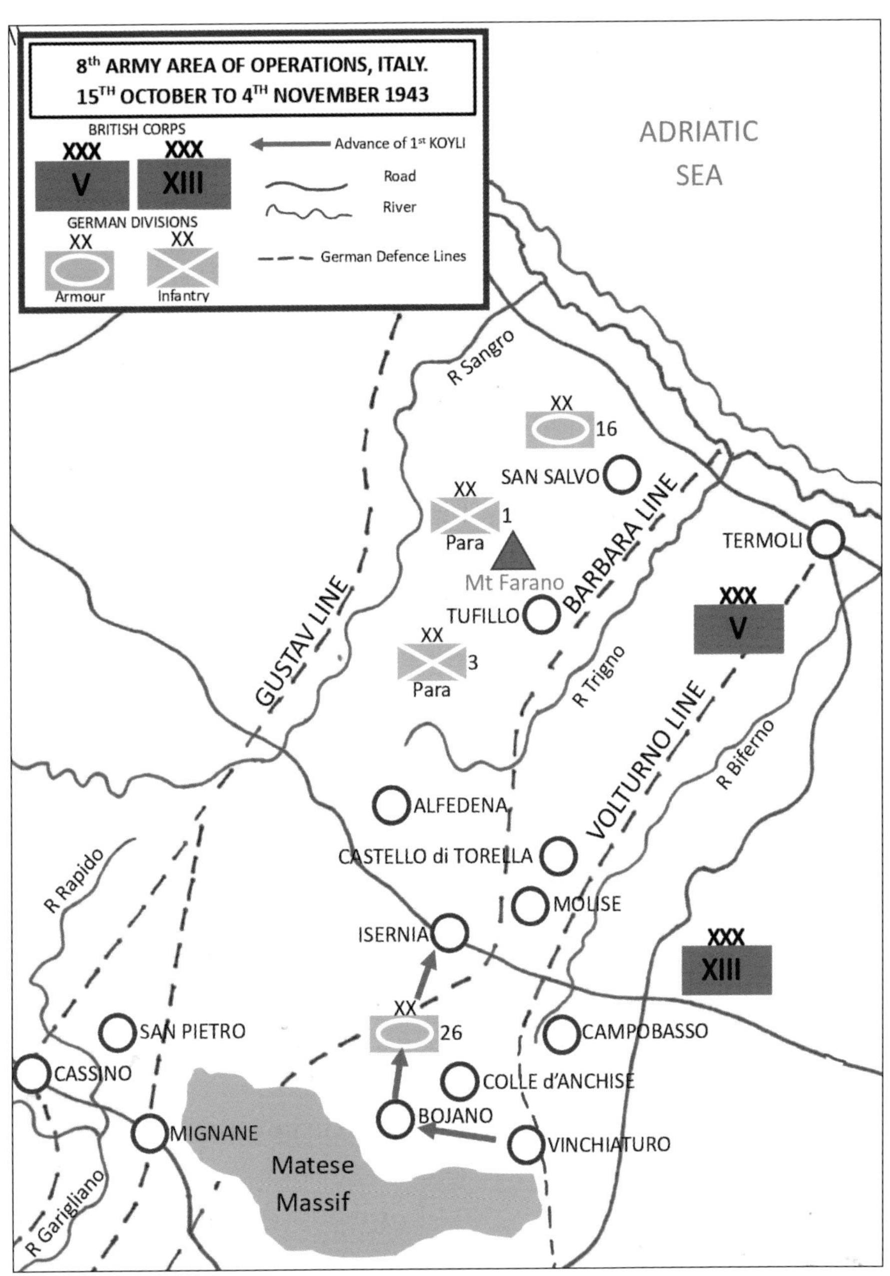

water and enemy gunfire. The battle for Mount Farano, and the town of Tufillo, turned into a vicious dogfight, in the darkness of a moonless night, which was pierced only by the blaze of flaming haystacks and scrub. The initial attack was repulsed, and this gave the enemy an opportunity to thin out their line and retreat to the Sangro, in accordance with the general plan. When this retreat became obvious to the British on 4th November, they poured forward to finally take Tufillo on the next day.

To the west, XIII Corps moved forward, in the knowledge that they were supposed to provide the bait that would lure some of the German forces away from V Corps and the main thrust of the offensive. By 24th October, they had battled their way to Colle d'Anchise, and taken up position on a hill from where they could observe both the Matese massif, and the valley of the Biferno. The town of Bojano had been cleared during the advance down the Vinchiaturo- Isernia Road, as 1st Canadian Brigade moved along the right flank to tackle the heights that stretched from Molise to Castello di Torello. 5th Infantry Division followed up the initial advance to take the lead as they swept through Bojano on 28th October, before attacking the heights from which the Germans were attempting to hold up the entire advance of XIII Corps. Yet again, the infantry spearheads sent to clear the way, were faced with a succession of bloody slogs, up rugged slopes, and along exposed ridges, where mountaineering skills were learnt on the job, under intense fire from a well-entrenched enemy. Roads needed to be cleared of carefully constructed roadblocks and the massive holes that had been blasted into their surfaces had to be filled with material manhandled into position as collapsing hillsides were shored up, again and again. Despite all this, Isernia was taken on 4th November, after a two-day street battle, and the men of 1st KOYLI were able to rest, as they watched the full might of their new corps, envelop the captured town.

7.4.3 The Sangro and the Moro

So it was, that by 9th November, the men of 8th Army were able to look down at the swirling waters of the bolder-strewn River Sangro, from the steep hills that formed its south bank. Montgomery was determined to force a crossing as soon as possible, to maintain the impetus of the advance to the Pescara-Avezzano Road, from where they could support 5th Army's move on Rome.

Between Casalbordino and Torino di Sangro. Infantry advances along the main road to the north of Vasto. Unknown. (*National Army Museum Study Collection*)

The Sangro varied in width, from 300 to 400 yards, and could turn into a five-foot-deep torrent at the first sign of significant rainfall. All the bridges had been blown up, and the mined approaches were so soft that traffic would find it extremely difficult to reach the water, let alone cross through it. The northern bank was both steep and treacherous, and 2,000 yards of open plain led to a shallow ridge that was the gateway to a 400-foot-high escarpment, running parallel to the river. The Germans occupied this high ground, which gave them a complete view of the entire front, from a complex of deep bunkers and trenches stretching back almost three miles.

By 18th November, 1st KOYLI were dragging themselves through the thick mud of the scarred countryside that led to Castel di Sangro. As part of 5th Division, they were ordered to attack the high ground around Civitella, and in the usual torrential rain, they climbed the steep slopes, under a tremendous barrage of fire. By 22nd November they had reached the summit, and as they prepared to attack the nearby town of Alfedena, they received the order to halt. Other plans had been made for them.

The battle for southern Italy had devastated the land and destroyed villages and towns in its path. It became clear that the refugee situation was becoming critical, as the homeless tried to escape the carnage and find

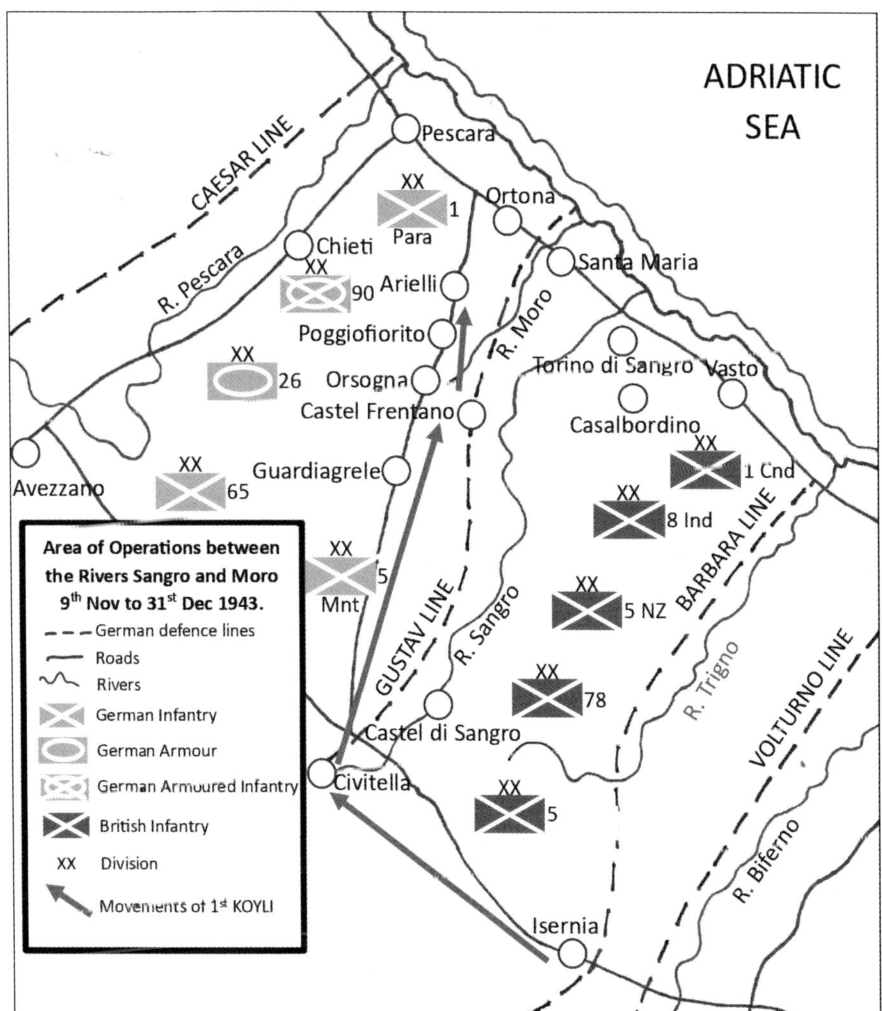

food and shelter. The infrastructure of society had broken down and the only possible source of hope for the estimated 4,000 people in need of help, was XIII Corps. They tried to set up shelters and provide food, using the already stretched transport that ground its way along the treacherous roads. Sanitation was a real concern, as was the provision of drinking water, because the local sources had been polluted by the swirling mud, driven down from the high ground by the never-ending rain.

The risk of disease was so bad that each transport vehicle had to be disinfected after every trip, as the Corps' medical services struggled to cope.

To the east, V Corps had reached the lower Sangro, ready to break through the enemy lines towards the next objective, which was the small port of Ortona. The advance of XIII Corps was supposed to be the signal for the main attack by V Corps, but in the event, the atrocious weather delayed the second part of Montgomery's plan until 27th November. Preceded by air attacks and an artillery bombardment, the assault swept towards Mozzagrogna, which was taken by the Gurkhas at nightfall. Next morning, a German counterattack pushed the 17th Indian Brigade out of the town when armoured support failed to arrive, but somehow they managed to regroup and retake the town later that day. On other parts of the front, the New Zealanders pushed towards Castel Frentano, whilst the Inniskillings, with armoured support, captured Santa Maria by late afternoon.

The advance continued, and on 30th November the German defences were breached close to the coast, as the town of San Vito was taken. By 4th December, V Corps had reached the River Moro, where the German forces had established their next line of defence.

Montgomery's next target was Ortona, five miles beyond the Moro, and after eight days of house-to-house fighting, the town was taken, on 28th December. As the Canadians had been battling their way towards Ortona, XIII Corps had been brought into action on the left of the line, at Orsogna.

Taking the town of Orsogna would threaten the right flank of the German defences and would also provide a secure basis for any advance that might take place towards Chieti, along the road from Guardiagrele. 5th Division had taken the town of Poggiofiorito on the 17th December, after a grinding battle in which 1st KOYLI was at the forefront of wave after wave of assaults on a series of limited objectives that were continually counterattacked. Ammunition was running low, and the fighting had often been hand-to-

Searching the ruins of Ortona for snipers. 1943. Unknown. (*National Army Museum Study Collection*)

hand, yet the KOYLI were back in action again on 23rd December, attacking toward Arielli. 2nd New Zealand Division were to move northwest, in an arc that would enable them to take the German defences at Orsogna from the north. This was to be the final attempt by the New Zealanders, who had made three previous attacks on Orsogna, resulting in many casualties as the Germans held on grimly. 1st KOYLI entered Arielli, along with the rest of 5th Division, on the evening of the first day, securing the flank of the New Zealanders, who attacked early the following morning. By the afternoon, it had become clear that the German defences were still holding firm against the onslaught of the exhausted Kiwis. As the Canadian advance from Ortona ran into a freezing blizzard that shut down all communications and air support, Montgomery called off any proposed further movement. The whole offensive was stalled, as the dog-tired 8th Army settled down to fight against the forces of nature. The opportunity to reach Pescara, and so to approach Rome along the Via Valeria, had been lost. On 31st December, Montgomery turned over command of 8th Army to General Sir Oliver

Leese, when he was recalled to Britain, in order to prepare for the invasion of northwest Europe.

In early January 1944, 5th Division was transferred to the west, to join X Corps as part of US 5th Army.

7.4.4 From the Bernhardt Line to the Gustav Line

As 8th Army had been battling its way north, to the east of the spine of Italy, in the west, 5th Army's first attempt to break the Bernhardt Line, had resulted in severe casualties, and an order to halt had been given.

On 24th November, General Clark issued his new plan for 5th Army's advance to Rome. Beginning on 2nd December, the offensive was to be divided into three phases.

Men of 15th Infantry Brigade trudge down a snow-covered hillside, 1st January 1944. Dawson (Sgt), No 2 Army Film & Photographic Unit. (*Wikimedia Commons*)

Phase I was to involve the capture of the critical terrain features of Mount Camino, Mount La Difensa, and Mount Maggiore. X Corps was to capture the Mount Camino hill mass, before carrying out a feint that would fool the enemy into thinking that it intended to cross the lower reaches of the River Garigliano. Meanwhile, II Corps would move against Mount La Difensa, and Mount Maggiore, as VI Corps carried out harassing raids along the entire corps front.

Phase II would involve the capture of Mount Sambucaro, as a secondary attack was being made along the Colli to Atina road. X Corps would consolidate its positions on Mounts Camino, La Difensa, and Maggiore, whilst continuing to give the impression of a planned offensive across the Garigliano, as II Corps forged on, to capture Mount Sambucaro with the help of VI Corps. One division would be spared to probe along the Colli to Atna road, towards the hill mass to the north of Cassino, and another attack would be made on the same objective, along the Filignano to San Elia road.

Phase III would be the main attack by X Corps, up the Liri valley, but only after II Corps had secured sufficient ground to enable the bringing up of bridging materials, so that a crossing of the River Liri could be made, and a bridgehead secured near San Ambrogio. Once established, it was Clark's intention to push II Corps along Highway 6 and surround the German forces at Cassino. From there, he hoped to open up the road to the west, and the prize of the Eternal City.

As was becoming very obvious, all depended upon the capture of Cassino, and in particular the mountains behind it, which dominated the route on which Clark had pinned his hopes of an armoured thrust towards Rome. The reality of events was to prove chastening for the ambitious general.

The battle for the Camino Massif began on 1st December, when X Corps moved into the attack. The forces involved were:

56th Division: 201st Guards Brigade.
6th Grenadier Guards.
3rd Coldstream Guards.
2nd Scots Guards.
167th Brigade: 8th and 9th Royal Fusiliers.
7th Oxfordshire and Bucks Light Infantry.
168th Brigade: 10th Royal Berkshire Regiment. 1st London Scottish.

1st London Irish Rifles.
169th Brigade: 2/5th, 2/6th, 2/7th Queen's Royal Regiment.
46th Division: 138th Brigade: 6th Lincolnshire Regiment.
2/4th KOYLI.
6th York and Lancaster Regiment.
139th Brigade: 2/5th Royal Leicestershire Regiment.
5th Sherwood Foresters.
16th Durham Light Infantry.

Opposing them, were:

129th Panzer Grenadier Regiment.
104th Panzer Grenadier Regiment.
115th Reconnaissance Battalion.

Mount Camino dominated the gateway to the Liri valley. To the west, the River Garigliano flowed through a narrow valley between a range of hills, and to the north, Highway 6 ran up to the town of Cassino, ten miles away. The massif was made up of two long and narrow ridges that were called, "Razor Back," and "Bare Arse," by the men who looked up at them, in dismay. A high point was crowned by a monastery, and to the west lay the Acquapendola Ridge.

An initial attack on Calabritto was ordered, as a diversion from the main thrust by 56th Division, and this began on the night of 1st December, with 5th Foresters on the right and 2/5th Leicesters on the left. In deep clinging mud, they pushed forward into a minefield, as the enemy guns opened fire, and the British artillery responded in kind. According to the British War Office report on the battle, 436 guns, fired 71,000 shells, at five enemy positions: a total of 1,329 tonnes of high explosive. Yet still the Germans held on, as 56th Division began to climb Razor Back and Bare Arse Ridges, towards Monastery Hill. They tried to utilise a series of mule tracks between the ridges, where the huge rocks made it impossible to lie prone, as mortar shells rained down between the crevices in which they huddled. Jagged shards of rock were sent spinning through the air, to cut down anyone unfortunate enough to be in the process of advancing from one outcrop to another, and casualties began to mount. It seemed that this attack would be repelled, like

Infantry moves towards the mountains south of the Gustav Line. Unknown. (*National Army Museum Study Collection*)

so many others in the grim and murderous campaign for Italy, yet somehow, the four brigades managed to drag themselves forward, towards the last ridge of Acquapendola, as 46th Division turned, to force their way through the pass below. 2/4th KOYLI were sent to create a diversion, by crossing the Garigliano to the south of the main battle, near the lower of two dams, but the enemy was deeply entrenched on the opposite bank and it was impossible to wade through the torrents of water and steel.

Yet the trap was closing, and Kesselring recognised that it was time to withdraw to a new line, to the west of the Garigliano and the Peccia, but his request for permission to do so was firmly rejected by Hitler. Even so, the tide of events proved more powerful than any command from Berlin, and 129th Panzer Grenadier Regiment was forced further back, as 104th Panzer Grenadier Regiment and 115th Reconnaissance Battalion, tried in vain to obey the Fuehrer's orders. The pressure was unceasing, and on the 8th, Kesselring ordered 15th and 29th Panzer Grenadier Divisions to withdraw. In the battle for Mount Camino, X Corps lost 941 men, whilst the 15th Panzer Grenadier Division lost 974.

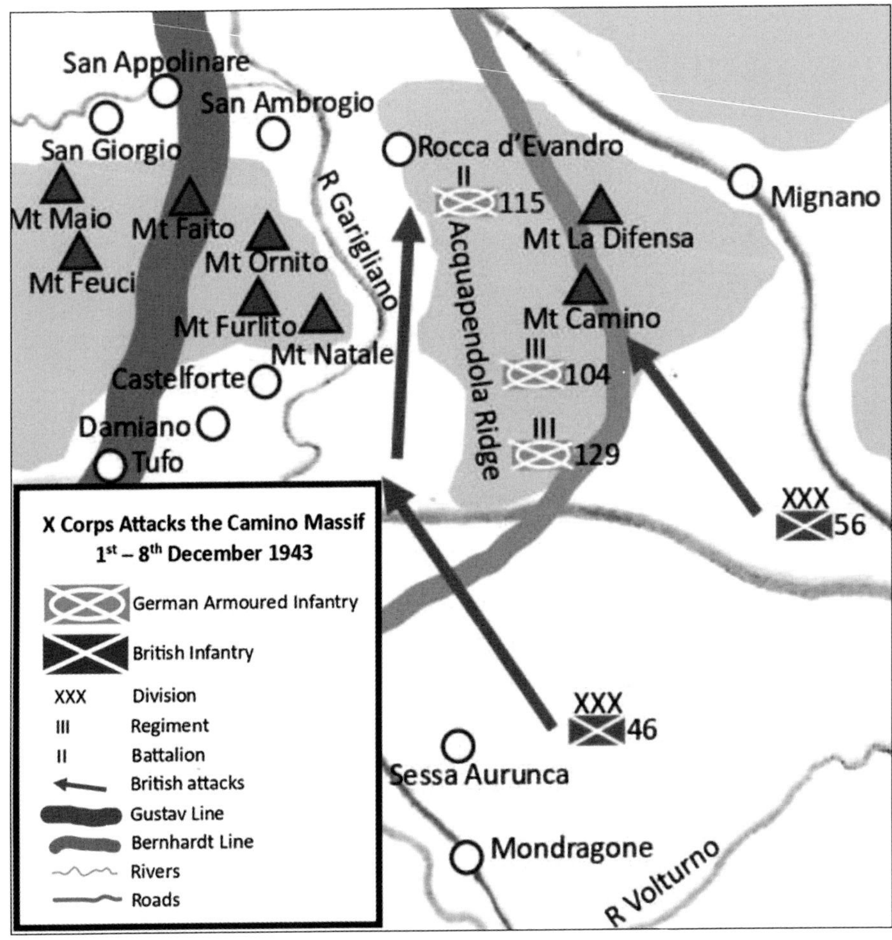

The tenacity of the German forces, together with the weather conditions that threatened to flood the river valleys, now resulted in a stalemate that caused the British Prime Minister to signal his Chiefs of Staff, on 19th December. He was outraged.

"There is no doubt," he stormed, "that the stagnation of the whole campaign on the Italian front is becoming scandalous. The C.I.G.S.'s visit confirmed my worst forebodings. The total neglect to provide the amphibious action on the Adriatic side, and the failure to strike any similar blow on the west, have been disastrous."

Their response must surely have reinforced his belief in his own strategic prowess. It may also have served to set his mind firmly on the plan that had been developing in his always-inventive mind, for some time. Of course, the

Chiefs of Staff were aware of Churchill's enthusiasm for amphibious landings, which had persisted, even after the disaster that had been his Gallipoli plan during the First World War. Now, in what seemed to be a blatant attempt to pass the buck for what would surely be an extremely dangerous project, they said that they were:

> "in full agreement with you that the present stagnation cannot be allowed to continue. For every reason, it is essential that something should be done to speed things up. The solution, *as you say**, clearly lies in making use of our amphibious power to strike round the enemy's flank and open up the way for a rapid advance on Rome."

Indeed, Churchill had been thinking about the possibility of another amphibious assault since October, when Alexander had given a situation update that painted a picture of a long and costly advance, which could not be speeded up by an outflanking move, owing to the lack of resources. Now, Churchill was determined that he should have those resources, as, in his view, an amphibious outflanking movement was the only way to break the deadlock in Italy and make the capture of Rome a possibility before the end of January 1944. Other allied leaders were at last reaching the same conclusion.

By the end of 1943, it had become clear that the Italian capital would not be taken by the original target date. Indeed, without an amphibious landing, it was difficult to see how it could be achieved in the foreseeable future. Any hope of a breakthrough, lay with 5th Army, as it pushed down the west coast, and a major reorganisation of 15th Army Group was undertaken, in order that this could be achieved.

To the east, 8th Army was on the verge of a coastal plain that stretched for 100 miles to Ancona, which was of little strategic value. To their left, lay a plateau that was split by three rivers which ran between a series of rugged ridges. On top of the ridges were several stone farmhouses that both armies used as defensive positions and had surrounded with minefields and foxholes. Behind the ridges rose the Apennine Mountains; a 6,000 feet high range. The area was swept by a gigantic blizzard, and as men sheltered in the villages that dotted the area, the next few weeks saw a succession of thaws, rain, mist, frost, and icy winds. Roads were impassable as the mud glued up the

* Author's emphasis.

wheels of any transport that managed to get within sight. Engineers toiled ceaselessly at the task of metalling roads, and infantrymen were constantly required to clean rifles, machine guns, and uniforms that were clogged with freezing mud. This was a war for survival, and both sides fought skirmish after skirmish to preserve a shelter, a bunker, or a high point. Nightly raids were conducted with the purpose of taking German prisoners for interrogation; it was important to find out any information on the opposing forces, and particularly any movements that might influence the situation facing 5th Army. At the same time, other intelligence revealed that German reserve forces in the Rome area were being moved south to reinforce the right flank of the Gustav Line, and Alexander ordered the newly reorganised 8th Army to be ready for a major offensive in the second half of January, to help 5th Army. General Leese argued that small attacks would be of little use to 5th Army and that the weather, together with the condition of his newly reorganised forces, meant that an effective assault could only begin in mid-February, at the earliest. He also argued that the reorganisation of 5th Army would make it difficult to arrange a coordinated plan of action before that time. As Alexander seemed to be priming Leese for a major attack, it must have been a source of puzzlement to his subordinate, when, on 30th January, he was ordered to send 4th Indian Division over to 5th Army and to do the same with 78th Division on 7th February. It was now obvious that any major operations by 8th Army were impossible, and any thoughts of a swoop through Pescara and Avezzano to support 5th Army were totally abandoned.

A high-level conference of allied leaders had identified the town of Anzio as the best location for the amphibious assault that would break the deadlock and open the path to Rome. 5th Army was to push towards Cassino to divert the German reserves away from the landing grounds, before attempting to link up with the Anzio force. It was recognised that the forces of 15th Army group had to be reorganised to meet the requirements of this new situation, and as a result, X Corps was restructured as follows: 5th Division, 46th Division, 56th Division, and 23rd Armoured Brigade. Both 1st and 2/4th KOYLI were now part of the same corps.

As 1st KOYLI moved across the Apennines, 2/4th were involved in the holding role that had been given to X Corps. In mid-December, the situation altered as II US Corps asked for protection on the right flank of their advance. 138th Brigade was furthest north and went to relieve the Americans on

A forward position during a blizzard. Winter 1944. February 1944. Unknown. (*National Army Museum Study Collection*)

Mount Maggiore and the hills to the west, which stretched as far as Carlo. On Mount Maggiore, the KOYLI and the York and Lancs, built sangars amongst the rocks and ledges, where they sheltered between regular patrols along the steep muddy slopes, in the rain and sleet that swept in each day to banish the dank mists rising from the Garigliano. They watched the never-ending stream of mules and porters that climbed towards them from the supply dump at Mieli. On 19th December, the German dive bombers put in another appearance, strafing, and bombing the frozen soldiers as they clung to their exposed position on the slopes of Mount Maggiore. This was one of the few instances of noise and fire during those eerie days when enemy patrols appeared like ghosts from the swirling mist, to take a few prisoners and a few lives before melting away into the grey shroud. Christmas Day was one of the few days when the sun managed to make an appearance, and at Campo, Galluccio, and Vandria, the men of 2/4th KOYLI tried to celebrate the day in the cold stone cottages, as the guns crashed outside.

The most likely pathway to Rome lay up the valley of the Liri, through which ran Highway 6, as the territory on either side of the valley was deemed unsuitable for a large, mechanised force. The first twenty miles or so were thought to be fairly easy-going, through pasture and woodland that was four miles wide at its narrowest. Of course, the Germans had also been aware of the advantages that an advance up the Liri valley might afford the allies, and they had been busy since November, constructing defences on Mounts Belvedere and San Croce, which would dominate the river valleys from the north. They had built a defence line that ran from Alfedena, through Mounts Rotondo and Cassino, San Ambrogio, and along the River Garigliano to Mount Scauri in the Gulf of Gaeta. Such was the extent of the Gustav Line. The many rivers in the area were also seen as important defensive features: the Rapido flowed from the east of Mount Rotondo, through the town of Cassino, and down to its junction with the Liri, south of San Angelo. At that point, it became the Garigliano, which flowed down to the sea. The towering Mount Cairo loomed over the Liri valley from the north, and the high ground continued all the way to Mount Cassino. To the south, the Aurunci Mountains were made up of a series of rugged ridges that ran between the mountains, Maio, Faito, Feuci, Ornito, Furlito, and Natale, providing a 3,000 feet backdrop to the lower reaches of the Garigliano. A secondary road, Highway 7, ran north along the coast and passed through several gorges on its way to the Pontine marshes south of Rome. On either side of the two roads, the Garigliano Plain was quite impassable to vehicles in wet weather, as it was split by several streams and channels, and both roads crossed the one hundred yards wide river over a single bridge. The banks were high, muddy, and impossible to negotiate, and two groups of hills, each 1500 feet high, looked down on the entire Garigliano Plain from Minturno, to Castelforte.

Alexander was well aware that Kesselring had placed his strongest defences along the Liri valley, but despite this, he urged his commanders on. The enemy, he said, would be forced to react to the landings at Anzio, and when they did, the two parts of 5th Army would join together and the road to Rome would be open.

By the beginning of January, the Americans were ready to attack the next enemy positions at Mount Porchia and San Vittorio del Lazio. To enable this, the British 46th Division was to be placed on their left flank, from where they would cross the River Peccia before securing the road that ran below the heights of Cedro Hill, which was being held by an experienced battalion from the 15th Panzer Grenadier Division. They would then wait, until the Americans had taken Mount Porchia, before climbing the hill and driving the panzer grenadiers from the summit. 138th Brigade was to lead the attack and had been rested at the end of December so that they could be in shape to do so.

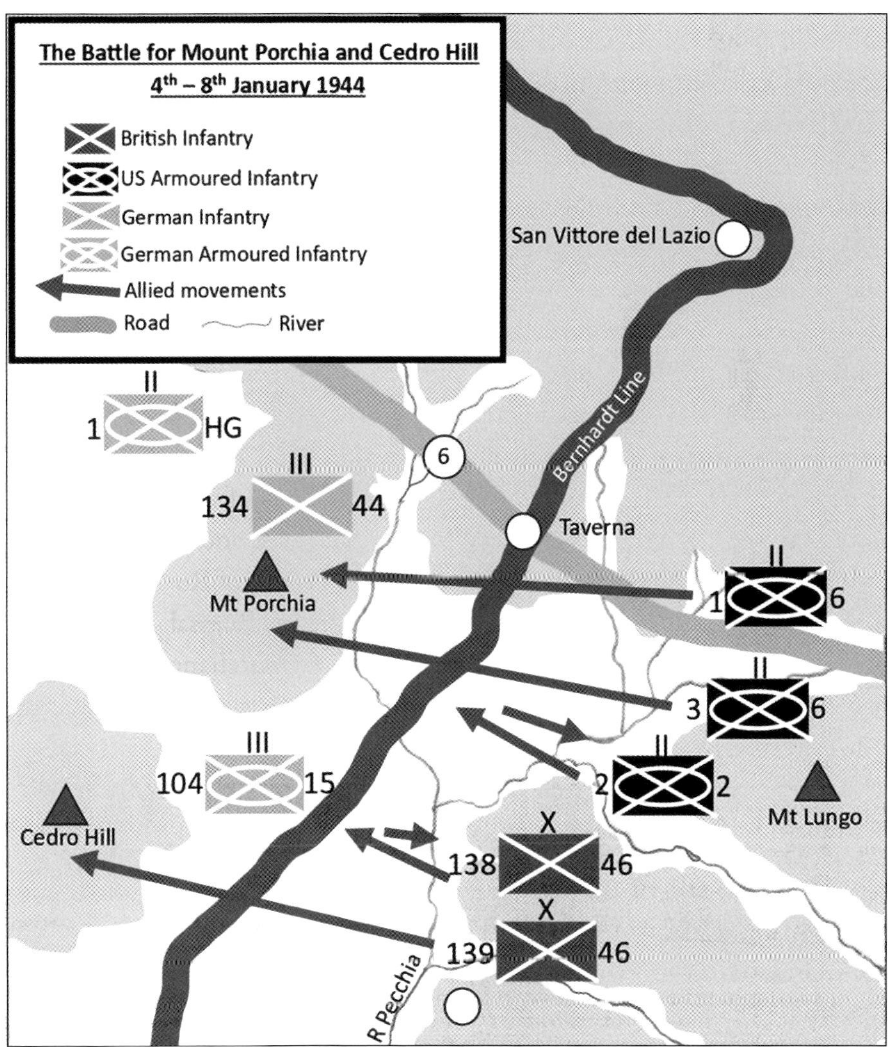

New Year arrived in the form of a blizzard, which swept snow into the faces of the waiting assault troops and created drifts that made communications almost impossible. Any movements were carried out in a nightmare of biting cold and penetrating damp. As Brigadier Harding arranged his troops in a blanket of swirling snow, the sappers began work on a ford across the Peccia. They were decimated by mortar fire. The squadron of tanks assigned to support the 138th, was stuck on a snowbound track, and a diversionary attack by the York and Lancs, was met with determined resistance so that it was nightfall before the main force caught up with them and the enemy fell back. Two farmhouses were cleared, and a patch of woodland became a temporary sanctuary for the weary attackers. A second attack on the left, resulted in the loss of an entire platoon, as the Lincolns managed to get one company across the river. A second company was caught in a storm of intense shelling, as they huddled in a gully, prior to an intended crossing. They never made it. The York and Lancs charged into an enemy counterattack with bayonets fixed, and thirty-five Germans were killed in the hand-to-hand fighting. 2/4th KOYLI were sent to fill a gap that had opened between 138th Brigade, and the nearest Americans, whose slow advance from Mount Lungo, had left the Lincolns in a very exposed position. So the 138th found themselves facing the main body of German forces in the area when they had only been given the task of creating a diversionary attack, but the American commanders were confident that the assault they had planned for that afternoon would enable the brigade to withdraw from Cedro Hill. Because of this, they held on, as, at midnight, the rest of the forces who had crossed the river began to carry their wounded back to their own lines.

Expecting to be relieved, 2/4th KOYLI began preparations to withdraw from their exposed position, but before they could begin to move, they were told that the American advance had now reached Mount Porchia, and they would have to go forward to Cedro Hill, in order to support the flank of the impending attack. A scouting party went forward and managed to scramble up to the summit, overrunning the machine gun post that had been firing down at them. They discovered several other enemy positions, before withdrawing to pass this intelligence on to Brigadier Harding.

As night fell on the 7th, the men of 138th Brigade went forward again. The battalions swept around the hill and came at the enemy positions from different angles, managing to overrun several emplacements before the German artillery spotted them and opened fire. It was impossible to find cover on the bare, rocky hillside, and they were forced to run back to a position where they were out of sight of the artillery spotters. Brigade HQ was unable to move quickly enough, and a direct hit killed the officer in charge of artillery control, effectively ruling out any attempt to hit back at the German guns. All hope for a breakthrough now rested with an armoured assault that would allow the infantry to move forward behind the advancing tanks. Unfortunately, the tank leading the force that had been ordered to the rescue broke down at a road junction and prevented the others getting through. 2/4th KOYLI were ordered to sit tight until the Americans had cleared Mount Porchia, as any further attempts to advance until this had happened, would be suicide for all the men of the 138th.

Finally, on 9th January, the Americans achieved their aim, and 138th Brigade was able to move into the town of Cedro, where they regrouped for another assault on the hill. Once again, 2/4th KOYLI sent out scouting parties, and to their utter relief, they found that the Germans had abandoned their positions, before withdrawing to the north. Their "minor diversion," in support of the main American assault, had turned into a devastating battle in its own right, and the 138th had lost over 250 men on that bare hillside, something from which they never really recovered.

The 200 prisoners taken by the Brigade were questioned by intelligence officers, who discovered that Kesselring had ordered the retreat on the 10th of January. In fact, the withdrawal plan had been drawn up well before anticipated losses had forced it to be implemented. In 10 days, the allies had lost over 2,000 men. Although the German losses were less, at just over 1,500, they could not afford such a rate of attrition without pouring in more reserves; something that would expose the southern flank of Germany to an unimaginable threat. Once again, the tide of the Italian campaign had been turned by the actions of individual battalions, companies, and platoons.

The British 5th, 46th, and 56th Divisions had been in constant action since the end of September, and there seemed little prospect of any relief forces coming to their aid, as casualties mounted, especially amongst the infantry units. Yet they were expected to go back into the fray once again on 17th January, as the crossing of the Garigliano was scheduled for that date. Once again, they were the bait that was to attract the attention of the German forces away from the US attack on the Rapido, near San Angelo, and whilst the 46th was given a little respite by being held back, in order to provide flanking cover for the US II Corps, when the time was right to cross the Garigliano near San Ambrogio, the 5th and 56th were told they were to cross the river in advance, to create a bridgehead that would be four miles deep and eight miles in length. Once the bridgehead had been secured, 5th Division, with 1st KOYLI, was expected to capture a gorge, southwest of San Giorgio, an advance of ten miles that would be the key to the Liri valley. To carry out their tasks, the division was allocated forty-five assault boats, several rafts and pontoons, a kapok footbridge, and a construction kit for an eighty-foot-long Bailey bridge. They were to go in on the left of 56th Division and attack towards the high ground of San Vito, Mount Natale, and Mount Scauri, with the intention of

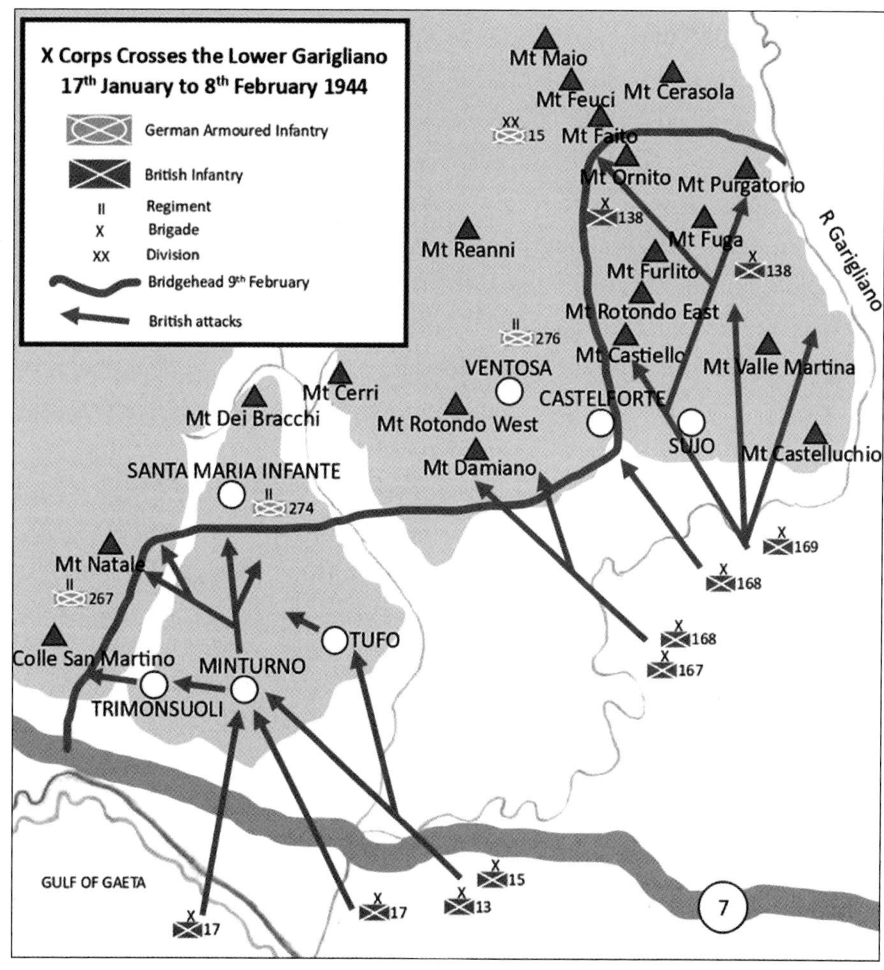

penetrating as far as Castellonorato. The attack was to be made without a preliminary artillery bombardment, to preserve the advantage of surprise. 2/4th KOYLI, with the rest of their division, was assigned to the task of creating a diversion a few miles upstream.

At 9 pm on 17th January, 5th and 56th Divisions began to cross the Garigliano in assault boats and rafts that had been brought forward and hidden close to the bank, over the previous few nights. The experience gained in the crossing of the Volturno now proved vital. "Beachmasters" were appointed to each crossing place, and controlled the flow of traffic, up to the water's edge and back again; another innovation that was to prove vital in the Normandy landings to come. The initial assault by 17th Brigade ran into serious trouble as the assault craft that were intended to support the crossings from the sea were unable to navigate the eleven-mile stretch of waterway with sufficient accuracy, mainly due to a failure to set up navigation lights in sufficient time. The result was that the bridgehead was much smaller than had been envisaged, and the 17th found themselves trapped in minefields that stretched from the beaches to the landing grounds. 5th Division's second assaulting brigade managed to cross, and began to advance towards Tufo, despite some confusion caused by navigation issues, but exhaustion, caused by the fact that they had been required to carry heavy equipment as well as fighting off the German counterattacks, was setting in. Despite this, on the morning of the 18th, the assault brigades had formed up and were attacking everywhere, enlarging the bridgehead. Casualties had been heavy, and it was realised that such a rate of attrition could not be sustained for too long.

On the night of the 18th, the three battalions of 15th Brigade were sent in. Brigadier Martin led the crossing of 1st KOYLI, 1st Green Howards, and 1st York and Lancs, on a motley collection of boats and rafts, as the enemy observation posts directed artillery fire onto them. Three rafts were destroyed. The engineers had been unable to construct a bridge because of that same fire, and although they managed to throw a boat bridge across the river by 2 am, the first vehicle to cross it struck a mine, and the wreckage took 3 hours to clear.

The established German practice of piecing together "battlegroups" from whatever troops were available, had led to a series of local counterattacks as these small units struck wherever they could. As a result, 15th Brigade found themselves in a battlefield that was constantly changing. On the

Infantry crossing the Garigliano River in assault boats, 18th January 1944. Bowman (Sgt), No 2 Army Film & Photographic Unit. (*Wikipedia*)

20th, Kesselring ordered a major counterattack by 29th Panzer Grenadier Division, with the objective of rescuing the 94th Infantry Division, which was trapped in the area of Castelforte, out of fuel and under constant attack. By that time, 13th Infantry Brigade had driven off a dawn counterattack, which allowed the 15th to pass them. 1st KOYLI were ordered to capture the town of Tufo, which is situated on the peak of a volcanic outcrop, and so dominates the surrounding area. Obviously, this fact was not lost on the Germans, and after a gruelling climb, 1st KOYLI were forced into a street battle, to clear the defenders out of the town. The Green Howards overcame the German defences at Minturno and Trimonsuoli, as the York and Lancs pushed towards Santa Maria Infante. 56th Division had reached

Men of the 1st KOYLI climb an Italian mountain. Dawson (Sgt), No 2 Army Film & Photographic Unit. (*Wikimedia Commons*)

the outskirts of Castelforte, where they discovered that the enemy was established in force. German counterattacks took place near Santa Maria Infante, but the British forces stood their ground, in a brutal encounter that surged back and forth. It was becoming clear to the German commanders that any hopes of throwing 5th and 56th Division back over the Garigliano were fading fast. Kesselring ordered that the British had to be ejected from the front line in the Minturno sector, although he probably knew that this was an impossible demand.

Meanwhile, 46th Division had been engaged at San Ambrogio. 128th Brigade had been selected to cross the Rapido on the night of 19th January, to support the left flank of US II Corps, when they crossed at San Angelo on the following day. From their position five miles to the south of the American landing zone, they were to occupy the village of San Ambrogio, and the low ridge that spread to the north and south of it. They were to cross in assault boats, just below the junction of the river with the Peccia stream, and once they had established a bridgehead, 138th Infantry Brigade was to cross, before pushing west to San Apollinare and San Giorgio, where they would join the northward thrust of 5th and 56th Divisions.

Throughout the first months of winter, the strain of fighting in such terrain had been steadily building. At heights of over 2,000 feet, the infantry clung to the rock faces, in their hastily constructed positions, as they huddled together in their jerkins, greatcoats and gas capes, against the biting cold. "Compo" rations were sometimes supplemented by "high altitude" rations that included chocolate, margarine, and biscuits, but these had to be dragged up the mule tracks by the incredibly brave porters, who also carried back the wounded on makeshift stretchers. Lighting a fire to make "a brew" was a dangerous activity, yet they still did it; some things were just worth the risk. Patrols sometimes discovered abandoned American positions where they could load their packs with leftover rations to take back to their mates, and they even came across a few unguarded supply dumps. Reinforcements had practically dried up since the Volturno crossing, and the men who had survived for months in such conditions were now asked to go back into battle, yet again.

The attack began at 8.30 pm, as the moonlight struggled to pierce the blanket of fog that clung to the Garigliano. The Germans had opened the sluices of a dam at San Giovanni, so that the irrigation water poured into the river at exactly the point where the crossing was to be made, sweeping away the fragile assault boats, and snapping the cables that had been set up so that they could be pulled across. Not for the first time in the history of river crossings during this campaign, the infantrymen tried to hold position by using the lightweight paddles that had been provided, but most were swept a long way downstream, where the boats were smashed against the shore. Swimmers who tried to reconnect the hand cables met a similar fate. By this time, the Germans had been alerted to the attack and were able to surround an isolated unit. A few survivors managed to get back across the river, and next morning, the attack was called off.

The assaults made by US 36th Division were similarly driven back, and General Clark decided that his main effort would now be directed towards Cassino. Between 18th and 22nd January, X Corps had lost almost 1,500 men, whilst the US Corps had lost almost 2,000.

The bridgehead that had been made by 5th and 56th Divisions, was coming under tremendous pressure, as Kesselring urged his forces to throw them back. However, because of the failure of the crossing further upstream, the units that would have been employed there were now available to be sent to reinforce and expand the bridgehead. Accordingly, 138th Brigade went to relieve the 169th, as 168th moved to take over from 167th, on Mount Damiano. Just as these changeovers were being made, the Germans threw in a massive counterattack.

13th Brigade was in the area between Tufo and Minturno, when the counterattack began on 20th January, and 15th Brigade was moving forward to take the ridge behind Trimonsuoli. For two days, 1st KOYLI, with 1st Green Howards, and 1st York and Lancs, stood firm against Kesselring's counterattack, which surged along the boundary of the bridgehead, and on

British infantry serving with 5th Army climb a steep path to their forward positions. Unknown. (*National Army Museum Study Collection*)

towards Mount Damiano, Mount Castiello, and the Sujo valley. The front line on the right of the attack moved back and forth, as the Germans fought to throw it back to the river, and the 138th, battled to hold it in place. As the casualties began to mount, the entire front started to stabilise into a position that was roughly the same as had existed when the German counterattack had been launched.

Although the battle had been exhausting, McCreery knew that if he waited too long, the Germans would get stronger, and because of this, he ordered his divisions into the attack once more. It was vital that the enemy forces in Castelforte, together with those on Mounts Fuga, and Dei Bracchi, be eliminated as soon as possible, as well as those in Castelforte and the northern part of Damiano.

138th Brigade, with 2/4th KOYLI, arrived in the Sujo valley on the night of 26th January and went straight into the attack towards Mount Fuga. In their way, were five bleak and boulder-strewn mountains: Rotondo East, Furlito, Fuga, Purgatorio, and Ornito, with an average height of 2,000 feet.

The brigade opened the attack in the face of an entrenched opposition when 2/4th KOYLI stormed past Mount Valle Martina, and onto the high ground to its north. As 6th Lincolns veered away to capture Mount Rotondo East, the KOYLI took on a powerful German emplacement that had taken up position in a group of sturdy farm buildings. At Ruffiano farm they were forced to clear each stone building, using the tactics with which they were, by now, becoming all too familiar: a sprint between one patch of shelter and another as every window poured fire into the open spaces that were the yard areas, a grenade thrown, another charge into the resulting smoke and flying debris, before kicking in a door, throwing another grenade, and spraying the inside of the room with machine gun fire.

After two days of fierce close-quarter fighting, Ruffiano Farm was clear, and the men of 2/4th KOYLI were on the move again, this time to the slopes of Mount Purgatorio. The enemy had set up a position in each of the many caves that dotted the rock face. They fired down, as 2/4th KOYLI crept towards them. Every move was countered by a crossfire that threatened to wipe the infantry from the face of the mountain, yet somehow, they kept coming. Gripping like lizards to the rough and crumbling surface, individual attackers made their way from one cave to the next. As each one came within grenade range, the pin was pulled, the bomb flew through the air, and the occupants were trapped in an exploding tomb. By 30th January, every enemy position had been cleared.

On the same day, 1st KOYLI had been part of the 5th Division's assault on the Trimonsuoli Ridge, which pushed the bridgehead out towards Colle San Martino, and Mount Natale. Between 46th and 5th Divisions, the 56th had poured across the river, and despite an attack that verged upon the suicidal, they were driven back with devastating losses.

138th Brigade, still pushing northeast, through the range of mountains, were now told that they would have to take Mounts Cerasola, Faito, and Feuci. On the night of 7th February, 5th Hampshires, who were reinforcing the brigade, found themselves on a ridge overlooked by German gun emplacements, after clearing those on Cerasola. The Germans knew that the loss of Mount Faito would open the floodgates for a British advance, and high command gave the order that it must be held at any cost. 2/4th KOYLI, and 6th Lincolns, were sent to take it.

Yet again, they fought their way to the summit, but there they were met by a fanatical resistance that conformed to the Fuehrer's wishes. The defenders could not be dislodged without risking two entire battalions, and so the KOYLI and the Lincolns withdrew to the British positions on Mount Ornito.

Now the Germans poured out from their fortress of Mount Faito, in the belief that they could recapture Mounts Ornito and Cerasola as the two British battalions retreated. Wave after wave of units from the 15th Panzer Grenadier Division swept towards the three battalions that now defended two mountains. Using up their ammunition at a worrying rate, 2/4th KOYLI knew that they had no alternative but to hold fast if they were to have any chance of surviving. Just when it appeared that they would be overrun, they saw the attackers begin to slow, to hesitate, and then to fall back.

At last, the isolated battalions were contacted and informed that 2nd Coldstream Guards were being sent to reinforce them. So they settled down in their makeshift sangars between the rocks, to wait for their resupply and deliverance, as the rain, sleet, and snow began to fall.

Mount Faito had not fallen, and the anticipated British rush had therefore not materialised. Now, the demands of the Anzio landings dictated that 56th Division be re-assigned to that area, and this move so weakened X Corps, that the advance units were ordered to stay on the defensive, as the rear echelons moved towards them, across the newly repaired bridges over the Garigliano, which the KOYLI had christened "Skipton" and "Pateley," during the time that they had climbed across their wreckage, several days earlier.

On 1st March, 2/4th KOYLI left Taranto in MS Batory, after the promised support from the Guards Brigade had first reinforced, and then relieved them. 138th Brigade was bound for the Middle East, having taken part in all the hardest battles of the Italian campaign up to that point: Salerno, the Volturno crossing, the Camino massif, and the battle of the lower Garigliano. Any pre-conceived ideas of "Sunny Italy" had disappeared amongst the rain, wind, mud, snow, and blizzards of the dark and inhospitable Apennine Mountains, and they were now being taken out of the front line for a period of respite that would be all too short.

General Clark's plans for the advance of 5th Army up the Liri valley, had run into trouble. Having crossed the River Rapido, they began to encounter a stiffening opposition in the area around Mount Cassino, where the Germans had set up their defences in territory that was ideal for defence.

Although Hitler, in one of his usual flights of fantasy, had demanded that all lost territory should be immediately retaken, Kesselring knew that the forces at his disposal were simply not up to the task of mounting any sort of offensive whatsoever: between 21st January and 10th February, XIV Panzer Corps had lost almost 6,500 men, and the survivors were in poor shape. Hitler insisted that National Socialist ardour was all that was needed to turn the course of the war, but Kesselring had long since ceased to listen to the ramblings of his deluded leader. He knew that the best, in fact, the only way to deliver the allies a blow that might cause them to think twice about the cost of the campaign in Italy, would be to create a deathtrap amongst the mountains, that they would not be able to outflank or overcome. From the monastery on top of Mount Cassino, he looked down upon the valley that spread out below him, and he knew that he had found such a place.

Certainly, the allies were under no illusions that Kesselring might ignore the defensive possibilities of Mount Cassino, and it became clear that the whole area was being turned into a fortress, as heavy guns were dragged up the mountainsides and embedded into steel and concrete emplacements, with similarly built bunkers for the infantry.

General Clark realised that if his ground forces were to have any chance of linking up with the Anzio landings, they would have to get past Cassino, and that would be an incredibly daunting task. He was very reluctant to send in a frontal attack and opted instead to try to outflank the German defences from the north. The ridges that formed the backbone between Mount Cairo and Mount Cassino were a nightmare of deep gulleys, steep rock faces, and small hollows, which held a variety of vegetation that could tear and cut the flesh of anyone unfortunate enough to stumble into them. Huge rocks blocked the way across the ridges, and some of these were so unstable as to be sent crashing down onto anyone below, at the slightest touch. Many promising routes through the rock maze, were later found to be blocked by a fall, so the tortuous pathway had to be retraced, all under fire from German gun emplacements.

And so it was, that attack after attack foundered in the shadow of Mount Cassino. The Germans had taken up positions in the ancient monastery at its peak, and the entire allied advance was brought to a standstill, from 17th January to 18th of May 1944. When the monastery was flattened by allied bombing, this action brought worldwide condemnation from those who saw it as both a desecration and a wanton destruction of ancient art treasures. The Germans simply set up again in the even better shelter of the rubble.

Alexander used the period from March to May 1944, as an opportunity to rebuild his forces and plan the final push on Rome. With this in mind, the 8th Army front had been extended westward, across the Apennines to Cassino. The twin objectives of the May offensive, which was codenamed Operation Diadem, were to capture Rome and to tie down German forces that would otherwise have been available to oppose the Normandy landings. General Clark objected to Alexander's plan, basically because he wanted American soldiers to be the first to take the Italian capital, yet the Commander-in-Chief insisted that, whilst British XIII Corps were crossing the Rapido, taking Cassino town and smashing into the northern flank of the new Hitler Line, and the Polish Corps were taking Mount Cassino, 5th Army was to be restricted to protecting 8th Army's flank as it drove to link up with the breakout from Anzio. US VI Corps would be assigned the tasks of breaking out from the beachhead, capturing the town of Valmontone, and cutting the German 10th Army's line of retreat.

Three times, the Allies tried and failed to break the Gustav Line, but at 11 pm, on 11th May, the entire front line, from Cassino to the Tyrrhenian

An infantryman fires a Bren gun in the ruins of Mount Cassino. Tanner (Capt) War Office official photographer. (*Wikimedia Commons*)

Sea, erupted into flame, as twenty-five allied divisions attacked. As usual, the assault on Mount Cassino was thrown back with devastating losses, but the Gustav Line was penetrated at several other points. Finally, on 17th May, the Polish Corps took the monastery on Mount Cassino, and hoisted their national flag over the ruins.

The Germans fell back, and 8th Army prepared for yet another assault, on yet another defensive line. As they did so, General Clark decided that the time was right to push his 5th Army forward, to link up with the forces who had now landed at Anzio.

7.5 Anzio

As we have seen, the reorganisation of allied forces in Italy resulted in 1st and 2/4th KOYLI finding themselves part of the same corps. However, on 16th March, 2/4th KOYLI had been pulled out of the line, along with the rest of 46th Division, owing to the devastating losses they had suffered. During their rest, refitting and retraining period in Palestine, the Division was to receive almost 3,000 replacements. 1st KOYLI, on the other hand, was destined for the beaches of Anzio, as were the 9th Battalion, who had been transferred from 1st Armoured to 1st Infantry Division.

Anzio had finally been chosen as the most acceptable site for the amphibious landings. Although the beaches had been popular with pre-war visitors from Rome, the gently sloping sand was not so attractive for the planners of an assault from the sea. Apart from the sand bars that lay just offshore, the gradient of the beaches meant that landing craft would have to deposit their contents well off dry land. A belt of soft dunes would make difficult going for heavy vehicles, but behind them lay two good roads that ran for 20 miles inland, to the Alban Hills, which had been identified as a strategic objective. 5th Army was only 70 miles away and it was hoped that a link could be made quickly. In view of these factors, three beaches were selected: "Peter," 6 miles to the north, "Yellow," just east of the harbour, and "X," 4 miles further to the east.

The town of Anzio is situated on a coastal plain that stretches all the way to the River Tiber. To the south, the land had been reclaimed as part of Mussolini's modernisation programme. Marshes had been turned into cultivated fields, watered by a large network of drainage ditches and irrigation channels. Woodland surrounded the town, in the shape of the Bosco di Padiglione. Beyond that, was an area of open flat ground that led all the way to the Alban Hills, which rose to a height of 3,000 feet and covered an area of 192 square miles.

For the Anzio operation, VI US Corps was placed under the command of Major General Lucas, and was to be composed of:

3rd US Infantry Division (Major General Lucian K. Truscott).
1st US Armoured Division (Major General Ernest N. Harmon).
1st British Infantry Division (Major General W. R. C. Penney) which included 2nd and 3rd Infantry Brigades, 24th Guards Brigade,46th Royal Tank Regiment, 2nd Special Service Brigade, and 9th and 43rd Royal Marine Commandos.

Between 17th and 19th January, a rehearsal was held on the Salerno beaches. It did not go well; forty DUKW amphibious vehicles and 10 artillery pieces went to the bottom of the Tyrrhenian Sea.

7.5.1 The Landings

The Anzio D-Day was set for 22nd January, despite the short time available for rehearsals, and as it approached, Lucas fine-tuned his initial assault formations as follows:

American 3rd US Division.
751st Tank Battalion.
1st, 3rd, 4th Ranger Battalions.
504th Parachute Infantry Regiment.
509th Parachute Infantry Regiment.
British 1st Infantry Division.
2nd Special Service Brigade.
46th Royal Tank Regiment.
No. 655 Air Observation Post Squadron (RCAF)

As previously mentioned, the assault beaches had been given codenames, and now the assault units were assigned their targets. Three infantry regiments

HMS 'Spartan' bombarding enemy shore positions as allied landing craft close in on the beaches. Tomlin, H W, (Lt) Royal Navy Official Photographer. (*Wikipedia Commons*)

of 3rd US Division, would make the assault on "X" beach, which would be followed up by 504th Parachute Regiment. The three Ranger Battalions would assault "Yellow" beach, to be followed by 509th Parachute Regiment. 2nd British Infantry Brigade would make the assault on "Peter" beach, with the follow-up provided by 2nd Special Service Brigade. It was decided that the remainder of 1st Infantry Division would be held in reserve.

Between 5 pm on the 20th January and noon on the 21st, the fleet carrying VI US Corps set sail from Naples and other ports in the area. At 2 am, the first landing craft touched down, and the first troops stormed ashore to be met by nothing but the cry of the seabirds that circled above them in the clear night air. Impossible as it seemed, the assault had taken the Germans completely by surprise. Intelligence had totally failed to identify Anzio as the location for the attack that they knew must come, and it was not until late morning that Kesselring received notification at his headquarters north of Rome. He immediately contacted Berlin and asked for permission to implement the plans that had already been drawn up, for the supplementation of his forces in Italy. These involved the following units:

The headquarters of LXXVI Corps, with three infantry regiments, and supporting artillery.
1026, 1027, 1028 Grenadier Regiments, with a regiment of artillery, and a battery of nebelwerfer rocket artillery.
715th Infantry Division from southern France.
1st Battalion, 4th Panzer Regiment, equipped with the new Panther tanks.
I and III Gruppen of Kampfgeschwader 26 from Luftwaffe bomber forces in southern France.
II Gruppe, Kampfgeschwader 100.
II Gruppe, Kampfgeschwader 40.
I and III Gruppen, Lehrgeschwader 1, equipped with Junkers 88 bombers.

Apart from a few scattered reserve units of the Hermann Goering Panzer Division in the Alban Hills, the only German ground forces between Anzio and Rome on 22nd January were:

1st and 2nd Battalions 200th Panzer Grenadier Regiment.
1st Battalion 361st Panzer Grenadier Regiment.

One battalion from each of 10th, 11th, and 12th Parachute Regiments.
2nd Battalion 71st Panzer Grenadier Regiment.
129th Reconnaissance Battalion.
One company of engineers.

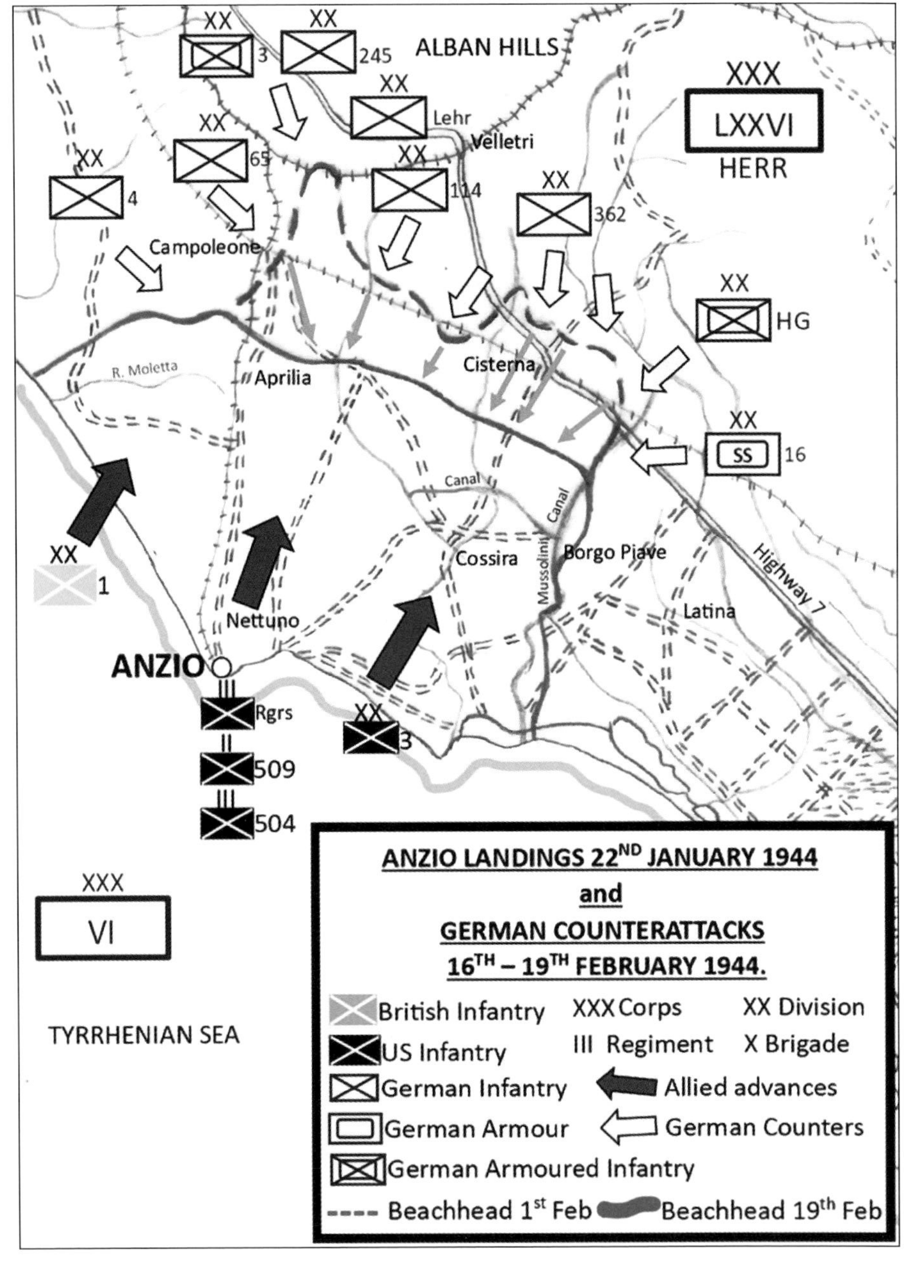

Meanwhile, the invaders had swept ashore, quickly overcoming the few bewildered enemy patrols, many of which, simply left their dugouts, with hands in the air. There had been no time for the harbour facilities to be destroyed, as all reserve troops had, they said, been sent to help hold back the allied assault on the Gustav Line. All the initial objectives had been reached for the loss of thirteen killed, ninety-seven wounded, and forty-four captured or missing. British 1st Infantry Division advanced 7 miles up the Albano Road as they moved towards the River Moletta.

American units seized the vital bridges over the Mussolini Canal, and in two days, VI US Corps had secured a beachhead that was over 7 miles deep. The German reinforcements started to arrive, and by the 24th, they were confident that they could hold the allied advance, and even hurl it back into the sea, once their forces had been fully established. That day, American units began to cross the canal towards Cisterna, as the British moved on Campoleone, both seen as important strategic points. By the 28th, only five miles separated the swelling German defences from the main beachhead line, and Clark now urged Lucas to make an all-out attack to take Cisterna and Campoleone. The Cisterna assault began at 1 am, on 30th January. The Germans were ready, and the US forces ran into a trap that led to 1st and 3rd Ranger Battalions being surrounded.

The Herman Goering Panzer Division claimed to have taken almost 650 prisoners, as the Americans advanced to just under a mile from Cisterna. 3rd US Infantry were forced to halt, in order to set up their own defensive line against the counterattack that seemed inevitable.

The attack on Campoleone began at midnight on the 29th, when two battalions of 24th Guards Brigade set out for their objective, which was the railway line just south of Campoleone Station. Once again, the Germans were ready to fight, and soon the night air was filled with the glow of tracer shells and burning vehicles. Despite the chaos, both battalions managed to take their objectives, before being overrun by a dawn counterattack. By 6 pm, 3rd Infantry Brigade had retaken the lost ground, after an intense battle, and continued to press forward against mounting enemy resistance, which caused the entire allied advance to come to a halt on 1st February.

The US 1st Armoured Division was pulled back into the corps reserve and the British 1st Infantry Division was left to hang onto the ground that had been won, with very little time to prepare for the impending counterattack.

A destroyed Sherman tank at Nettuno, Anzio. Koch. (*Wikimedia Commons*)

This appeared to have begun late in the afternoon of 3rd February, when the German artillery opened up to support a series of small infantry raids, which were fairly easily repulsed. Just before midnight, another artillery barrage began and this time it was far more concentrated, falling on the ground east of the Albano Road. The 24th Guards Brigade came under attack first, but as dawn began to light the scene, it became clear that the enemy was attacking at several points around the Campoleone salient, with the intention of cutting off the whole of 3rd Brigade. At least six enemy tanks managed to establish themselves on a ridge that commanded the Albano Road, as infantry swept in behind them, and more tanks arrived to complete the encirclement of 3rd Brigade. The 1st Irish Guards Battalion were forced to fall back and set up a defensive hedgehog position, as 3rd Brigade came under ever heavier attack.

The 24th Guards, together with the 6th Gordon Highlanders, battled the Germans to a standstill, from their isolated defensive positions, and by the afternoon of 4th February, the 1st Irish Guards had fought their way out of the trap. As the British brought up their anti-tank guns, the German attacks began to falter, before infantry with tank support was thrown in and drove them back. The isolated 3rd Brigade was rescued.

It was clear that 1st Infantry Division was dangerously exposed, and they were withdrawn to a more defensible position during the night of 4th February. 3rd Brigade, and 24th Guards Brigade, in particular, continued to take heavy casualties.

Although the Germans had effectively destroyed the Campoleone salient, they had paid a heavy price. Nevertheless, they were on the attack, and by 16th February, moving forward on a four-mile front that was centred on the Anzio-Albano Road and led by 3rd Panzer Grenadier Division, with the 715th Motorised Infantry. The allies were split, and the entire beachhead was threatened. Gunfire from the ships anchored offshore, together with the heaviest ground support attacks ever conducted by the allied air forces, managed to halt the almost suicidal rush of the German troops after two days of fighting. Yet again, on 18th February the enemy surged forward, forcing the allied command to issue a "no retreat" order which resulted in 500 German corpses in front of the defensive line. Although the attacks continued until 22nd February, the German commanders recognised that they could not afford the loss of almost 5,500 men since the counterattacks had begun. The thirty-five miles of beach perimeter had been held by the entire allied force of 96,500, against ten German Divisions totalling 120,000 men.

On 4th March, the last German attack petered out and both sides collapsed into an exhausted stalemate.

7.5.2 The Beachhead

9th Battalion KOYLI had landed at Anzio in mid-February, as part of 18th Infantry Brigade, which had been called upon to replace the 24th Guards, who had borne the brunt of the fighting, suffering terrible losses. Now under the command of 1st British Infantry Division, the battalion went into the line for the first time on 6th March, and from then onwards they were in the line for periods varying from six to nine days, in reserve for four days, and resting for four days.

The situation at Anzio was one of deadlock, and each side settled down into a daily routine, not unlike that of the trenches of the First World War. Of course, both sides kept a careful eye on what the other was up to, but apart from the occasional clash of scouting parties and the daily exchange of artillery shells, nothing much was happening. As on the western front thirty years earlier, the living conditions of those trapped in the shell holes,

On patrol at Anzio, 20th–21st March 1944. Loughlin (Sgt), No 2 Army Film & Photographic Unit. (*Wikimedia Commons*)

bunkers and tents that covered the beaches and surrounding land were atrocious. Even though there was an almost complete lack of movement, both sides found it impossible to get enough sleep, which led to a dramatic increase in stress-related illnesses as the Germans fired their heavy artillery, and the allies replied with the guns of the big ships out in the bay, and the strafing of the fighter bombers that roared overhead in regular attacks. The opposing trenches were very close in some areas, which meant that the threat of sniper fire was always present for those who were assigned to these forward positions, and the times when relief units took over, were especially dangerous.

The units were rotated, so that, occasionally, they were able to fall back to the rear, where there was the opportunity to clean up in the canvas shower

The Anzio Ritz Cinema, March 1944. Spittle (Sergeant) No 2 Army Film & Photographic Unit. (*Wikimedia Commons*)

tents, or to swim in the sea. Sometimes, American army bands played concerts, and there was even an "Anzio Ritz," where Hollywood films were shown.

Under shellfire, the supply ships kept ploughing through the heavy seas with their precious loads, which were passed on to the unit Quartermaster Sergeants who were responsible for the safekeeping of stores in their canvas tents; not a very secure warehouse, under the circumstances.

Kesselring had recognised the need for his forces to be reorganised, in order to fulfil their new defensive role. In particular, he needed to reduce the number of units that were stationed directly around the beachhead, and the first to leave was the Hermann Goering Division when it was sent to Leghorn for rest and refitting. Following this, 114th Light Division was posted to the Adriatic front, and 26th Panzer and 29th Panzer Grenadier Divisions went

Landing ships unloading supplies in Anzio harbour, 19th–24th February 1944. Radford (Sgt) No 2 Army Film & Photographic Unit. (*Wikimedia Commons*)

south, to become army group reserves, ready for any eventuality. Although some units were transferred to the bridgehead boundary, these were mostly inexperienced, and it was generally recognised that, by early April, only 3rd Panzer Grenadier Division could be regarded as a first-class fighting unit. Even so, the number of German forces opposing any breakout was much greater than had been the case during the previous month's fighting.

The changes undertaken by 5th Army involved the relief of 56th Infantry Division by 5th Infantry Division, which included 1st KOYLI, whilst the British Commando units were also withdrawn. As we have seen, the devastated 24th Guards Brigade had been replaced by 18th Infantry Brigade, which included 9th KOYLI, and it now came under the command of 1st

Infantry Division. During March, a total of 14,000 replacements had brought up the strength of VI Corps to the equivalent of six divisions, and those 90,000 men now outnumbered those of the German 14th Army.

Back on the beach, the mole-like existence of the troops was further disturbed by the arrival behind German lines, of a giant K5 290 mm railway gun, which was to be christened "Anzio Annie" by the British contingent. On 24th March, she fired for the first time, devastating the beachhead once more, as shell fragments ripped through tents and trees, and anything else that rose above ground level. It was not until April, that VI Corps was able to bring up heavier artillery guns and howitzers which, because of the work of incredibly brave artillery spotters who had managed to infiltrate forward trenches, finally put an end to "Annie."

The allies brought up smoke generators in an effort to reduce the accuracy of enemy artillery and bombing. The German 88 mm anti-aircraft guns were lethal in their role as ground attack weapons, particularly as a tank killer, and they now targeted the bulldozers that tried to carve out shelters for the infantry and pits for gun emplacements. Those bulldozers which were allocated to rear areas tried desperately to build up mounds of soft sand around the piles of fuel tanks and ammunition boxes, as these arrived on

Anzio Annie being loaded by its crew, May 1944. Micheljak. (*Wikimedia Commons*)

shore. The holes that had been carved out for the infantry became sodden stinking water traps during wet weather, and it became almost impossible to dig alternative shelters when the weather improved, and the sun baked the surface into the consistency of rock. More and more casualties arrived at the hospital tents that had now been reinforced with masses of sandbags. It took amazing courage on the part of the medical staff, to continue to perform surgical operations as sirens blared and everyone else took cover. During the time of the Anzio beachhead, ninety-two medical personnel were killed in action, 387 wounded, nineteen captured, and sixty reported missing in action.

German propaganda was, as usual, on top form. Hastily built radio sets were able to tune in to "Axis Sally," who bombarded the eager listeners with an imaginative selection of bawdy broadcasts that were delivered in conjunction

4.2-inch mortar of 15th Brigade Mortar Support Company in action in the Anzio bridgehead, Italy, 16th March 1944. Lambert (Sgt), No 2 Army Film & Photographic Unit. (*Wikimedia Commons*)

with her partner, a certain "George." Sally spoke with a deep throaty voice, which tempted and threatened, seemingly as the mood took her. Promises of wonderful food, and nights of pleasure with the local "Venuses," seemed to have little effect. It was probably Sally's selection of the latest American music that had the greatest influence on the mood of her listeners. Homesickness mingled with pleasure, but everyone recognised that Sally was simply part of the grim and deadly existence that was Anzio. The casualties sustained by both sides during the four months of action on and around the beachhead were ample confirmation of the horrors experienced there. In that period, VI Corps lost approximately 30,000 men, and the German 14th Army suffered almost exactly the same number of casualties.

Private Phillip Johnson of the 2/6th Queen's Regiment inspects British graves at Anzio, 1st March 1944. Lambert (Sgt), No 2 Army Film & Photographic Unit. (*Wikimedia Commons*)

Amongst those losses, were 170 members of 9th Battalion KOYLI, who had set out on a raid into enemy territory on the night of 13th March. The battalion had already experienced losses on the beach itself, and more had been sustained as they had gathered on the starting line, yet still they had reached their designated objective, and dug in. Unfortunately, at that moment, the Germans had been in the process of relieving the position, and so there were double the number of occupants than had been expected. The leading sections of 9th KOYLI had been cut off and, after running out of ammunition, were forced to surrender. There were no reinforcements for those who made their way back to the allied line, and this meant double duties for the remainder of their stay at Anzio, as casualties continued to mount, and the battalion strength dropped to 475. "C" Squadron (9th Battalion still used the unit designation that had been part of their life as a cavalry regiment) ceased to exist. In early May, however, reinforcements arrived from England, and 9th KOYLI were up to strength again, with a complement of seven hundred.

7.5.3 The Breakout

On 22nd May, British 1st and 5th Infantry Divisions were transferred to the direct control of 5th Army. 1st Division now consisted of 2nd, 3rd, and 18th Infantry Brigades, whilst 5th Division was made up of 13th,15th, and 17th Infantry Brigades. They were to take part in the spring offensive, codenamed "Operation Diadem," that had been launched on the night of 11th May, by a 5th Army now released from its duties at Cassino by 8th Army. Despite the offensive launched by 5th Army, the Germans were still convinced that another seaborne landing would be attempted, possibly north of Anzio and near the River Tiber. As a result, Kesselring was not inclined to reinforce the Anzio boundary by releasing his reserves. It was also believed that any thrust out of Anzio would be made up the Albano Road, so the 65th Infantry, and 3rd Panzer Grenadier Divisions, who were considered to be the strongest of the available forces, were held in that area, whilst the Cisterna and Mussolini Canal sectors were held by the weaker 362nd and 715th Infantry Divisions. Kesselring's view was further strengthened by the activities of British 1st and 5th Infantry Divisions who had been ordered to conduct raids against the right flank of the German positions.

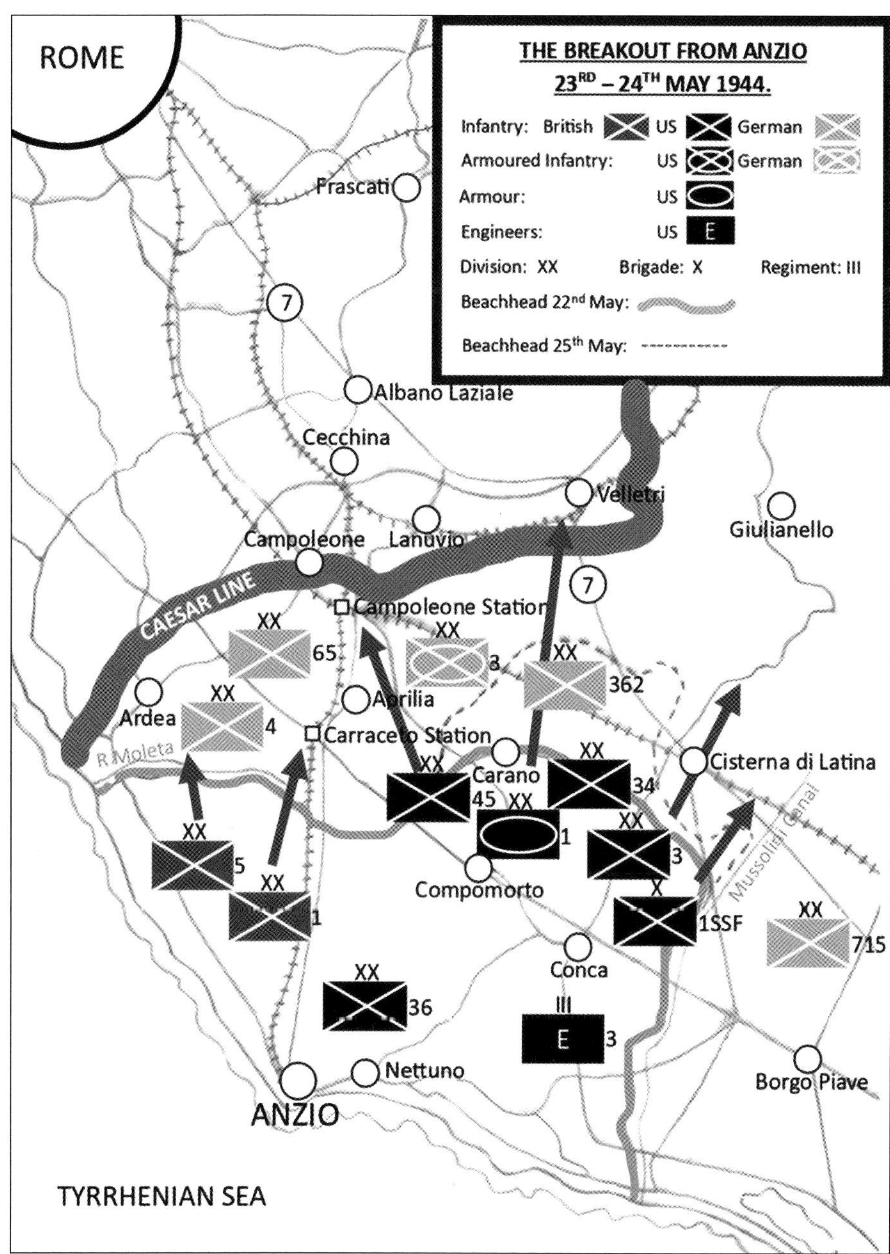

At 5.45am on 23rd May, the Cisterna front was engulfed in flame, when every one of the allied artillery pieces opened fire on the enemy positions. As the barrage abated, the defenders peered into the drifting smoke, to see a swarm of infantry advancing in the wake of a mass of tanks that stretched all the way from Carano to the Mussolini Canal. The minefields took their

British infantry occupies a captured German communications trench during the breakout from Anzio, May 1944. Radford (Sgt) No 2 Army Film & Photographic Unit. (*Wikimedia Commons*)

inevitable toll, but nevertheless, the entire US 1st Armoured Division had broken through the main line of resistance, leaving the enemy survivors reeling, and bewildered by the power of the assault. The Hermann Goering Panzer Division was rushed to the front, from its rest area at Leghorn, but attempts to move reinforcements from the Albano Road sector were frustrated by the intervention of British 1st and 5th Infantry Divisions. General Mackensen, commanding the German forces at Anzio, pleaded with Kesselring to allow him to pull his left flank back to the Lepini Mountains. The Commander in Chief refused. On 25th May, Cisterna was captured, and the enemy fell back into chaos. Nearly 1,000 prisoners were taken, as the allied wave smashed into the base of the Lepini Mountains.

A British soldier guards a group of German prisoners at Anzio, 22nd January 1944. Menzies (Sgt), No 2 Army Film & Photographic Unit. (*Wikimedia Commons*)

On 26th May, reconnaissance units from US 3rd Division, reached Artena, only three miles from the objective of Valmontone, but the Hermann Goering Panzer Division had now regrouped and were holding off 3rd Division's probing attacks. The first stage of the breakout from Anzio had been a great success, but the cost had been high. In 5 days, the attackers had lost 4,000 men, and eighty-six armoured vehicles. German casualties were higher. Even though no official figures exist, it is today estimated that 4,800 men surrendered, and 2,700 vehicles were destroyed.

On the 25th, units from II Corps made contact with a scouting party from Anzio, and the breakout was complete.

7.5.4 To Rome

General Clark now intended to "crush the 14th German Army," but he was not inclined to share the glory with anyone but his American forces from Anzio. Although the advance to Rome now seemed to be a relatively routine matter, he was secure in the knowledge that the British would be at the back of it, as they had to move through the more difficult territory. They would, he decided, get their opportunity to go sightseeing in the Eternal City, once the Americans had taken it.

However, the American Caesar was unaware of just how much the German defences had been strengthened during the time that the allies had spent trying to break the Gustav Line at Mount Cassino, and on the 28th, Kesselring was able to call for defiance from both 10th and 14th Armies, with their reinforcements from the north.

The 8th Army continued to push forward, meeting less resistance, as more and more German units were withdrawn to the Caesar Line, which was the name given to the last defences before Rome. On 4th June, Piglio and Paliano, to the northeast of Valmontone, were occupied, and this was to be the 8th Army's last contribution to the battle for Rome.

Clark was determined to split the German line between Lanuvio and Campoleone before moving on the capital city, so he ordered British 1st

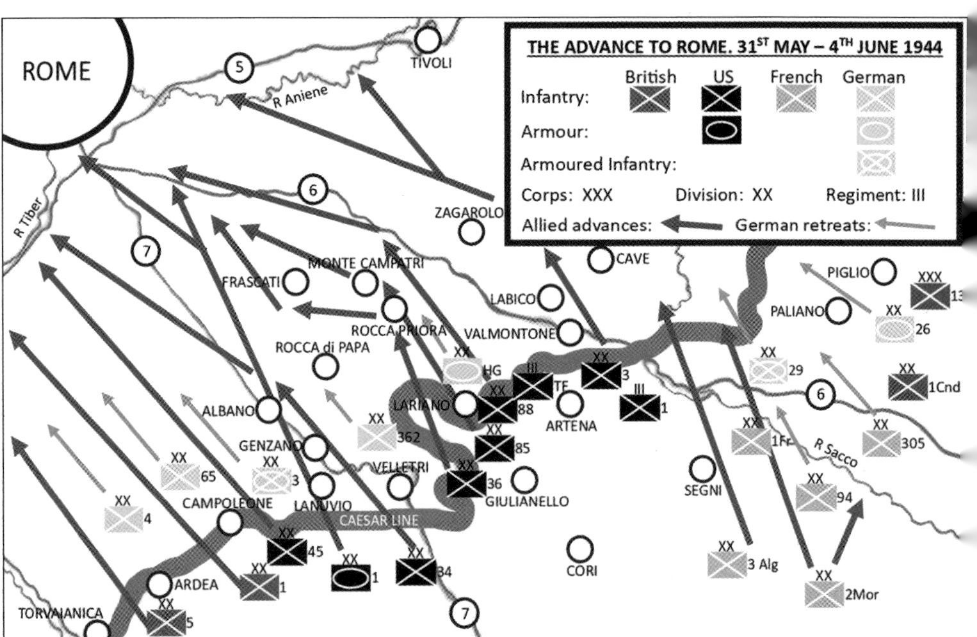

The 8th Army advances through Aquino, southeast of Rome. 19th May 1944. Unknown. (*National Army Museum Study Collection*)

and 5th Infantry Divisions to attack the Caesar Line along the coastal front, where the German 1st Parachute Corps were waiting for them. As 1st KOYLI joined in the assault by 5th Division, 9th KOYLI were pitted against a battalion of 4th Parachute Division in an effort to open one of the roads into Rome for the American forces who were now advancing along them. "A" Squadron was given the objective of taking a vital bridge, whilst "B" Squadron was ordered to take a series of three successive ridges, to the right of the road. The German paratroopers were part of a crack division, and they were fighting both for their pride and for the benefit of their comrades who were now retreating towards the mirage of a safe haven north of Rome. Bullets and mortar shells rained down on "B" Squadron as they climbed the first ridge. Unlike their fellow KOYLI in 1st Battalion, they had little experience of the jagged ridges of southern Italy, but they learnt as they climbed, finding shelter behind an outcrop in the rough ground, before leaping to another as covering fire was provided. They battled with the defenders on the first of the ridges and there was no time to take prisoners before they began the assault on the next obstacle. Major Harris St. John was awarded the Military Cross for his leadership that day, and others went to Major MacKenzie Smith and Lieutenant Philips. Military Medals were awarded to Sergeants Hutchings, Taylor, Riley and Woolnough. Meanwhile, "A" Squadron were scrambling over the open ground towards the bridge. Once again, the enemy had set up defensive positions in a way that only experienced and battle-hardened troops could. The KOYLI crawled and slid their way from one depression in the ground to another, throwing hand grenades as they went. One by one, the German emplacements were overcome, until, in a final charge, the Yorkshiremen swarmed over the final gun emplacement, which had been set up on the bridge itself. 100 prisoners were taken, and the roadblocks cleared, just in time for the armour to pass over the bridge and go roaring on to Rome. The ridges had all been cleared and the survivors of "B" Squadron simply sat on the final summit and waved the tanks through. Brigadier Loewen, acting Commander of 1st Infantry Division, knew the importance of that action by 9th KOYLI, and he made a point of congratulating them when he visited them the next day.

Rome fell on 4th June. During the fighting from Anzio, 9th KOYLI had lost sixty-seven men, with ninety-three wounded, and 153 missing or taken prisoner.

7.6 The Gothic Line

As Clark had always planned, the capture of Rome was an all-American affair. The British infantry divisions attached to US VI Corps were held back on the south bank of the Tiber, where they went into billets and watched the taking of the capital city from a distance. After a programme of training, 9th KOYLI were once again placed under the command of 1st Armoured Division, along with the rest of 18th Infantry Brigade, and went back into the line on the outskirts of Florence. Towards the end of August, it was decided that all those members of 9th KOYLI who had completed almost five years abroad, would be repatriated, and they left for home on 31st August.

5th Army tanks in Rome, 4th June 1944. Unknown. (*National Army Museum Study Collection*)

The 1st Armoured Division now comprised: 2nd Armoured, 43rd Gurkha, and 18th Infantry Brigades.

46th Infantry Division returned to the theatre, and 2/4th KOYLI, as part of 138th Infantry Brigade, formed part of the reorganised unit, along with 128th and 139th Infantry, and 25th Tank Brigades. Both divisions became part of V Corps, under the overall command of 8th Army.

Along with the rest of 15th Infantry Brigade, 1st KOYLI was detached from the Italian campaign and deployed to garrison duties in the Middle East. It was destined to re-enter the fighting on 3rd March 1945, as part of the allied forces in northwest Europe.

Clark's fixation with ensuring that 5th Army was first to enter Rome had resulted in the escape of the remaining German forces in Italy. Now Kesselring had been allowed the time to organise a succession of masterly delaying operations that, in turn, had given him the opportunity to bring in gangs of slave labour to work on the construction of a new defensive line. The allied advance across the River Arno was held up for over a month, between 23rd July and 31st August, and by the time the "Arno Line" was eventually stormed, the formidable "Gothic Line" was nearing completion. The Apennine Mountains formed the bulk of the line, and these were, in places, fifty miles deep and 7,000 feet high. Along its length were nearly 2,500 machine gun posts that had been expertly placed to provide an intense crossfire. Concrete pits and trenches had been built to house the infantry, and 480 anti-tank and artillery positions had been carved into the mountainsides, behind a forest of barbed wire and a maze of anti-tank ditches.

Public attention had turned towards the invasion of France, which took place two days after the fall of Rome. The allied high command now saw

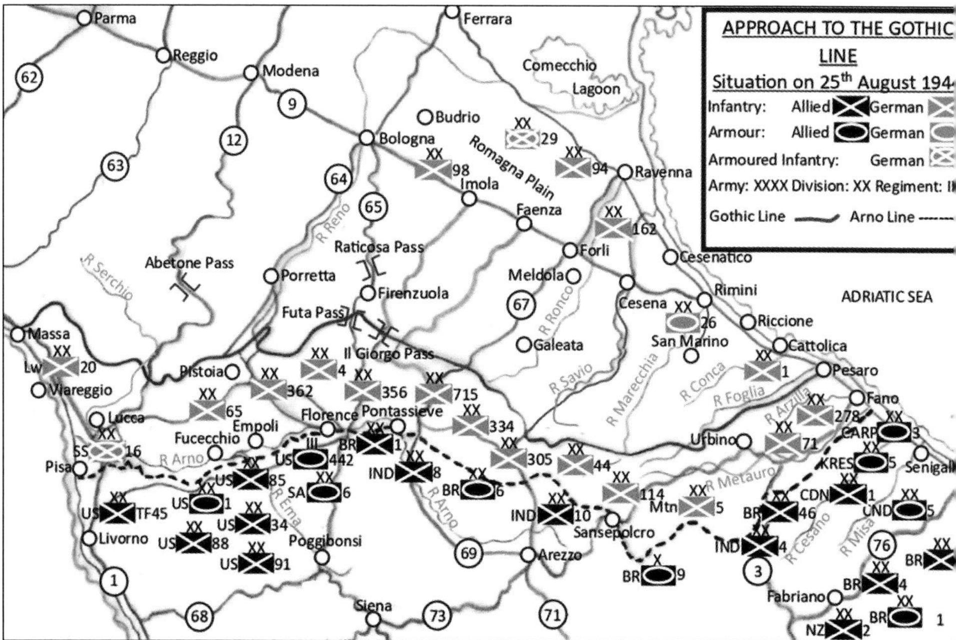

the Italian campaign as being of secondary importance to the one that was unfolding in France, and as a result, seven American divisions were withdrawn from Italy to take part in "Operation Dragoon;" landings in the south of France that were designed to pull some of the German forces away from Normandy. The taking of the Gothic Line would now be down to 8th Army, and it was important, argued Churchill, because the threat of an invasion of Germany from the south would tie down enemy forces that would otherwise be available in France. Although the US Chiefs of Staff wanted to shelve the Italian operations, Churchill finally got his way, and the attack on the Gothic Line was given the green light.

"Operation Olive," was to be focussed on the Adriatic coast, and would involve all the forces available to 8th Army:

Polish II Corps:	5th Kresowa Division.
	3rd Carpathian Division.
Canadian I Corps:	1st Infantry Division.
	5th Armoured Division.
British V Corps:	46th Infantry Division.
	4th Indian Infantry Division.
	56th Infantry Division.
	1st Armoured Division.
	7th Armoured Brigade.
	25th Tank Brigade.

British X Corps would protect the left flank of 8th Army's offensive.

The German 10th Army was given the task of repelling 8th Army. It now comprised:

1st Parachute Division.
71st Infantry Division.
278th Infantry Division.
51st Mountain Corps (five divisions).
162nd Infantry Division.
98th Infantry Division.

7.6.1 Operation Olive

As we have seen, 2/4th KOYLI had been withdrawn to the Middle East on 1st March, having been involved in the hard fighting all the way from Salerno to the northern banks of the Garigliano. Now they had returned, and after landing at Taranto, had been loaded into cattle wagons for the two-day journey to Capua. They had passed through the wreckage of Cassino and

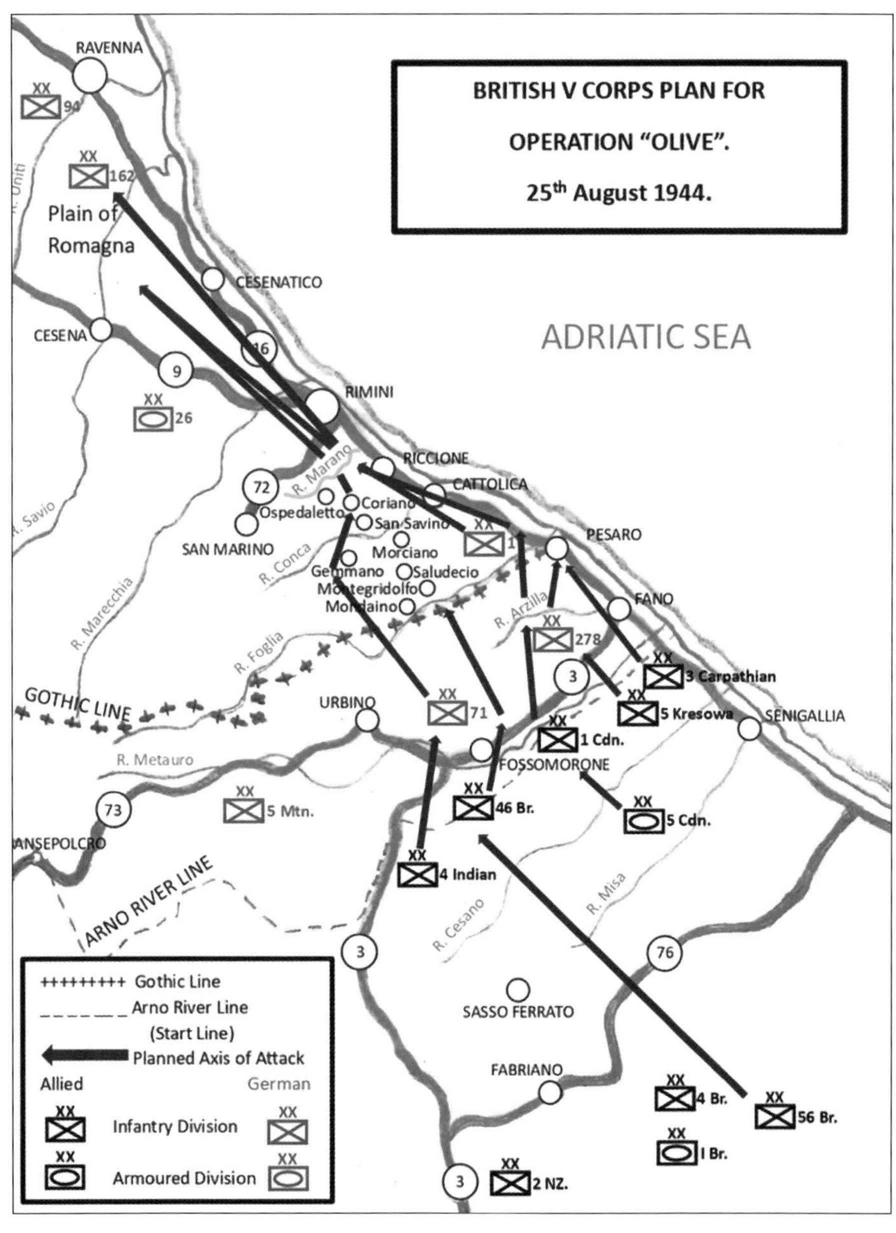

the magnificence of Rome, before finally halting in the rolling countryside around Bevagna. The training schedule had been tough, but by 1st August, they were deemed fit to return to the fighting. This news served to dampen the celebrations of Minden Day, an anniversary celebrated on 1st August by those regiments whose predecessors had taken part in the Battle of Minden in 1759, but the KOYLI were at least able to help themselves to the local Italian wine.

As part of V Corps, 46th Division was concentrated around Sasso Ferrato, which they reached after a silent night journey that was completed in total blackout conditions. They travelled slowly, aware that their vehicles could throw up a cloud of dust that would identify their position to the observation posts of the German 71st Infantry Division, who stood in front of them. As it happened, the 71st were conducting a clandestine move of their own: retreating towards the River Foglia and another fearsome line of defences. When Kesselring realised what was happening, he ordered reinforcements to the area, but by the time they arrived, the Canadian and British Corps had reached the defence line that ran along the northern bank of the Foglia, and by the 3rd, the allies had pierced a second line near Riccione. Just when it seemed that a breakthrough to Rimini was about to happen, the left wing of the German 10th Army managed to retreat behind the River Conca, where they regrouped and organised a formidable defence.

V Corps began to enter the high ground overlooking the Foglia, where they discovered a series of barren hills that had been heavily mined by an enemy who was in position to spray machine gun fire into any infantry that attempted to advance across the open grassland.

The villages of Montegridolfo, Mondiano, and Saludecio, were perched 1,200 ft above the river and provided ideal locations for holding up the advance of the men of 2/4th KOYLI, as they negotiated the winding and unstable tracks that were the only way up the mountainside.

On 1st September, 138th Infantry Brigade was brought forward to support 142nd Royal Tank and 46th Reconnaissance Regiments. As part of this move, 2/4th KOYLI were called upon to push into the low ground east of Montegridolfo, where they might join up with the Canadians. They went into action at midday and were involved in heavy fighting that lasted until well after nightfall.

Troops of 128th Brigade move up to their last objective before the Gothic Line, 27th August 1944. Menzies (Sgt), No 2 Army Film & Photographic Unit. (*Wikipedia*)

7.6.2 The Conca

On 2nd of September, 2/4th KOYLI fought its way into Morciano, driving the German defenders in front of them as they captured the town bridge at about 10 pm. This allowed two battalions of 128th Brigade to cross in troop carriers. Although they were exhausted, they went on to take part in the capture of the vital bridge over the River Marano, at Ospedaletto.

On the night of 3rd September, 138th Brigade set off towards Coriano, but at dawn they were hit by a barrage of artillery fire, during which 2/4th KOYLI took their full share of the heavy casualties. Along with 128th Brigade, they managed to capture the town of San Clemente, as 46th Reconnaissance Regiment penetrated along the ridge as far as Castelleale. At that point, German artillery fire smashed into 128th and 138th Brigades, again taking a heavy toll on the attacking 2/4th KOYLI, as they waited for the leading tanks of 1st Armoured Division to cross the Conca and catch up with them.

By now, air reconnaissance had discovered a new German line, running from Rimini to San Marino, as Kesselring rushed to reinforce his defences with 356th Infantry Division, stationed to the north. He also called upon the services of two battalions of Tiger tanks, one battery of 88 mm anti-tank guns, and one of Nebelwerfer rockets.

9th KOYLI were part of the lorried infantry support attached to 2nd Armoured Brigade, when just after midnight on 3rd/4th September, they crossed the Conca and raced to the support of 46th Division, which was still under heavy fire in the area around Castelleale, from the ridge that ran from San Savino to Coriano. After being appraised of the situation, the commander of 2nd Armoured decided to push on and seize the crossing

1st Armoured Division advance to the Gothic Line, 27th-28th August 1944. Lupson (Sgt), No 2 Army Film & Photographic Unit. (*Wikimedia Commons*)

over the Marano. The German artillery observers on the Gemmano heights, now began to direct fire onto the attacking forces, as the crossing was taken and the lorried infantry began to climb the Coriano Ridge, in support of the tanks which began to struggle on the difficult slopes that caused them to slide, shed tracks, and overturn as the artillery shells smashed into them. There was nothing for it but to retreat to the shelter of the San Clemente Ridge, where the survivors fell into an exhausted sleep.

Next day, 9th KOYLI, together with other units of the lorried infantry support, managed to fight their way into the village of San Savino, at the end of the Coriano Ridge. They had to fight it out with the Germans who had taken up position in the houses, and that night, the rest of 18th Lorried Infantry Brigade came to their aid. They captured the German commander and forty-six of his men before they were forced to pull back.

7.6.3 Gemmano and Coriano

During this time, 56th Division had crossed the Conca and had tried to take two enemy positions, at Croce and Gemmano. Again, the weather was atrocious, as a storm caused the rivers to overflow and turned the ground into a sticky mess. Bailey bridges were washed away and the whole advance came to a halt.

It was 12th September before conditions eased sufficiently for the offensive to begin again. Following the reorganisation of the attacking forces it became obvious that V Corps held the key to success, as they tried to clear the high ground on 8th Army's left flank.

The next assault on the Coriano Ridge began on the night of the 12th, after an artillery barrage by 700 guns. As the Canadians attacked Coriano itself, 1st Armoured Division began the treacherous climb towards the summit of the ridge, and 18th Infantry Brigade became part of a two-brigade attack. Each brigade sent two battalions to the front of the assault, whilst holding a third in reserve, and 9th KOYLI were selected to lead a second attempt to drive the enemy out of San Savino. The German defenders had taken the time provided by the short break in fighting, to turn the rubble into a hedgehog position, in which each machine gun post was able to support those around it by setting up a crossfire through which the enemy infantry would have to pass in order to move through the town. As the British at Waterloo had lured the French cavalry into a charge that took them between "squares" of

Outside the village of Gemmano, 6th September 1944. Dawson (Sgt), No 2 Army Film & Photographic Unit. (*Wikimedia Commons*)

infantry that bristled with muskets on all four sides, so the Germans at San Savino thought they could lure the men of 9th KOYLI into the death trap of a hedgehog position. But the Yorkshiremen had learnt a lot since their conversion to lorried infantry. They knew how to support an armoured force brought to a halt by infantry that had taken up position in a built-up area, and they had become experts in clearing positions that would have devastated any unsupported tank attack. Using these learnt tactics, they crawled, sprinted, and dived their way through the remains of the little town, taking out the fearsome gun posts as they went. Hurling grenades and pieces of rubble, they came to grips with the desperate defenders, who swung at them with sharpened entrenching tools, in the close confines of buildings where the use of bayonets was restricted. Boots smashed into shins and groins, helmet rims were butted into faces, and men struggled to win individual wrestling matches, where death awaited the loser of each bout, and where the winner tried to find some dark hole, that would allow him to catch his breath, or tend to the wounds of a friend.

The fighting went on throughout the day and the following night, until on 14th September, the Germans cracked. Those who were still able to do so, crawled out of their blood-soaked holes and stumbled forward with arms outstretched towards the men in khaki, who were scarcely in condition to recognise that they had won the battle. Nevertheless, 600 prisoners were taken in the small, previously insignificant town of San Savino, on 14th September 1944, and Colonel Kelly, back in command of 9th KOYLI after being hospitalised, was awarded the bar to his DSO, whilst Lieutenant Brierley received the Military Cross, and Lance-Corporal O'Meara the Military Medal.

On 9th September, 138th Brigade had been ordered to relieve the 168th, who were having a rough time in the fight for the Gemmano Ridge. 2/4th KOYLI had been in Morciano, resting in the shell of a factory, when they were told of their next objective. They had been allowed to finish their brew-up, before marching out in the direction of the forbidding ridge. In the distance, they could see a mass of hills and ravines, where a series of small villages clung to the slopes and peaks. An officer pointed towards the eastern end of the ridge and the village of Villa. Further on they could just make out the grey shapes of Gemmano and Borgo. Beyond their range of vision, was Zollara, at the extreme west of the ridge. The officer pointed towards a particularly high spot, between Borgo and Zollara, that was topped by a single white farmhouse, and any of them who glanced down at the tactical map in his hand, would have seen that this had been designated as Hill 414. Nearby was Hill 449, and the giant, rusting cross that had been placed at its summit, cast an ominous shadow, which cut across a neglected cemetery, before disappearing into the darkness of a ravine.

The KOYLI were told that their mission was to climb the ridge to rescue the two battalions of 169th Brigade, who had been badly mauled in the fighting for the heights. A third battalion of 169th was still relatively intact and was trying to forge on, to take the town of Farneto, at the extreme end of a spur that jutted out of the ridge itself. It was intended that the taking of Farneto would allow 6th Lincolns to pass through and take Hill 449.

The Farneto attack was repulsed as 2/4th KOYLI were climbing Hill 414, on their way to the rescue of the stranded battalions of 169th Brigade. This meant that they found themselves spread out and vulnerable on the bare slopes, as the enemy machine guns tried to sweep them away. Two companies managed to reach Gemmano, as another struggled into Villa and a third went on to try to clear the houses at the western end of Borgo. The all too familiar pattern of bloody house-to-house fighting, resulted in the loss of half the force, in yet another battle of small, isolated units, where the course of a whole campaign hung in the balance. As night fell, men took shelter in any deserted house they could find, counting the losses and bandaging the wounded, sometimes in the full knowledge that their efforts would be in vain.

The 6th Lincolns had been faced with trying to take Hill 449 without the strategic point of Fameto having been secured. As they moved forward towards Gemmano, they were met by devastating artillery and mortar fire that cut them to pieces before they had even reached Hill 414, from which their attack was to begin. It was midday before a single depleted company managed to charge through a blanket of smoke, under heavy fire from their right flank, to reach the lonely cross.

It was obvious to those watching from the valleys below, that more support was desperately needed if the troops of the 169th were to be rescued. The 2/4th KOYLI were released from their support role so that they could move on to help 6th Lincolns as they clung to their exposed positions on Hill 449. The importance of this high point was obvious to both sides, and this resulted in more vicious fighting, in which the summit changed hands several times. One company of 2/4th KOYLI took cover in the ominous surroundings of the cemetery, as the shelling increased and wave after wave of enemy attacks were repulsed. The losses were mounting, and on the night of 12th September, the 6th York and Lancs were sent in to help the rest of 138th Brigade clear Gemmano, as part of the plan to break German resistance along the hills between Coriano and Gemmano.

From across the river, the 6th York and Lancs tried to take the ridge from which the enemy was shelling Gemmano, but they were held up in more fighting that involved the now familiar groups of small units, amongst the rocks and crevices of a dark mountain. The battalions of the Austrian 100th Mountain Regiment were experienced in this kind of fighting, but even these determined and fanatical men had no answer to the heavy artillery fire that battered the slopes, on which soldiers of both sides, clung and died.

A British 17 pdr shelling the village of Gemmano. Unknown. (*Wikimedia Commons*)

As the Austrians hung on to their positions amongst the death-filled crevices, the men of 138th Battalion began to filter their way through the tiny ravines that ran between the enemy gun posts. When they had crawled their way into a slightly less exposed area were able to redirect the artillery fire, so that it fell more accurately, onto the enemy positions.

The exhausted 2/4th KOYLI were still in the cemetery, where they sheltered behind gravestones that rang and shattered, under the almost constant fire of the counterattacking Germans. Eventually, the more precise artillery fire began to have a real effect on the men of 100th Mountain Regiment, and the KOYLI became aware of a slackening in the attack on their graveyard fortress, as the Austrians fell back to take up more defensive positions. Carefully, they crept from behind the tombs, and moved forward, towards the summit of Hill 449, where they found the body of a soldier from the 6th Lincolns. He had fallen at the foot of the giant cross, and his dead hands were gripping tight to the rusting metal that his incredible bravery had enabled him to reach.

The advance became a slow, mile-by-mile slog, to the last of the Gothic defence lines, at Rimini. British V Corps now faced 356th Infantry Division, with the Canadian Corps up against 1st Parachute and 29th Panzer Grenadier Divisions. 1st Armoured and 56th Infantry Divisions were sent to clear yet another ridge, this one called the Ripabianca.

The assault on the ridge began when 1st Armoured Division crossed the Marano at Case del Monte, and 56th at Mulazzano, both to the west of Ospedaletto. 46th Division would follow up, by crossing the Conca and taking the dominating heights of Monte Colombo and Montescudo.

The all-out offensive drove the German line back in confusion, and by the afternoon of the first day 9th KOYLI were with 18th Infantry Brigade on the Ripabianca Ridge as 56th Division smashed through the reconnaissance battalions of 44th Infantry and 114th Jaeger Divisions, who had been sent to support 356th Infantry Division.

46th Division, with 2/4th KOYLI, took Monte Colombo, and found themselves marching along roads where the stench of rotting bodies, both human and equine, told the story of the artillery bombardment that had gone before them. 8th Army was now ready to attack the Rimini Line.

7.6.4 The Rimini Line

On the night of 17th September, the assault on the Rimini Line began, and both 56th and 46th Divisions ran into severe opposition as they tried to clear Mount Olivo and Colle di Montelupo, respectively. 1st Armoured Division, meanwhile, had sent its infantry force to take Mount dell'Arboreta, and during the night of 18th September, 9th KOYLI became involved in heavy fighting, when 18th Brigade attacked their objective. Under intense fire, "A" Squadron had battled their way up to the summit, and were in the process of regrouping when the defenders counterattacked. Instinctively, they tried to set up defensive positions, as the Germans charged out of the smoke, yelling and shouting like demons. As a few men struggled to set up the Bren gun, the rest tried to hold off the assault, with bayonets and fists. The squadron leader, Major Dawson, was killed in that encounter, which drove the KOYLI back to the edge of the summit. As they tried to keep their footing on the edge of the precipice, they heard another shout, and "D" Squadron swept in, to smash into the German flank, and send the enemy reeling backwards. "B" Squadron were given the chance to reach their objective, and they took it, as "D" Squadron charged on, to drive the Germans from the peak for the last time.

Next day, 9th KOYLI came under intense artillery fire again, and although the majority of them managed to spread out and take cover, the command post received a direct hit. One man was killed, and two others seriously wounded, including Colonel Kelly, who had to be evacuated down the mountain, as Major Tarrant took command and was promoted to Lieutenant Colonel.

On the morning of 20th September, 2nd Armoured Brigade came under heavy fire from the German 88mm guns, and 18th Lorried Infantry Brigade had to dig in, as all but three tanks were destroyed. They were expecting that more tanks would follow as night fell, but again the rain made the ground impassable for armour, and all they could do was hold on.

That afternoon, Kesselring ordered the whole of LXXVI Panzer Corps to retreat across the River Marecchia, and Rimini was evacuated on 21st September after all the port installations had been destroyed. At dawn on the 22nd, the men of 8th Army collapsed in exhaustion, on the banks of the Marecchia. They were out of ammunition and supplies, but they had broken the Rimini Line, and with it, the morale of the Nazi forces in Italy, who shrank back to the wilderness of the Romagna Plain and knew that their next stop would be Germany.

Had they known the extent of the losses that 8th Army had sustained during Operation Olive, the German high command may still have been able to stir their beaten forces into action once again, but those soldiers had been fed Reichminister Goebbels' propaganda lies, all the way from Alamein to the foothills of the Alps, and they would surely have doubted the accuracy of any more "good news" that might have been put to them. Still, 8th Army certainly had no reinforcements, as all the fresh troops that were available, had been sent to northern France, along with the best equipment. They were forced to stop and wait for any developments the winter might bring.

Such was the shortage of reinforcements, that it was decided to break up 18th Infantry Brigade so that its remaining men could be used to bolster other units. As the former Queen's Own Yorkshire Dragoons Regiment, 9th KOYLI was placed in what was referred to as, "suspended animation", and the majority of its officers and men, were posted to 2/4th KOYLI. In an open letter addressed to them, under their previous title as Queen's Own Yorkshire Dragoons, Field Marshall Alexander wrote:

> "You may be proud of the part your Regiment has played in our great victories out here, and I shall always feel very proud to have had the Yorkshire Dragoons under my command."

A great many of the original Yorkshire Dragoons who had arrived home in September and October went on to join in the fight in northwest Europe. Regimental Sergeant-Major Roberts was awarded the MBE, for his distinguished service since before the battle of El Alamein.

By the end of September, the Po Valley and the Alps were within sight, but the Plain of Romagna was an obstacle too far. As winter set in, 8th Army was forced to halt, in the inhospitable landscape that was perfectly suited to defensive warfare. In terrible conditions, the men of 2/4th KOYLI, and the former members of 9th KOYLI who now found themselves in other regiments, huddled in their freezing and sodden dugouts, and waited for spring. By their endurance, they ensured that none of the enemy who stood in their way, could be released to take part in the battles for northwest Europe, and when spring finally arrived, General Clark's 5th Army, not the 8th, would be the one to clear Italy of the remaining German forces.

Chapter 8

Northwestern Europe 1944–5

8.1 Normandy

On 11th June 1944, 1/4th KOYLI landed at La Riviere in Normandy, to the east of Arromanches-les-Bains. From there, they marched inland for several miles, until they reached the area around Coulombs, where the Divisional Command Centre was to be located. On

British infantry on the lookout for a sniper. Normandy, June 1944. Christie (Sgt), No 5 Army Film & Photographic Unit. (*Wikimedia Commons*)

the 14th, they sent out two patrols: one towards Tilly-sur-Seulles, and another towards the small village of Le Hamel. This was "Bocage country," where narrow roads with high hedges on both sides, snaked through open fields and provided ideal territory for defenders. The patrols soon came into contact with enemy units hidden in the hedgerows, from where snipers fired at any attempt to move out of the roadside ditches. The casualties started to mount, as the KOYLI tried to pick out the sniper positions in the trees, and amongst the thick bushes. If a head was raised too far, there would be the crack of a rifle shot, followed almost instantaneously by the dull sickening sound of a bullet against helmet, and a comrade would be dead in a Normandy ditch. The survivors had no alternative but to wait until the enemy position had been flanked by other units, keeping their heads buried in the damp earth until they heard the sound of fighting up ahead.

Just north of Tilly-sur-Seulles, the KOYLI were engaged by a hidden enemy gun emplacement, which they were able to destroy with a barrage of accurate mortar fire, before charging in to take the survivors prisoner.

Still, the casualties mounted as the enemy continued to bombard the KOYLI positions, yet on the 16th they were ordered to attack and disable the German-held position in the village of Cristot. Under cover of a rolling barrage from both artillery and naval guns, the battalion crept towards the silent buildings, through the ripening wheat. They had almost crossed the field when the enemy opened fire, and they quickly took shelter behind the Sherman tanks that had been sent to support them. They pressed on, and several of the tanks were hit before the KOYLI found themselves fighting their way through the houses, as the Germans were pushed back. A counterattack was repelled, and the battalion held on until relieved, when they withdrew to lick their wounds and count their losses.

As the KOYLI tried to rest before the next battle, which they knew must come before too long, the powers-that-be were putting the final touches to "Operation Martlet," a plan that included the taking of the high ground south of the town of Fontenay, which was held by elements of 12th SS Panzer Division (Hitlerjugend). On 25th June, 1/4th KOYLI found themselves in the second wave of the attack, with instructions to infiltrate an area of forest, known as Tessel Wood. They were drawn up beside a ditch that ran along one side of an area of open meadow, waiting for the order to charge forwards, towards the dark trees in the distance. The air was still, except for

Fontenay-le-Pesnel, Normandy, 25th June 1944. Handford (Lt), No 5 Army Film & Photographic Unit. (*Wikipedia*)

the far-off sound of shellfire, and the occasional rattle of a machine gun, and in any other circumstance they might have enjoyed such a calm country scene. But they knew that the wide field of meadow grass and wildflowers would be a hellish area to cross, under fire from the cool shadows that beckoned them on.

The officer's arm went down, and the advance began. They had covered the first 50 yards before the shooting began and the men started to fall, but there could be no stopping, even though the deep grass seemed to promise a degree of safety, as the bullets flew above it. They charged on, and the distance between them and the flashing lights beneath the trees, grew smaller and smaller. Then they were there. The Germans had turned to run deeper into the trees, leaving behind their heavy machine guns, and for a while, it seemed as if they had abandoned the wood altogether. The KOYLI set up a command position and quickly spread out to form a defensive perimeter, and it was then that they realised that the enemy had only retreated to the far side of the wooded area. For three weeks, the isolated KOYLI held off a series of counterattacks that threatened to break their defences. At night, supplies were brought forward, across the meadow, and they were able to keep fighting; carrying out nightly patrols which almost always resulted in contact with enemy forces. On 14th July, one company was sent to attack a group of buildings known as Barbee Farm, as part of a larger assault on the village of Vendes. They fought their way into the farm but were soon surrounded, and pinned down by heavy fire. When the enemy was seen to be pulling the noose tighter around their position, they radioed the commander of the Hallamshire Battalion force that had penetrated Vendes itself, informing him of the situation. They were pinned down, had many wounded, and had little hope of being able to escape the trap that was closing around them. Immediately, the Hallamshire's CO requested an artillery barrage that would surround the farm, and drive the Germans back. Before the shells came raining in, a half-tracked vehicle sped out from the British line, towards the beleaguered farmhouse. Even though it was marked with the red cross of a medical vehicle, the KOYLI who huddled behind the wrecked walls,

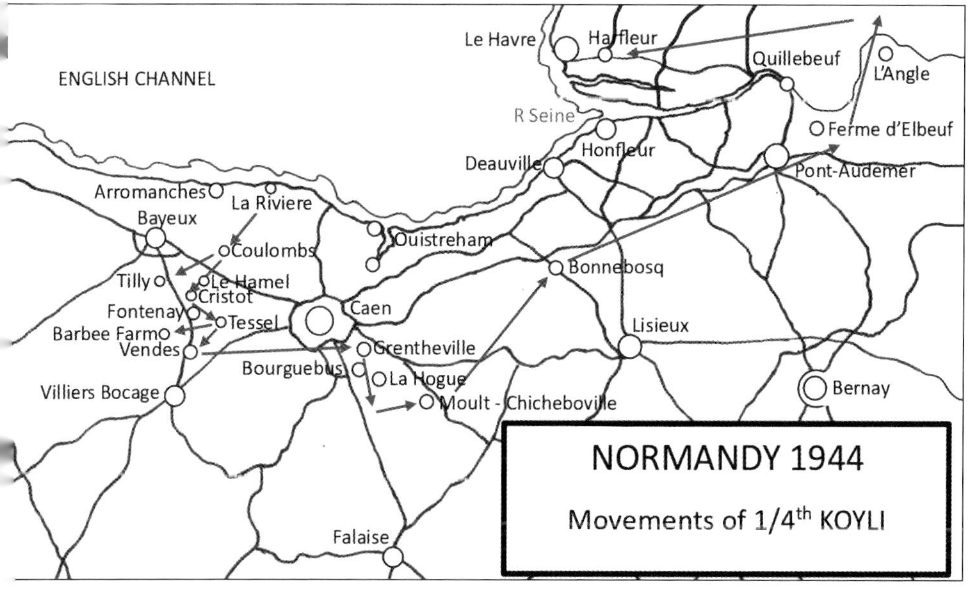

were still amazed that the German guns failed to score a hit, and the hero at the wheel brought it to a skidding halt at what now remained of the front door. Under the cover of the artillery bombardment that had now begun, they loaded the wounded onto the half-track, and together made a dash for safety, through the cloak of smoke and fire.

Three days later, after another artillery bombardment, the rest of 1/4th KOYLI, joined in the attack that took back the village of Vendes and found that the corpse-strewn wreckage that had once been Barbee Farm had been abandoned by the Germans.

They were next in action at Grentheville, on 21st July. In the "Falaise Pocket," the Germans had suffered a crushing defeat, yet they had held open a gap through which many of their men had managed to escape. Now the allies were intent on following up their victory before the enemy had time to reorganise. However, the German army's ability to react to what should have been a devastating defeat, soon became evident, and now 1/4th KOYLI were called upon to carry out probing missions that would test the strength of the enemy at a range of points, along what was thought to be their new line of defence, to the north of Falaise. Over the next few weeks, small units went out into the "no man's land" in front of the allied position, to creep forward in the darkness, listening for the sounds of activity, and German voices. Sometimes, these sorties resulted in an exchange of gunfire and a hasty withdrawal, with a prisoner where possible.

Finally, the advance began again, and 1/4th KOYLI were part of an arcing manoeuvre that was designed to push north, towards Le Havre. Many villages lined the route, and most of them hid an enemy detachment, determined to hold up this thrust towards Holland, and the German border itself. At Grentheville, Bourguébus, La Hogue, Moult-Chicheboville, Bénouville, and Bonnebosq, the KOYLI were called upon to clear out the enemy emplacements. Each engagement was a hellish battle against a determined enemy, for a spot on the map that was significant only to those who fought there, but the victors continued to move north, as the vanquished lay dead by the roadside.

As they approached the River Seine, the KOYLI were detached from the main force, which was moving to attack the town of Quillebeuf, on 25th August. Their assignment was to nullify a German unit that had created a strongpoint in yet another farm, this one to the south of Quillebeuf. On the

27th, they attacked the Ferme d'Elbeuf, under the covering fire of mortars and machine guns. Storming into the farmyard, they were hit by a deadly crossfire that came from the buildings on all sides, and they spread out to take cover behind the abandoned farm machinery, and piles of hay that had been left to rot in the rain. Hurling grenades, and firing from the hip, the companies charged forward towards the muzzle flashes that lit up the darkened windows and barn doors. Within seconds, the German defenders began jumping from their positions. Some tried to fight with bayonets, but most made a run for the gaps in the far wall of the yard. Few survived. The KOYLI were in no mood to stop their headlong charge, and they continued to spray bullets after the fleeing Germans until there was no one left to run. Those few prisoners who were taken must surely have considered themselves very lucky indeed.

The KOYLI advanced further into the Forêt de Brotonne, and a few miles south of a great bend in the river, they settled into the village of L'Angle. Nearby, they discovered a huge abandoned stache of weapons and equipment. They searched amongst the detritus, for any food supplies, but the Germans had managed to escape with them all.

On 2nd September, they crossed to the north bank of the Seine, in boats that were swept along by the strong current, as the engines failed, and the rain poured down. The next major objective was Le Havre, and they quickly began to link up with other elements of the force that had been assigned to take the great port, which was held by elements of 226th and 245th Infantry Divisions, together with a few other units that had been gathered together into a "Festung Stamm Abteilung," one of the last examples of Hitler's flawed "fortress" strategy.

About 3 miles to the east of Le Havre lies the town of Harfleur, which Henry V had struggled to capture in 1415. Over five centuries later, the defenders again knew the importance of holding on to this gateway to the port, and they had constructed a huge roadblock that 1/4th KOYLI were now called upon to break. As they approached, the KOYLI were hit by a wall of gunfire that drove them into cover in the roadside ditches, from where they called for tank support. When this arrived, they crept out of their shallow refuge, and fell into step behind the steel giants as they pressed forward, towards the concrete emplacements and abandoned vehicles that blocked the road into Harfleur, and Le Havre beyond. The tanks took a battering,

British infantry on the outskirts of Le Havre, September 1944. Collins (Sgt), No 5 Army Film & Photographic Unit. (*Wikimedia Commons*)

but they continued to fire into the German bunkers, as the KOYLI swarmed out from behind them, to clear out each enemy gun post as they reached it. There were four main enemy positions, and as darkness descended, the survivors of the assault began to enter Harfleur, where they stopped, to tend to the wounded.

A single road ran into the city of Le Havre, which is built on the peninsular where the Seine flows into the English Channel. The area to the north of the road was very boggy, and this meant that there was only one realistic route to their target. More defensive positions had been built all along the way to the main fortifications in the city itself, and when the attack began, it once again developed into a fight for each street, each pillbox, and each gun position. 1/4th KOYLI had to cross a deep minefield where they lost many men, even before coming into contact with enemy troops. When a unit of mine-clearing tanks arrived, they managed to reach the far side of the minefield, where they came to grips with the defenders in their concrete bunkers and machine gun posts. All were taken.

On 12th September, the German garrison in Le Havre finally surrendered, and six days later, the KOYLI began their journey north again, along roads packed with celebrating civilians, all the way to northern Belgium.

8.2 Belgium and Holland

On 22nd September, the advanced units of the newly christened "British Liberation Army," came within sight of the Albert Canal, and when the sappers arrived, they went to work on the construction of Bailey bridges.

The German forces in what Hitler had dubbed "Fortress Holland," had been divided into "battle groups," and these semi-autonomous units were, as had been seen in Italy, very effective in a defensive role, being both flexible and highly manoeuvrable. They had been ordered to fight to the last man, in defence of the "Fortress."

1/4th KOYLI were able to cross the canal on the 24th, and their next objective was to be Rijkevorsel, a small town about 15 miles northeast of the city of Antwerp. They entered the town and set up an observation post in the church tower, before coming under fire from a strong force of German troops who swept in from the north. The tower was blown to pieces as the KOYLI battled to hold on, and ammunition started to run out. Although a section of "B" Company was forced to surrender, the rest of the KOYLI managed to hold out until a relief force came to their rescue, in the form of the 2nd Battalion of the Essex Regiment, and they were allowed to fall back.

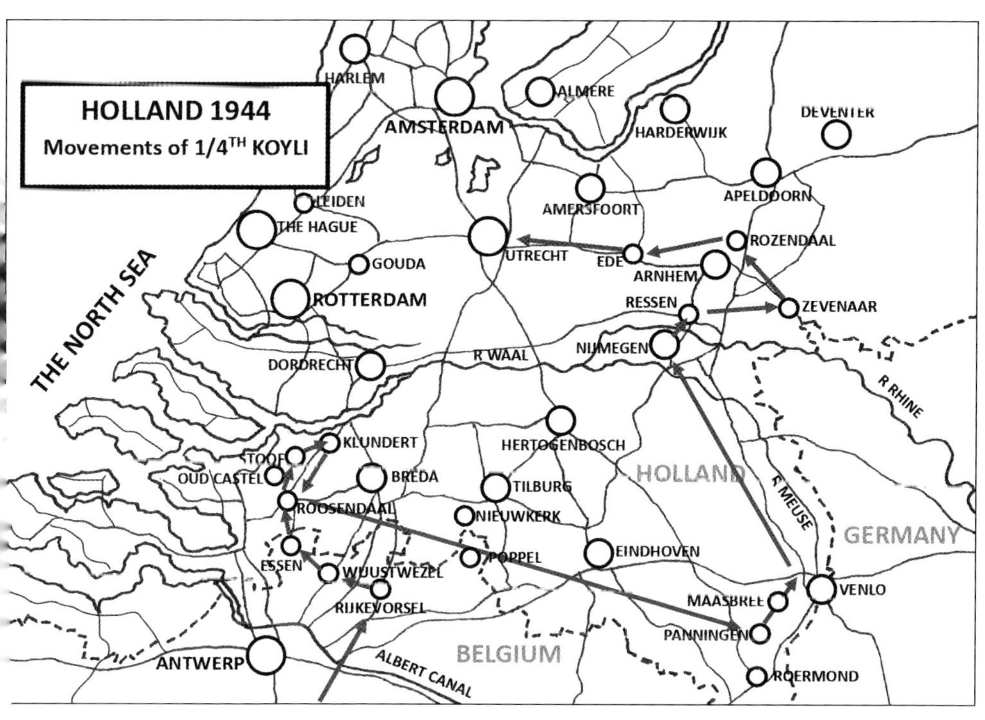

On 3rd October they were back in action as they advanced towards Poppel, just over a mile from the Dutch border. Once again, they came under heavy fire, but along with other units, they eventually took the town and pressed on towards Nieuwkerk. During the 7th, the 2nd Lincolnshires came under heavy gunfire, as they moved along the main Poppel to Tilburg road, and they were forced to dig in. They tried to fight back against a well-positioned and superior force, and it was the afternoon of the following day before 1/4th KOYLI arrived to tip the scales of the encounter. With artillery support, the KOYLI held that position for two weeks, occupying a strong enemy force, as the area around Antwerp was cleared.

After moving back to Rijkevorsel, they finally began a move to the northeast, on 20th October, as they set off to negotiate the road to Roosendaal, about 10 miles east of Breda. As they approached Wuustwezel, they once again came under heavy artillery fire, but managed to fight their way through and continue the advance towards Essen. They passed through the wrecked town on the 26th.

By the 28th they were on the outskirts of Roosendaal, and were ordered to rest until the German gun positions had been cleared, at which point they got to their feet and charged through the gaps between the shattered anti-tank guns, into a town that now erupted with joy. Long hidden bottles of every sort of spirit imaginable were pushed into the hands of the bewildered KOYLI, as girls hung around their necks, and old men came forward to shake their hands, beneath the fluttering banners of red, white, and blue. A detail was ordered to bypass the celebrations and make sure that all the Germans had left. They most certainly had.

On the night of 3rd November, 1/4th KOYLI were ordered north, towards the wide stretch of water, known as Hollands Diep. They passed through Oud Gastel before one company was detached to deal with an enemy position in the tiny village of Stoof. Three men were lost in that brief engagement. They pushed on towards their objective, and from some distance away, they could see that the town of Klundert was a mass of flames. They passed through the burning streets, towards the glowing waters of the Hollands Diep, at which point it became clear that the Germans had gone.

After the heavy fighting of the last few weeks, 1/4th were now granted rest, and took great pleasure in helping to distribute the food that now began to arrive for the starving population, but by the 14th, they had made

A fighting patrol of the KOYLI, armed with rifles, Bren gun, Sten guns and a PIAT, Elst, Holland. 2nd March 1945. Laing (Sgt), No 5 Army Film & Photographic Unit. (*Wikimedia Commons*)

their way to Panningen, to the west of Venlo, from where they set out for Maasbree, and the west bank of the River Meuse. Just south of the town, they were ambushed and lost several men, but they pushed north towards their next objective: Nijmegen.

Upon reaching the city on 1st December, it became clear that it had been ravaged by the earlier armoured attack towards the bridge at Arnhem, and there was little for them to do, now that the Germans had fallen back to the "bridge too far." So, they set up camp in Ressen, on the north bank of the River Waal, and began to carry out patrols in the area, as winter began to set in.

The wait continued until early April, and on the 10th, they reached Zevenaar, to the southeast of Arnhem. The Germans had positioned their

Arnhem, 14th April 1945. Author: Hewitt (Sgt), No 5 Army Film & Photographic Unit. (*Wikimedia Commons*)

artillery on the high ground to the east of the city and were able to fire down on the advancing troops. Nevertheless, the KOYLI and their comrades fought their way along the suburban streets, before battling through the city centre, and on 17th April, Arnhem was liberated.

A new camp was set up in the town of Rozendaal, just northeast of Arnhem, as the next move took place: an assault on the town of Ede. The town was held by a formation of the Dutch SS, some of whom had been part of the force that had defeated the earlier attack on Arnhem, during "Operation Market Garden". But although they were battle-hardened and experienced, they were also exhausted and running out of ammunition, as they cowered in their bunkers, under a constant rain of artillery shells. This time, there was to be no victory for the SS, and the British infantry took their surrender, when they finally crawled out of their dugouts, and into captivity.

On 7th May, 1/4th KOYLI left Ede, in the advance towards Utrecht. There was no opposition as they entered the city, to be met by thousands of cheering people, who mobbed their lorries and carriers.

8.3 Germany

On 2nd March 1945, 1st KOYLI, as part of 5th Division, arrived in northwest Europe, after their refitting in North Africa. They had been transported to Italy, and from there to Marseilles, where they had boarded a troop train that took them to the Belgian town of Sotteghem. There, they had been told that, in view of the fact that they had been overseas for over 3 years, they would be allowed a short period of home leave. Whether this was eventually felt to have been a good move, or not, depended upon each individual's point of view, as all too soon they were called back to Divisional HQ at Ghent, and the war.

Towards the end of March, they moved over the German border, to Xanten, before crossing the River Rhine, into a devastated landscape, where children stood at the roadside, begging for food, as their parents sat amongst the rubble that had been their homes. Cities had been razed to the ground,

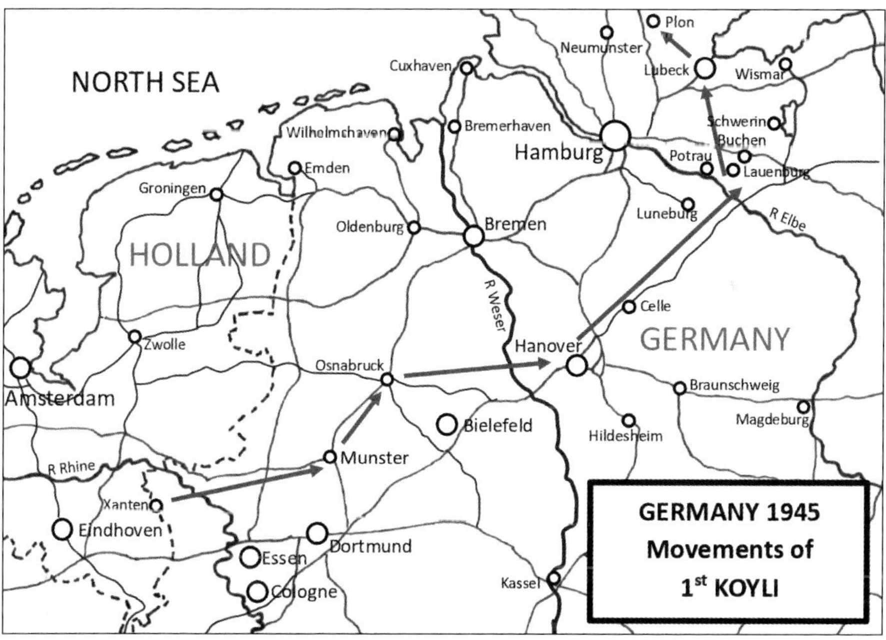

and the lines of women who had already started to clear away some of the rubble, in order to create some semblance of order amongst the desolation, made a pitiable sight.

After passing through Celle, they moved out into the Luneburg Heath, where thick patches of trees hid small groups of youngsters, unable to accept the inevitability of their country's defeat, after a lifetime of Nazi propaganda had left them indoctrinated with an absolute belief in its invincibility. These "werewolves," as Propaganda Minister Goebbels had named them, took many allied lives in those desperate last days of the war, and they received very little mercy from the war-weary soldiers, who tended to shoot them on the spot, whenever they were cornered.

By 21st April, 1st KOYLI were in position to cross the River Elbe, at a point just below Lauenburg, where a collection of German infantry faced

British VIII Corps moves up to the Elbe on 30th April 1945, prior to the advance on Lübeck. Unknown. (*National Army Museum Study Collection*)

them from the opposite bank, behind a screen of battered anti-aircraft guns. That night, the Allied artillery opened fire, and when the smoke cleared, the far bank was a smouldering heap of bodies and metal.

The KOYLI were in the second wave of the crossing, and by the time they reached the other side of the river, the Germans who had survived the bombardment, were running across the fields, weapons thrown away in terror.

As they raced on towards their final destination at Lübeck, the KOYLI listened to the first reports of the death of Adolf Hitler and thought that their war was over. But one more nasty surprise awaited them. Approaching the railway track that ran from Buchen to Potrau, they were fired upon by the remnants of a regular army unit, and once again they were called upon to fight it out amongst the ditches and roads of a foreign field, where more young men died in the last convulsions of the Second World War.

They moved on, to occupy Plon in Schleswig-Holstein, and continued to be involved in sporadic fighting until the German surrender on 8th May, after which they were transferred to XXX Corps and became part of the occupation forces.

Chapter 9

Greece, 1944–5

9.1 Patras

46th Infantry Division, including 2/4th KOYLI, were transferred to Greece before the start of the spring offensive that finally brought about the end of the war in Italy.

Towards the end of 1944, events in Greece were proving very concerning for the Western allies. As the German army in the Balkans collapsed under the immense pressure of a new Soviet thrust, the potential for a communist takeover in the area was becoming very real, and it was deemed vital to prevent a Greek Communist victory in the civil war that had erupted in the country.

On 18th October, British forces had protected the members of the Greek Government in Exile,, as they returned to Athens, but their position had been made very difficult by Britain's wartime support for the EAM, a socialist/communist party that had formed the main resistance to the German occupation, through its military wing, the People's Liberation Army, or ELAS. During the war, the communist partisans had tolerated the existence of a rival group of non-communist resistance, called the National Republican Greek League, or EDES, as their hatred of the Germans was stronger than their hatred of the Republicans. However, as the invaders began to melt away, both parties began to recognise that the long-term political future of Greece would be decided in the next few months, and this resulted in the eruption of a civil war in early 1944. Now, the return of the Government in exile served to increase the level of violence, as ELAS tried to carry out a coup, and the British sent 46th Infantry Division to prevent it.

At the end of January 1945, the men of 2/4th KOYLI found themselves in the coastal town of Patras, on the northern shore of the Peloponnese peninsular. Along with the rest of 138th Brigade, they were ordered to carry out house searches in order to identify ELAS supporters, disarm any that might be capable of fighting, and locate any hidden arms stockpiles. Of course, this was bound to cause resentment amongst those who thought

British tanks during operations against members of ELAS in Athens, Greece. Powell-Davies (Lt), No 2 Army Film & Photographic Unit. (*Wikimedia Commons*)

that they had a right to decide their own future after having fought against the German army for so long, but the KOYLI carried out their orders with a great deal of sensitivity, and four months later 138th Brigade had been relieved by 23rd Armoured Brigade and were on their way back to Italy.

By the time 46th Division arrived in Italy again, the spring offensive was already underway. Nevertheless, 2/4th KOYLI began to ready itself for action. As they moved towards the front on 2nd May, news came through of the German surrender in Italy, and the war in Europe ended six days later. Instead of fighting, 2/4th KOYLI found themselves transported to Austria, where they joined the occupying forces and waited to go home.

After the War

As was the case with all infantry regiments in the British Army, the KOYLI was reduced to a single battalion in 1948, when it was deployed to Malaya as part of the peacekeeping and counter-insurgency forces.

In 1954 it was sent to Kenya, before moving to Aden in 1955, Cyprus in 1956, Germany in 1958, Malaya in 1962, Borneo in 1964, and West Berlin in 1967.

In 1968 it was merged with The Somerset and Cornwall Light Infantry, The King's Shropshire Light Infantry, and The Durham Light Infantry, to form The Light Infantry.

Bibliography

Alexander, Harold (1948) The Conquest of Sicily from 10th July 1943 to 17th August 1943. The London Gazette. Source: Page 1009 | Supplement 38205, 10 February 1948 | London Gazette | The Gazette Accessed: 10th June 2023.

Anderson, K.A.N. Lieutenant General. Operations in North-west Africa from 8th November 1942 to 13th May 1943: The London Gazette 1946. Supplement 37779. Source: www.thegazette.co.uk/London/issue/37779/supplement/5449 Accessed: 29th May 2023.

Blumberg, A. Warfare History Network: Crushing Counterattack at Salerno (2016) Source: Crushing Counterattack at Salerno – Warfare History Network Accessed: 13th June 2023.

Britannica. World War II – Maginot Line, invasion of Low Countries and France | Britannica Accessed 3rd June 2023.

British Military History: France Norway 1940: Lines of Communication: 46th Infantry Division. Source: www.britishmilitaryhistory.co.uk/wp-content/uploads/sites/124/2020/09/46-Infantry-Division-1940.pdf Accessed: 23rd May 2023.

British Military History. Italy 1943 -1945: British Armoured Divisions. Source: Docs – Italy 1943 – 1945 – British Armoured Divisions – British Military History Accessed: 7th October 2023.

British Military History. Italy 1943 -1945: British Infantry Divisions. Source: Docs – Italy 1943 – 1945 – British Infantry Divisions – British Military History Accessed: 7th October 2023.

British Military History: 46th Infantry Division: http://www.britishmilitaryhistory.co.uk/webeasycms/hold/uploads/bmh_document_pdf/46-Infantry-Division-1940-.pdf Retrieved 29th May 2023.

British Military History. 5th Infantry Division (1945). Source: 5 Infantry Division (1945) (britishmilitaryhistory.co.uk) Accessed: 12th October 2023.

Case, G.C. "Trial by Fire: Major General Christopher Vokes at the Battles of the Moro River and Ortona, December 1943." Canadian Military History 16, 3 (2007) Source: Trial by Fire: Major General Christopher Vokes at the Battles of the Moro River and Ortona, December 1943 (wlu.ca) Accessed: 21st September 2023.

Center of Military History, United States Army. Anzio Beachhead. Washington DC. 1990. Source: ANZIO BEACHHEAD (22 January-25 May 1944) (army.mil) Accessed: 27th September 2023.

Center of Military History, United States Army. Anzio 1944. ANZIO 1944 | US Army Center of Military History Accessed: 27th September 2023.

Cooper, J. Animals in War. London: Corgi (1984) ISBN-10: 0552990914

Derry, T.K. The Campaign in Norway. HyperWar: The Campaign in Norway (ibiblio.org). Retrieved 28th May 2023.

Delaforce, P. The Polar Bears. Monty's Left Flank. From Normandy to the Relief of Holland with the 49th Division. London: Chancellor Press. ISBN 0 75370 265 7.

Ellis, L.F. Victory in the West. Vol. I. The Battle of Normandy. Victory in the West: The Battle of Normandy (archive.org) Retrieved 22nd December 2023.

Ellis, L.F. Victory in the West. Vol. II. The Defeat of Germany. Victory in the West: The defeat of Germany (archive.org) Retrieved 22nd December 2023.

Hudson, E R B. A Close View of the Disaster at the Sittang Bridge (2010). Michigan War Studies Review. Source: www.miwsr.com/2010/downloads/20100706.pdf Accessed: 12th December 2023.

Jackson, W. G. F.; Gleave, T. P. (2004) [1988]. Butler, Sir James (ed.). The Mediterranean and Middle East: Part III – November 1944 to May 1945. History of the Second World War United Kingdom Military Series. Vol. VI (Naval & Military Press, Uckfield ed.). London: HMSO. ISBN 1-84574-072-6.

Live Journal: Harry Pynn: The Ballad of the D-Day Dodgers: Harry Pynn, 'The Ballad of the D-Day Dodgers' (livejournal.com) Retrieved 26th May 2023.

British Military History: British 1st Infantry Division. Source: 1 Burma Infantry Division (1941-42) (britishmilitaryhistory.co.uk) Accessed: 10th December 2023.

British Military History: Italy 1943-1945: British Armoured Divisions. www.britishmilitaryhistory.co.uk/docs-italy-1943-1945-british-armoured-divisions/ Retrieved 27th May 2023.

British Military History: Italy 1943 – 1945: British Infantry Divisions. www.Docs%20–%20Italy%201943%20-%201945%20–%20British%20Infantry%20Divisions%20-%20British%20Military%20History.html Retrieved 27th May 2023.

Delaforce, P. (1995). The Polar Bears: Monty's Left Flank: From Normandy to the Relief of Holland with the 49th Division. Stroud: Chancellor Press. ISBN 9780753702659.

Ellis, J. (2003) [1984]. Cassino, The Hollow Victory: The Battle for Rome, January-June 1944. London: Arum Press. ISBN 1-85410-916-2.

Ellis L.F. Major. The War in France and Flanders 1939-1940 Source: HyperWar: The War in France and Flanders 1939–1940 [Appendix I] (ibiblio.org) Accessed 3rd June 2023.

Forty, G. (1998). British Army Handbook 1939–1945. Stroud: Sutton Publishing. ISBN 978-0753703328.

Frederick, J.M.B. Lineage Book of British Land Forces 1660–1978, Vol I, Wakefield: Microform Academic, 1984, ISBN 1-85117-007-3

Generals dk. Source: www.generals.dk/general/Fisher/Arthur_Francis/Great_Britain.html Accessed: 7th June 2023.

Generals dk. Source: www.generals.dk/general/Holworthy/Alan_Wilmot_Wadeson/Great_Britain.htm Accessed 1st June 2023.

Hastings, M. Overlord. D-Day and the Battle for Normandy 1944. London: Guild Publishing. ISBN 10:9999-999241 0665.

Hirst, C.J. Col./ Warde-Aldam R. Maj./Hanwell Col. (eds.) A Short Record of The Queen's Own Yorkshire Dragoons. 1794 – 1954. Gale and Polden, 1954.

Hunt, Sir David. (1990) A Don at War. London. Routledge. ISBN 9780714643748

Imperial War Museum: The Song that Ruled the Airwaves During the Second World War. Source: The Song That Ruled The Airwaves During WW2 | Imperial War Museums (iwm.org.uk) Accessed 20th May 2023.

IWM: Collection: McIntyre H M J (Brigadier) Collection. www.iwm.org.uk/collections/item/object/205303561 Retrieved 27th May 2023.

Jackson, Sir William. Butler Sir James (Ed.) History of the Second World War. United Kingdom Military Series. London 1987. Her Majesty's Stationery Office. SEN 01

630946 6. The Mediterranean and Middle East Vol. VI. Victory in the Mediterranean. Part 2: June to October 1944.

Johnson, B. Evacuation of Dunkirk. Source: The Evacuation of Dunkirk – May 1940 (historic-uk.com) Accessed 3rd June 2023.

Joslen, H. F. (2003) Orders of Battle: Second World War, 1939–1945. Uckfield, East Sussex: Naval and Military Press. ISBN 978-1-84342-474-1.

Jewish Chronicle: Who was Nancy Astor?: www.thejc.com/news/uk-news/who-was-nancy-astor-the-first-woman-to-take-her-seat-in-parliament-was-also-branded-virulently-ant-1.493848 Retrieved: 20th May 2023

King, C. Operation Husky 70 years later: When the allied forces landed in Sicily. Italy Magazine 2013. Source: Operation Husky 70 Years Later: When The Allied Forces Landed in Sicily | ITALY Magazine Accessed: 10th June 2023.

Laurie, C.D. Rome – Arno 1944. US Army Centre of Military History. Source: ROME-ARNO 1944 | US Army Center of Military History. Accessed: 29th September 2023.

Litchfield, N.E.H. The Territorial Artillery 1908–1988 (Their Lineage, Uniforms and Badges), Nottingham: Sherwood Press, 1992, ISBN 0-9508205-2-0.

Lynch, T. (2015). Dunkirk 1940 'Whereabouts Unknown': How Untrained Troops of the Labour Division were Sacrificed to Save an Army. Stroud: The History Press. ISBN 978-0-75096-453-1.

Mead, R. (2007). Churchill's Lions: A Biographical Guide to the Key British Generals of World War II. Stroud: Spellmount. ISBN 978-1-86227-431-0.

Molony, C.J.C. Brigadier. Butler Sir James (Ed.) History of the Second World War. United Kingdom Military Series. London 1973. Her Majesty's Stationery Office. SEN 11 630064 7. The Mediterranean and Middle East Vol. VI. Victory in the Mediterranean. Part 1: 1st April to 4th June 1944.

Moorehead, A. (2009) [1944]. The Desert War: The Classic Trilogy on the North African Campaign 1940–43 (Aurum Press, London ed.). London: Hamish Hamilton. ISBN 978 1 84513-391-7

Moorhead, A. Eclipse. London. Hamish Hamilton 1946. Source: Eclipse (archive.org) Accessed: 9th June 2023.

National Army Museum: The King's Own Yorkshire Light Infantry: The King's Own Yorkshire Light Infantry | National Army Museum (nam.ac.uk) Retrieved 26th May 2023.

National WWII Museum, New Orleans (2012): The Allied Campaign in Italy, 1943-45: A Timeline, Part One. Source: The Allied Campaign in Italy, 1943-45: A Timeline, Part One | The National WWII Museum | New Orleans (nationalww2museum.org) Accessed: 11th June 2023.

Orgill, D. (1986) The Gothic Line. New York: Kensington Publishing. ISBN-13: 978-0821719169.

Oland, D.D. US Army Centre of Military History. Source: http://www.history.army.mil/brochures/nap/72-34.htm Accessed: 11th October 2023.

Patriot Files: British Northern Command on 3rd September 1939. British Northern Command on 3 September 1939: The Patriot Files: Dedicated to the preservation of military history Retrieved 27th May 2023.

Playfair I.S.O. Major General et al. Butler Sir James (Ed.) History of the Second World War. United Kingdom Military Series. London 1973. Her Majesty's Stationery Office. SEN 11 630064 7. The Mediterranean and Middle East Vol. II. The Germans come to the help of their Ally (1941).

Playfair I.S.O. Major General et al. Butler Sir James (Ed.) History of the Second World War. United Kingdom Military Series. London 1973. Her Majesty's Stationery Office. SEN 11 630064 7. The Mediterranean and Middle East Vol. IV. The Destruction of the Axis Forces in Africa.

Reynolds, B.E. (1994). Thailand and Japan's Southern Advance, 1940-1945. Palgrave Macmillan US. ISBN 978-0-312-10402-3

Richards, D/Saunders, H. St. G. History of the Second World War. The Royal Air Force 1939-1945. Vol. II: The Fight Avails. Chapter XII Torch and Tunisia. Source: HyperWar: Royal Air Force 1939-1945: Volume II: The Fight Avails [Chapter 12] (ibiblio.org) Accessed 8th June 2023.

Rickard, J. (28 November 2018) Battle of Gemmano, 4-15 September 1944. Source: http://www.historyofwar.org/articles/battles_gemmano.html Accessed 7th October 2023

Rickard, J. (14th August 2018) Battle of the Moro River – 4th December 1943 to 4th January 1944. Source: Battle of the Moro River, 4 December 1943-4 January 1944 (historyofwar.org) Accessed: 22nd September 2023.

Rickard, J. (3rd August 2018) Battle of the Sangro – 20th November to 4th December 1944. Source: Battle of the Sangro, 20 November- 4 December 1943 (historyofwar.org) Accessed: 21st September 2023.

Rickard, J. (23rd August 2018) Battle of the Winter Line or Gustav Line, 12th January -18th May 1944. Source: http://www.historyofwar.org/articles/battles_winter_line.html Accessed: 7th August 2023.

Rothwell, S. The Burma Campaign. 17th Indian Infantry Division 1941-1942. 17th Indian Infantry Division 1941-1942 (indiaburmasoldiers.co.uk) Accessed: 10th December 2023.

Russell, J. Theirs the Strife: The Forgotten Battles of British Second Army and Armeegruppe Blumentritt, April 1945. Warwick: Helion and Company (1921) ISBN -10: 1914059395

Slim. W.J. Defeat into Victory: Battling Japan in Burma and India, 1942–1945 (NY: Cooper Square, 2000) ISBN: 9780815410225

Sutton, D.: week 212: Ballad of the D-Day Dodgers by Harry Pynn/Hamish Henderson. Source: Harry Pynn | David Sutton (davidsuttonpoetry.com) Accessed 20th May 2023.

Unit Histories: 5th Infantry Division. Source: 5th Infantry Division [British] 1939-1945 (unithistories.com) Accessed 23rd May 2023.

US Army Center of Military History. Source: WWII Campaigns: Sicily | US Army Center of Military History Accessed: 9th June 2023.

Wayback Machine: The Battle for Kvam: Battle for Kvam (archive.org) Retrieved 28th May 2023.

Whitehead, D. Combat Reporter. New York: Fordham University Press. Source: Combat Reporter: Don Whitehead: Free Download, Borrow, and Streaming: Internet Archive. Accessed May 2023.

Whiting, C./Taylor, E. Fighting Tykes. An Informal History of the Yorkshire Regiments in the Second World War. Barnsley: Pen and Sword. ISBN 978 1 84415 6 450.

Woodburn, K.S. The War against Japan. Vol. II. India's Most Dangerous Hour. Source: ia902300.us.archive.org/11/items/war-against-japan-vol-2/WarAgainstJapanVol2.pdf Retrieved: 1st December 2023.

Ziemke, E.F. The German Northern Theater of Operations 1940-1954. Source: www.history.army.mil/html/books/104/104-23/CMH_Pub_104-23.pdf. Accessed: 23rd December 2023.

Zimmerman, D.W. (2013): The Surrender of Italy: The Allies' Bungled Opportunity. Source: The Surrender of Italy: The Allies' Bungled Opportunity | Defense Media Network Accessed: 11th June 2023.

Zimmerman, D.J.: Churchill's Blunder: Anzio. Defense Media Network, 2014. Available at: www.defensemedianetwork.com/stories/churchils-blunder-anzio/ Accessed: 16th April 2022.

46th Infantry Division 1946. The Story of 46 Division 1939–1945. Naval & Military Press (9 July 2020) Uckfield. ISBN 978-1783316564

94th Light AA Regiment. web.archive.org/web/20160331000331/http://www.ra39-45.pwp.blueyonder.co.uk/laa/page88.html Accessed: 21st December 2023.

Index